Wandering & Feasting

A WASHINGTON COOKBOOK

Wandering & Feasting

A WASHINGTON COOKBOOK

MARY HOUSER CADITZ

Washington State University Press
Pullman, WA 99164-5910
(800) 354-7360

Washington State University Press, Pullman, Washington 99164-5910

Cover: Asahel Curtis photograph, courtesy Washington State Historical Society.

Library of Congress Cataloging-in-Publication Data

Caditz, Mary Houser.
   Wandering and feasting : a Washington cookbook / Mary Houser Caditz.
      p.   cm.
   Includes bibliographical references and index.
   ISBN 0-87422-138-2 (pbk.)
   1. Cookery, American—Pacific Northwest style. 2. Cookery—
Washington (State). 3. Washington (State)—Description and travel.
I. Title.
TX715.2.P32C33   1996
641.59797—dc20   96-13943
                                                              CIP

Washington State University Press
PO Box 645910
Pullman, Washington 99164-5910

Phone: (800) 354-7360
Fax: (509) 335-8568

For my daughters,
Kari and Kristine

SPECIAL COLLECTIONS, UNIV. OF WASHINGTON LIBRARIES, NEG. #12305

CONTENTS

Olympic Peninsula

Southwest Washington

North Puget Sound and San Juan Islands

Puget Sound

Cascades

Central Washington

Inland Empire

ACKNOWLEDGMENTS

To acknowledge all the people who helped with this book seems an impossible task, for so many joined and supported me along my journey. However, a few dear ones were close to the project all along the way. My husband, Syl, traveled throughout Washington with me, helped with research, acted as the chief tester for all recipes, and enthusiastically supported me. Daughters, Kari and Kris, and their husbands, Jim and Eric, tested recipes, gave ideas for new recipes, read my manuscript, and constantly gave me inspiration. My sister, Caroline Houser, encouraged and even prodded me, edited writings, gave positive suggestions, and always believed in the project. Gary Houser, my brother and a Washington state farmer, directed me to people, agencies, and commissions with whom I should consult.

My everlasting gratitude goes to the staff at Washington State University Press for their enthusiasm in guiding this, their first cookbook, to publication. Keith Petersen, my editor, has been helpful and enthusiastic about the project from the beginning. His informative and pleasant manner, coupled with a dry wit, makes him a joy to work with. I would also like to thank Jo Savage for the book and cover design, and Beth DeWeese for her marketing expertise.

Jan Grant, the former King County extension agent, checked recipes for safety. When Jan retired from her job, the Seattle Times described her as a food safety guru. She is just that and I am deeply appreciative of her knowledgeable input.

My heartfelt thanks to the following people who either edited copy, tested recipes, shared recipes, gave advice, or in some way contributed to Wandering and Feasting in Washington: Waleta and Boyd Rupp, Rachel Simpson, Bonnie Stuart Mickelson, Bruce and Heather Heibert, Mally Haight, Cindy Lang Caditz, Terri Caditz, Mary Lynn Baird, Chris Gittins, Janie Lanier, Joanie Staiger, Debra Holland, Sally Larson, Marie Williams, Cindy Breihl, Belle Rogers, and members of SAUTÉ.

I was assisted in locating old photos by: Susan Parish from her personal collection, Joy Werlink and the staff at the Washington State Historical Society Museum, Patrice Benson from the Puget Sound Mycological Society, the staff at the special collections department at the University of Washington Allen Library, and my cousin Robert Larson.

And my profound gratitude goes to the many Washingtonians who shared with me their knowledge of our state and its wondrous array of foods.

HOUSER MILL, COURTESY ROBERT HOUSER LARSON

INTRODUCTION

The passion I have for the state of Washington is embedded in my roots. in 1868, Levi and Mary Courtney, my great-great-grandparents, crossed the plains and rugged mountains in a covered wagon with their children to settle on the Pataha Prairie, in what is now southeast Washington. Their daughter, Florence (my great-grandmother), wrote in her journal, "Father and Baxter worked on our cabin, laid the floor, and then we moved in. The first thing after our house was completed was to plow sod for the garden."

In the same year, my maternal great-grandparents, Newell and Mary Patterson, also came west. Traveling by wagon they left Kansas to find new land to farm, eventually homesteading in Washington Territory.

Some years later, my great-grandfather, John Houser, developed a flour mill near the banks of the Pataha Creek. There he processed into flour wheat from the surrounding fields and sold it throughout the Western states and to some Asian countries. Great-grandmother Marie Houser made loaves of graham bread to give to friends, neighbors, and anyone in need. The old Houser Flour Mill, now deserted, is listed on the National Register of Historic Places.

I grew up on a wheat farm not far from the old mill. There, the color of the grain ushered in the seasons. In spring, the fields were grass green, soon turning to amber in summer before the harvest, then back again to green in late autumn when the newly planted fall wheat sprouted. By December, a winter white usually covered the ground, insulating the wheat from the bitter cold. Planting time and harvest time were ceremonies of the seasons. I grew up observing these seasons and rituals, and I learned to respect the land and those who tilled it.

Now I am settled in western Washington and have come to respect the water as well as the land. Lakes, bays, beaches, inlets, and the ocean offer a harvest of sea treasures. Eagerly and awkwardly, I dig for razor clams on ocean beaches, fish for salmon on rough waters, and search for oysters and other mollusks on island shores; sometimes I cast my line into the small lake by which I live to see whether I can lure a wary trout.

Trips back and forth across the state to visit the family farm often turn into excursions to all parts of Washington. My husband and I have watched the harvest of apples and other fruit, talked with vintners in wineries, picked mushrooms and berries on mountain slopes, and marveled at the beauty and diversity of the state.

The recipes in this book highlight products that are indigenous or cultivated near the communities featured. My keen interest in cooking and love for the state of Washington inspired me to write this book. May you, too, enjoy wandering and feasting in Washington.

A Word about the Recipes

Temperatures for the foods prepared are registered in Fahrenheit. If you wish to convert to Celsius, use the following approximate conversions:

275°F	140°C
300°F	150°C
325°F	170°C
350°F	180°C
375°F	190°C
400°F	200°C
425°F	220°C
450°F	230°C
475°F	240°C

Since most ovens in the United States are conventional (standard), that is what I used when preparing foods for this book. If you use a convection oven, the temperature of the oven and the time needed to cook the foods should be altered. Refer to the owner's manual, but in general, the temperature of the convection oven is reduced and cooking time is shortened. For example, a beef roast that cooks in a conventional oven at 325°F for 1¾ hours will cook in a convection oven at 300°F for 1¼ hours. A few recipes call for a microwave oven, though conventional oven instructions are usually also included. A microwave oven works well when poaching or cooking fruit, heating liquids, and melting chocolate.

All-purpose, unbleached white flour was used in the recipes, unless otherwise specified. Best-for-Bread flour has a higher content of gluten (protein) than all-purpose flour and is great for making bread and hard rolls. However, all-purpose flour is best for pastry, because the gluten development needs to be limited and a more tender product is desired. Cake flour has less gluten than all-purpose flour and is recommended for some cakes.

Eggs used in the recipes are large ones that measure about ¼ cup. Extra large or medium eggs may be used in some recipes, but for making batter that needs exact measurement, large eggs are recommended.

Happy reading and cooking!

OLYMPIC PENINSULA

Cathedral-like rain forests blanket wild mushrooms and berries. Icy Pacific waters harbor fish. Tranquil inlets are home to oysters, clams, and Dungeness crabs.

Neah Bay

Port Angeles

Sequim

Dungeness

Port Townsend

Discovery Bay

Hoodsport

Shelton

Aberdeen

Hoquiam

Ocean Shores

Copalis Beach

Pacific Beach

Quinault

Forks

NEAH BAY

Sea winds sculpt branches leeward, hurl waves onto steep, rugged cliffs and drive surging waters to dance around the off-shore rocks at Cape Flattery. This dramatic spot is the most northwesterly corner of the 48 states and was visited early by European explorers. Captain James Cook sailed past and named the cape in 1778. Seventeen years later, a Spanish explorer and his crew stopped long enough to set up a fort, the first European settlement in Washington. The encampment was brief, however, lasting only a few months.

Ancestors of the Makah Indians have lived in this area for more than 2,500 years, and a remarkable collection of Indian artifacts is on display at the cultural center at Neah Bay, a fishing village about 12 miles east of Cape Flattery.

Today, Neah Bay is a town busy with sport and commercial fishermen who find the waters off the western and northern shores of the Olympic peninsula excellent for **salmon, halibut, rockfish, Lingcod, Black cod,** and **Dover** and **Petrale sole. Clams** and other mollusks are found on beaches.

SUSAN PARISH COLLECTION

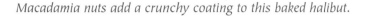

Halibut with Macadamia Nut Crust

SERVINGS: 4

Macadamia nuts add a crunchy coating to this baked halibut.

**4 halibut filet pieces,
about 5-6 ounces each**

1 cup shelled Macadamia nuts

1 tablespoon olive oil

**⅛ teaspoon dried thyme,
crumbled**

lemon wedges

1. Preheat oven to 450 degrees. Pat fish dry. Finely grind ¾ cup of the nuts in a food processor or by hand, add olive oil and thyme and combine. Spread nut mixture on top of fish filets.

2. Place filets in medium-size, broiler-safe baking dish and bake, uncovered, for 10-12 minutes or until centers are opaque. Meanwhile, coarsely chop rest of nuts. Remove fish from oven and turn on broiler. Top fish with coarsely chopped nuts and place fish under broiler to brown for about one minute, watching carefully. Serve with lemon wedges.

Shelled Macadamia nuts are found in jurs In supermarkets and have been roasted and salted. Or, look for them in markets that sell bulk food. If fresh unsalted Macadamia nuts are used, some salt should be sprinkled on fish.

Whole Baked Salmon with Medley of Three Dill Sauces

SERVINGS: 10-12

To please a crowd, serve this moist salmon with a medley of three dill sauces.
When visitors from out of town come, this is one of my favorite recipes to bring out.

SALMON

¾ **cup dry white wine**

1½ **teaspoons chopped fresh basil or ½ teaspoon dried**

¾ **teaspoon chopped fresh rosemary or ¼ teaspoon dried**

½ **cup chopped onion**

1 **unpeeled lemon, sliced**

½ **unpeeled orange, sliced**

1 **salmon (5-7 pounds) cleaned and boned (butterflied and left whole, head removed, optional)**

¾ **teaspoon salt, divided**

1 **tablespoon butter, cut in pieces**

1. Make one or all of dill sauces (to blend flavors) and refrigerate. Recipe on following page.

2. In a small saucepan combine wine, herbs, chopped onion, 2 slices lemon, and 2 orange slices. (Reserve remaining orange and lemon slices.) Place over medium low heat and simmer for 20 minutes to reduce slightly and incorporate the flavors.

3. Preheat oven to 400 degrees. Place cleaned salmon on a long, heavy sheet of foil. (Foil needs to be large enough to seal salmon.) Remove any remaining bones. Place rest of orange and lemon slices and ¼ teaspoon salt in cavity. Bring edges of foil up and pour wine mixture over. Sprinkle with remaining ½ teaspoon salt and butter pieces. Press foil edges together to seal and place in a large baking pan.

4. Put pan in oven and bake one hour. Remove from oven, take off foil and place salmon on large platter. Serve with dill sauces.

Penny Rawson is now the culinary director of Columbia and Paul Thomas Wineries.
For many years, she had a catering business and often served salmon
accompanied by her special dill sauce. Following is her recipe.

PENNY RAWSON'S SOUR CREAM DILL SAUCE

1 cup light sour cream

1½ tablespoons white wine vinegar

1½ tablespoons Dijon mustard

7 teaspoons light brown sugar

2 teaspoons dry dill weed

TO MAKE SAUCE

Mix ingredients together in a bowl and refrigerate several hours.

CRÈME FRAÎCHE, CUCUMBER, AND DILL SAUCE

1 cup crème fraîche (recipe on page 312 or use commercial)

3 tablespoons minced fresh dill

3 tablespoons grated cucumber, seeded

½ teaspoon white wine vinegar

slice of cucumber, for garnish

TO MAKE SAUCE

Mix first four ingredients in bowl, refrigerate, and bring to room temperature before serving. Serve with a slice of cucumber on top for guests to identify.

YOGURT DILL SAUCE

1 cup plain yogurt

¼ cup mayonnaise, regular or light

2 tablespoons minced fresh dill

Sprig of fresh dill for garnish

TO MAKE SAUCE

Mix first three ingredients in bowl, refrigerate, and bring to room temperature before serving. Serve with a sprig of fresh dill on top to identify.

Filet of Sole Turbans with Shrimp Sauce

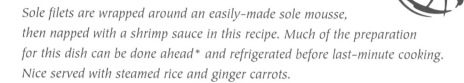

SERVINGS: 6

Sole filets are wrapped around an easily-made sole mousse, then napped with a shrimp sauce in this recipe. Much of the preparation for this dish can be done ahead* and refrigerated before last-minute cooking. Nice served with steamed rice and ginger carrots.

8 large filets of sole, about 6 ounces each (Petrale sole filets are sometimes large enough to divide in two)

1 egg white

¾ cup heavy or light cream (for light cream, see page 322)

¾ teaspoon salt, divided

⅛ teaspoon white pepper

3 dashes Tabasco sauce

1¼ cups milk

2 tablespoons butter or margarine

2 tablespoons all-purpose flour

⅛ teaspoon nutmeg

1 cup cooked baby shrimp

3 tablespoons dry sherry, divided

*Turbans (rolled-up and filled filets) and sauce can be made hours before serving, refrigerated separately, and taken from the refrigerator ½ hour before cooking.

1. Preheat oven to 350 degrees. Remove any bones from filets. Cut two sole filets into 1-inch pieces and place in a food processor with steel blade inserted, or blender, along with egg white, cream, ½ teaspoon salt, white pepper, and Tabasco. Blend until mixture is smooth. Lay remaining 6 filets flat on work surface and spoon fish mixture onto each, dividing evenly. Spread over filets. Roll up filets (turbans) and place seam down in baking dish, set aside or refrigerate, covered.

2. Make sauce by heating 1¼ cups milk over low heat in a small saucepan. Melt butter in separate saucepan over low heat, stir in flour, and cook, stirring for 3 minutes. Take off burner, add warmed milk all at once. Return pan to heat and stir constantly over medium heat until thickened. Add ¼ teaspoon remaining salt, nutmeg, and shrimp, and combine. Keep sauce warm on low heat, or remove from heat, refrigerate, then bring to room temperature.

3. Sprinkle 1 tablespoon sherry, and salt and pepper to taste, over filets (turbans) in baking dish. Place in 350 degree oven and bake, uncovered, for 15-20 minutes or until done (fish will be opaque throughout). Rewarm sauce if necessary. Lift filets (turbans) out of baking dish onto serving platter. Stir reserved 2 tablespoons sherry into sauce and pour sauce over filets and serve.

PORT ANGELES

An early Spanish explorer, cruising through the Strait of Juan de Fuca, sailed into a harbor and named it, "Porto de Nuestra Senora de los Angeles." Those who followed were more practical and a bit less poetic, shortening the name to Port Angeles. Today, both the harbor and town on its shore bear the name. Many sport fishermen set out for deep sea or reef fishing from this port. Ferries leave the harbor daily, making the voyage to Victoria, Canada, in about an hour.

South of Port Angeles is mile-high Hurricane Ridge, offering spectacular views of the Olympic Peninsula and Canada. On clear days, climbers see Mt. Olympus, the Strait of Juan de Fuca, and Canada's Vancouver Island.

Fishermen from Port Angeles seek their catch in the Pacific Ocean, Puget Sound, or the Strait of Juan de Fuca, all within range. They return with **Pacific rockfish, Lingcod, Black cod, halibut, salmon, Dover** and **Petrale sole.** The famous large **Beardslee trout** make their home in nearby Lake Crescent.

Easy and Elegant Baked Pacific Rockfish (Snapper)

SERVINGS: 4

Use this recipe on other fish such as halibut or cod. Pacific rockfish are sometimes called snapper. Many rockfish varieties are found in Northwest waters; one of the most common is the Yelloweye.

4 rockfish (snapper) filets, about 6 ounces each

2 tablespoons fresh lemon juice

½ cup freshly grated Parmesan cheese

2 tablespoons sour cream, regular or light

3 tablespoons mayonnaise, regular or light

3 tablespoons chopped scallions

1. Preheat oven to 375 degrees. Remove bones from filets and place filets in shallow baking dish. Sprinkle with lemon juice. Combine rest of ingredients in bowl. Spread mixture on filets evenly.

2. Bake, uncovered, for 15-18 minutes or until fish is opaque throughout. Lift out filets and serve.

Steamed Lingcod with Ginger Cream Sauce

SERVINGS: 4

Fish is kept moist by steaming, which works well with Lingcod. Serve with rice, snow peas, and Cucumber and Rice Vinegar Salad (page 121).

Water

4 Lingcod pieces, about 6 ounces each

2 tablespoons soy sauce

1 lemon, very thinly sliced

¼ cup fish stock or chicken stock (recipe page 313) or canned low-sodium chicken broth

¼ cup dry vermouth

1 cup heavy or light cream (for light cream, see page 322)

1 tablespoon minced fresh ginger or 1 teaspoon powdered ginger

chives for garnish

1. Place water in steamer or in sauce pan with steamer tray. The water should come to about ½ inch below tray. Bring water to simmer over medium heat.

2. Sprinkle fish with soy sauce and cover with lemon slices. Put fish on steamer tray. Cover and steam over medium heat for 12-15 minutes, or until fish is opaque throughout.

3. Meanwhile, make sauce by heating stock (broth) and vermouth in a medium saucepan over high heat and reduce to 2 tablespoons. Add cream and boil down again over medium heat until slightly thickened and reduced to about ⅔ cup. Add ginger and incorporate. When fish is cooked (opaque throughout), take off lemons and place fish on warm serving plate. Top with sauce and chopped chives to serve.

Sole Parmesan with Sun-dried Tomato Sauce

SERVINGS: 4

Crusty-coated tender sole is topped with a sauce bursting with flavor and color. The sun-dried tomato sauce is also good on veal and grilled or poached fish.

2 pounds Petrale or Dover sole filets

¾ cup all-purpose flour

½ teaspoon salt

freshly ground pepper

2 eggs, beaten with two tablespoons water

1½ cups bread crumbs

5 or 6 ounces freshly shredded Parmesan cheese (grated into thin toothpick-like pieces)

2 tablespoons vegetable oil

2 tablespoons butter or margarine

1. Wipe filets dry. Place flour on plate (or waxed paper) and season with salt and freshly ground pepper. In shallow bowl, put egg-water mixture. In third plate (or on waxed paper), mix bread crumbs with freshly shredded Parmesan cheese. First, dredge filets in flour, then dip in egg mixture, and finally coat filets liberally in cheese-bread mixture. Allow filets to rest for 20 minutes to set coating. Sauce may be made at this time. Refer to step 3.

2. Heat oil and butter in a large non-stick pan. When hot, add fish filets, without crowding, and sauté on both sides until golden brown and cooked throughout (about 4-6 minutes in all). To prevent overcrowding in pan, the filets may need to be done in two skillets or in batches and kept warm. (Rewarm sauce if necessary over low heat, and if too thick, thin with drops of water or white wine.) Place filets on serving dish and spoon sauce over.

SUN-DRIED TOMATO SAUCE

10-12 sun-dried tomatoes in oil, drained and patted dry

3-4 sprigs parsley

1½ cups heavy or light cream (for light cream, see page 322)

2-3 dashes Tabasco sauce

salt to taste

TO MAKE SAUCE

Puree sun-dried tomatoes and parsley in a food processor. Heat cream in medium saucepan over medium-high heat to boiling, reduce heat to low, and continue cooking, stirring frequently, until cream is reduced by about one-third. Stir in tomato-parsley mixture, Tabasco sauce, and salt to taste. Combine and set aside off heat.

SEQUIM AND DUNGENESS

Sun seekers, including many retired people, find balmy weather in Sequim. Clouds coming in from the coast shower rain on the Olympic Mountains, so when they get to Sequim most of their moisture has dissipated. Only 16 inches of rain fall on the Sequim area yearly, making it the driest coastal region north of California. Conversely, Mt. Olympus, about 35 miles southwest of Sequim, is deep in the rain forest. There, 140-200 inches of precipitation fall per year, making it the wettest spot in any state except Hawaii.

Dungeness, facing Canada on the northern coast, is less protected than Sequim and receives more rain. In 1792, when George Vancouver explored this area, he thought the low sandy land here resembled Dungeness in the British Channel, and gave the town its name. Now a harbor, a river, and even a type of tasty crab, also bear this name. Because many Northwest crabs were originally harvested here, they were named **Dungeness.** These **crabs** thrive on the sandy beaches near Dungeness as well as locations all the way from northern California to Alaska.

Clams, especially **littlenecks,** flourish on the local beaches. A valley south of Dungeness, once a thriving dairy region, now blooms with **strawberry** and **raspberry** fields. Some picturesque old weathered barns left over from the dairy farming days still stand amid the fields.

Dungeness Crab with Sauces

SERVINGS: 4

Fresh crab, a green salad, and hot garlic bread is a Northwest favorite meal and a traditional Christmas Eve supper at some homes.

FOR COMMERCIALLY COOKED CRABS:

Purchase 2 large or 4 medium precooked Dungeness crabs, cleaned and cracked. When home, loosen wrap and refrigerate until ready to use.

LIVE DUNGENESS CRABS:

2 large or 4 medium live crabs

salt, preferably Kosher or sea salt

1. Place live crabs in pan of ice before cooking. Fill a large stock pot or kettle (you may need two pots) about ⅔ full of water along with salt. (About ¼ cup salt per gallon of water.) Bring to boil, place crabs in water, return water to gentle boil, and cover pot. Boil 15-20 minutes or about ten minutes per pound of crab. Remove pot from heat.

2. With tongs take out the crab immediately and place under cold running tap water or in a bowl filled with ice water. When crabs are cool enough to handle, remove top shells. Rinse crabs under cold running water and discard viscera and feather-like gills. Separate legs from body if desired. (Claw "toes" make good picks for removing meat from other parts.)

3. Crack crab sections with wooden mallet. Cover crabs and refrigerate until serving. Make sauces.

4. To serve: place cooked crabs on platter with hand nutcrackers and picks for removing meat from shells, and offer sauces. Melted butter may also be offered for dipping.

(Sauces follow on next page.)

(Dungeness Crab with Sauces continued)

TARRAGON MAYONNAISE

1 cup mayonnaise, regular or light

1 teaspoon Dijon or
Dijon-style mustard

¼ teaspoon dried tarragon
softened in ½ teaspoon
lemon juice

1 teaspoon minced shallots

2 dashes Tabasco sauce

TO MAKE MAYONNAISE

Combine ingredients in bowl and chill.

SPECIAL CRAB SAUCE

1 cup mayonnaise, regular or light

1 cup chili sauce

1 teaspoon Worcestershire sauce

1 tablespoon lemon juice

¼ cup finely chopped celery

2 scallions, finely chopped

4 sprigs parsley, finely chopped

1 tablespoon granulated sugar

TO MAKE SAUCE

Combine all ingredients in bowl, chill,
and serve.

Chocolate Glazed Meringues with Raspberries and Cream

SERVINGS: 8

The marriage of raspberries and chocolate is always a success, and when served in these meringues the result is heavenly. The meringues are made the way they do at the Cordon Bleu in London and are light and crisp.

parchment paper for baking

4 egg whites

1 cup granulated sugar, divided

vegetable cooking spray

6 ounces semi-sweet chocolate, cut in small pieces, or good quality chocolate chips

3 tablespoons water

1½ cups heavy (whipping) cream

1 teaspoon vanilla

1½ cups raspberries (if frozen, thaw)

confectioners' sugar

1. Preheat oven to 250 degrees. Cut parchment paper to fit 2 large cookie sheets and draw 8 rounds on sheets of paper, about 5½ inches in diameter. (Do not cut out rounds.)

2. Beat egg whites until stiff, add 4 teaspoons sugar, and continue beating for ½ minute. Fold (do not beat) in the remaining sugar with whisk.

3. Place parchment paper on cookie sheets, upside down so pencil marks will not come off on meringues. Lightly spray with vegetable cooking spray. Spoon the meringue evenly onto the rounds and bake for 50 minutes or until lightly colored. Remove from oven and immediately remove meringues with large spatula and place them on wire racks to cool. (If a meringue cracks, it can still be used, as the whipped cream will keep it together.) Meringues now may be kept at room temperature for a couple days, or covered and frozen for a week.

4. A few hours before serving: melt chocolate pieces with water in top of double boiler over simmering heat, or in microwave oven on high for about 2 minutes, checking every 30 seconds, until chocolate is almost melted. Remove from heat and stir until smooth. Spread chocolate over the meringue disks and let cool.

5. Before serving, whip the cream and whisk in vanilla. Layer the whipped cream over cooled chocolate on meringues. Place well-drained raspberries on whipped cream and dust with confectioners' sugar, using a sieve.

PORT TOWNSEND AND DISCOVERY BAY

When Captain Vancouver explored Washington's coast in 1792, he named many of the inlets, bays, islands, and harbors that caught his eye. On the northern coast, he christened a large harbor after his friend, the Marquis of Townshend. A century later, a thriving seaport hugged the harbor, keeping the name Port Townsend, although the spelling was modified somewhere along the way. By the 1890s, this bustling, lively town was a port to ships from all over the world. At the docks, the streets were boisterous and wild, while up on the bluff, respectable women shopped, had tea parties, and anxiously paced widow's walks. Port Townsend had bright potential to become Puget Sound's commerce and trade center, but the failure of a proposed hook-up with the Union Pacific transcontinental railroad dashed the prospects.

Today, the city retains the look and feel of a small Victorian seaport. Bed and breakfasts in Victorian homes and inviting shops lure many visitors. Others are attracted to the cultural life in Port Townsend, the site of the Summer School of the Arts, the Summer Arts Festival, and the Pacific Northwest Music Festival.

Discovery Bay, named after Captain Vancouver's ship *Discovery,* lies southwest of Port Townsend. Its beaches abound in **oysters, crabs, shrimp,** and **clams.** One important clam found here is the **geoduck,** a large grotesque specimen that makes surprisingly fine eating. The bay also offers good **salmon** and **bottom fish.** Aqua farms for both **shell** and **fin fish** are located near Port Townsend, while inland are a large **herb farm** and a few **dairy** producers.

14

Seafood Lasagna

SERVINGS: 4-6

Fresh seafood is layered with pasta and sauces in this scrumptious lasagna. Serve with a green salad, Italian bread, and fresh fruit or Càffe Latté Frozen Mousse (page 137) for dessert.

2 tablespoons olive oil

1 cup chopped onion

2 cloves garlic, minced

1 (14½-ounce) can chopped tomatoes, with juice

¼ cup tomato paste

2 bay leaves, divided

⅛ teaspoon dried thyme

1 tablespoon minced parsley

1 teaspoon salt, divided

freshly ground pepper, to taste

lasagna (8 ounces, or about 8 large 2-inch wide strips)

2½ cups milk

⅛ teaspoon mace

6 peppercorns

slice of onion

3 tablespoons butter or margarine

4 tablespoons all-purpose flour

½ pound Dungeness crab meat, drained

½ pound small cooked shrimp, drained

8 large scallops, sliced in about ¾-inch rounds, drained (or 16 small scallops)

2 cups sliced mushrooms

⅓ cup Parmesan cheese, freshly grated

1½ cups mozzarella cheese, grated

1. Make tomato sauce by heating olive oil in a large saucepan over medium heat, add onions, and cook until soft. Add garlic, cook lightly, add tomatoes with juice, tomato paste, and 1 bay leaf, thyme, parsley, ½ teaspoon salt, and pepper to taste. Partly cover and simmer gently for 20 minutes.

2. Cook pasta in salted boiling water according to directions on package. Place under cool running water. Drain and lay pieces on clean towel to dry.

3. Make white sauce (Béchamel) by heating milk over low heat for about 10 minutes with 1 bay leaf, mace, peppercorns, and onion slice. In another saucepan, melt butter over low heat, add flour and cook, stirring constantly for about 3 minutes. Take butter mixture off heat, add heated milk through a sieve to catch peppercorns, onion, and bay leaf. Return to medium heat and stir constantly until slightly thickened. Add reserved ½ teaspoon salt or to taste. Cover sauce with buttered waxed paper to prevent a skin forming, and set aside.

4. Preheat oven to 375 degrees. Lightly butter 8x8 or 9x9-inch square baking dish. (Before mixing seafood with tomato sauce, be certain that all seafood is dry. If not, dry completely with paper towel.) Mix the crab, shrimp, and uncooked scallops and mushrooms with tomato sauce.

5. Spread about 1 tablespoon white sauce on bottom of pan. Layer ½ lasagna in bottom, cutting off ends that do not fit. Spoon ½ of the tomato sauce on pasta, cover with about ½ of white sauce and sprinkle with all the grated Parmesan cheese.* Repeat layers. Sprinkle top with grated Mozzarella cheese. Bake, uncovered, in 375 degree oven for 30-35 minutes. Remove from oven, cover with loosely vented foil, and let stand for 10-12 minutes. Serve.

Alternate method: sprinkle first layer with ½ of the Parmesan cheese and reserve the rest to sprinkle over Mozzarella cheese on top layer.

Sautéed Geoduck with Toasted Almonds and Homemade Tartar Sauce

SERVINGS: 2; MORE IF SERVED AS APPETIZERS

Geoduck, pronounced "Gooey duck," is an adaptation of the original Native American name for the clam "Gweduc." Geoducks are huge clams, averaging 3 pounds each, with a body too large for its shell so its long neck protrudes out, making it a strange-looking creature. When cooked briefly, Geoduck clam slices are tender and delicious. Dig for Geoducks along beaches, or look for them at local seafood markets. Fish-mongers at the Pike Street Market delight in selling these clams and staging a show for onlookers. A huge geoduck is wrapped and bound securely, then tossed into the crowd by the seller who shouts, "Here's one duck for the lady in blue."

Geoduck siphon (neck), about ½ pound

boiling water

⅓ cup all-purpose flour seasoned with ½ teaspoon salt and freshly ground pepper

2 tablespoons butter or margarine

1 tablespoon vegetable oil

⅓ cup sliced almonds, toasted

lemon wedges

1. Make tartar sauce and refrigerate until serving.

2. Pour boiling water over Geoduck neck to loosen skin. Peel off skin and slice Geoduck into ⅛-inch slices. Set aside. Coat Geoduck slices lightly with seasoned flour.

3. Melt butter and oil in large skillet over medium heat and sauté slices for 1-2 minutes on first side. Turn and add toasted almonds and cook for 1-2 minutes. Remove clam slices and nuts from pan and place on serving dish. Taste and add more salt and pepper if needed. Serve with lemon wedges and tartar sauce.

TARTAR SAUCE

1 cup mayonnaise, regular or light

2 tablespoons minced shallots

2 tablespoons minced dill pickle

2 tablespoons pickle juice

1 tablespoon minced parsley

1 tablespoon capers

TO MAKE SAUCE

To mayonnaise, add shallots, pickle, juice, parsley, capers, and combine in bowl. Refrigerate.

SPECIAL COLLECTIONS, UNIV. OF WASHINGTON LIBRARIES, NEG. #5784

Herb Roasted Chicken and Vegetables

SERVINGS: 4

There are many herb farms throughout the state, including one near Port Townsend. If fresh herbs are unavailable, use dried ones. In this recipe, the vegetables have a roasted and herbal flavor, complementing the chicken.

1 (3 to 3½ pound) whole chicken, without giblets or neck

½ lemon

salt and freshly ground pepper

2 medium onions, peeled and cut in quarters

1 bay leaf

sprig of parsley

1½ tablespoons olive oil, divided

1 tablespoon finely chopped fresh rosemary or 1 teaspoon dry rosemary, divided

2 teaspoons finely chopped fresh basil or ¾ teaspoon dry basil, divided

2 teaspoons finely chopped fresh thyme or ½ teaspoon dry thyme, divided

4 medium carrots, peeled, cut in 1-inch chunks

3 celery ribs, cut in 1-inch chunks

4 medium red potatoes, quartered (or 8 small whole ones)

1 green pepper, seeded and cut in eighths

1 red pepper, seeded and cut in eighths

1 sweet potato, peeled and cut in 1-inch chunks

8 cherry tomatoes, stemmed

1. Preheat oven to 350 degrees. Trim chicken of excess fat and pat dry. Rub inside of chicken with lemon half, sprinkle with salt and pepper, and place one quartered onion, bay leaf, and parsley in cavity. Brush outside with about ¼ tablespoon olive oil, reserving the rest. Sprinkle chicken with about ¼ of each herb, reserving the rest.

2. Place chicken in large baking pan, about 16x14.

3. Brush prepared vegetables with reserved olive oil (about 1¼ tablespoons). Add vegetables (except cherry tomatoes) around chicken, sprinkle with remaining herbs, and season with salt and pepper. Place in oven and roast about 1 hour, turning vegetables over once. Add cherry tomatoes and bake 15 minutes longer. Chicken should register 180-185 degrees near thigh bone when done. Serve chicken on large platter surrounded with vegetables.

HOODSPORT

Hoodsport, a small community, took its name from Hood Canal, the 80-mile long tidal channel on which it lies. Captain Vancouver decided to name this body of water in honor of the Honorable Lord Samuel Hood, a British admiral. Hood's friendship with Vancouver is not his claim to fame, however. During the Revolutionary War, Hood won many victories at sea, but failed to carry out a plan to pick up General Cornwallis's troops at Yorktown, leaving the general to surrender to colonial troops in that decisive battle. As a result, Hood has been called, "The Englishman who won the war for the colonies."

The protected waters of Hood Canal at the town's doorstep provide good fishing, swimming, sailing, and scuba diving. Seafood found in the canal includes **clams, crabs, oysters,** and for a few weeks, the delicious Alaskan **spot shrimp.** These shrimp, with average lengths of three to six inches, are sweet and meaty.

19

Hood Canal Spot Shrimp in Lemon Butter Sauce

SERVINGS: 4

These are impressive served as appetizers and also delicious
as a main course over rice.

1½ to 2 pounds spot shrimp
(large shrimp)

4 tablespoons butter or margarine

1 teaspoon salt

5 cloves garlic, minced

⅛ teaspoon dried thyme

2 tablespoons minced parsley,
divided

1½ tablespoons lemon juice

1 teaspoon grated
lemon zest (peel)

Cooked rice, optional
(about 2 cups)

1. Clean and shell shrimp, leaving tails on. (Spot shrimp do not need deveining.) Pat completely dry. Refrigerate if done ahead and pat dry again.

2. Before cooking, preheat oven to 400 degrees. In small saucepan, melt butter and add salt, garlic, thyme, and 1 tablespoon parsley. Pour butter mixture into large baking dish and top with shrimp.

3. Place dish in oven and bake for 5 minutes. Remove from oven, turn shrimp over, pour lemon juice over, and sprinkle grated lemon zest on top of shrimp. Return to oven and bake 7 more minutes.

4. Remove from oven, place on serving dish, and spoon butter sauce over shrimp so they are covered. Sprinkle remaining parsley on top. May be served on cooked rice.

Pacific Clam Chowder

SERVINGS: 6

Fresh chowder is one of the best ways to enjoy clams!

4 dozen clams, well scrubbed (use butter, littleneck, or Manila clams—often referred to as "steamer" clams)

2⅔ cups clam juice, or 2 (9.6-ounce) cans

3 pieces sliced bacon, cut in ¼-inch pieces

1 cup finely chopped onion

½ cup finely chopped celery

¼ cup all-purpose flour

1 bay leaf

1 teaspoon dried thyme

3 cups red potatoes, cleaned, unpeeled, and cut in small cubes

2 cups milk

1½ cups heavy or light cream (for light cream, see page 322)

salt and pepper to taste

chopped chives for garnish, optional

1. Place well-scrubbed clams in large, heavy-bottomed saucepan with clam juice. Bring to simmer over medium heat. Cover and simmer for 5-8 minutes or until clams open. Remove from heat, discarding any clams that do not open. Cool slightly and remove clams from shells, chop the meat, and set aside. Strain clam juice through sieve or 2 thicknesses of cheese cloth and reserve in bowl.

2. Return heavy saucepan to heat, add bacon, and cook over medium heat until crisp. Remove bacon pieces and set on paper towel. To bacon fat in saucepan add chopped onion and celery and cook until tender. Add flour and cook for 3 minutes over medium low heat, stirring frequently. Add strained clam juice, bay leaf, thyme, potatoes, milk, and cream, and stir together. Raise heat to bring to boil, stirring frequently. Reduce heat, cover, and simmer until potatoes are tender, about 10 minutes.

3. Add reserved bacon, chopped clams, and salt and pepper to taste. Serve with chopped chives on top, if desired.

SHELTON

The Christmas tree industry is so big in Shelton the town has been nicknamed "Christmas Town, USA." During the height of the season, Shelton sponsors an annual Christmas parade and a two-day holiday bazaar.

Oysters provide an equally important industry, and are the reason for another festival. Both the Pacific and the indigenous Olympic oyster thrive near Shelton. Aqua farming augments the natural fund of oysters to provide a rich harvest, celebrated by the Oyster Fest and Seafood Festival. Every fall, large crowds gather in Shelton for this seafood extravaganza that includes the West Coast oyster shucking contest. Contestants pry open shells as fast as most people open a sealed envelope. Onlookers marvel at their speed and wish a contestant would come around when they shuck their oysters.

Oyster Bisque

SERVINGS: 4 AS MAIN COURSE; 6 AS FIRST COURSE

This bisque makes a wonderful prelude to a special dinner or may be served as the main course for a light meal.

12 fresh oysters, scrubbed and shucked with liquid, or 10-ounce jar oysters with liquid

1½ tablespoons butter or margarine

4 shallots, peeled and sliced

1½ cups milk

1½ cups half-and-half

½ teaspoon salt

¼ teaspoon white pepper

1-2 tablespoons dry sherry (optional)

chopped chives for garnish

1. Place shucked oysters and liquid in a large saucepan. Bring to boil and cook for 2-3 minutes or until the oysters' edges curl. Place oysters and liquid in food processor with steel blade inserted, or blender, and blend until smooth.

2. Melt butter in large saucepan over medium heat, add shallots, and sauté until soft and transparent. Add milk, half-and-half, and oyster mixture, and heat gently. (Do not boil.) Season with salt and pepper. Add optional sherry just before serving. Garnish with chopped chives.

ABERDEEN AND HOQUIAM

Aberdeen means, "the meeting of two rivers" in Gaelic. In Aberdeen, Washington, the two rivers that join are the Wiskah and the Chehalis. Both these rivers flow into Grays Harbor at Aberdeen, and a nice view of the port can be seen from atop a hill near St. Joseph's Hospital.

Streets lead directly from Aberdeen to Hoquiam, merging the two cities into a single community where lumbering is the economic mainstay. Wood has always been an important part of this community's history—even the Indian word "Hoquim" refers to the driftwood at the mouth of the nearby river.

The American Captain Robert Gray explored Grays Harbor in 1792. Today from this port, the *Lady Washington,* a replica of Captain Gray's flagstaff schooner, offers cruises out to the ocean and up and down the coast.

Up until a few years ago, many commercial fishermen used Aberdeen and Hoquiam as their home ports. Now, most boats are kept at nearby Westport during the fishing season. Today, trucks carry fish from the Pacific into Aberdeen and Hoquiam.

Wild blackberries flourish in the wooded areas near these communities. The **Himalayas** are profuse, and the smaller native **Pacifics** are treasures available to those who can find them. These native berries have a unique sweet-tart taste and are worthy of the search. Pacific blackberry hunters are as secretive and cunning as mushroom hunters, so don't expect a guided tour from the locals.

Blackberry Tart

SERVINGS: 6-8

Blackberries top a pecan filling in this tasty tart.

CRUST

1⅓ **cups all-purpose flour**

¼ **cup granulated sugar**

½ **cup butter or margarine, chilled and cut in small cubes**

1 **egg yolk**

FILLING

½ **cup butter or margarine**

2 **eggs**

¾ **cup granulated sugar**

¼ **cup all-purpose flour**

¼ **cup finely ground pecans**

1 **teaspoon vanilla**

3 **cups fresh blackberries (or frozen and thawed)**

½ **cup red currant jelly**

whipping cream for garnish

1. To make crust: combine crust ingredients in a food processor with steel blade inserted, or with a pastry blender in bowl until just crumbly. With hands, press into ball then press dough evenly into an ungreased 9-inch tart pan with a removable bottom. Refrigerate for about 30 minutes. Preheat oven to 350 degrees.

2. To make filling: melt butter in a small saucepan over medium heat, take off heat, and reserve. Blend eggs and sugar in a bowl and add flour, pecans, and vanilla and combine. Stir in reserved melted butter until just combined. Pour filling into unbaked pastry shell. Bake in oven for 30 minutes. Place on rack to cool.

3. Place blackberries (completely drained and dry) on cooled filling. Over low heat in a small saucepan, melt currant jelly. Brush jelly over berries and let tart stand until jelly is set. Remove sides of tart pan. Whip cream and place a dollop of whipped cream on each serving.

Eldean's Pacific Blackberry Pie

SERVINGS: 6

I fondly remember visiting Jack and Eldean Adams in Aberdeen during blackberry season. Jack would rise early and before going to the office, sneak off to his secret spot to gather wild Pacific blackberries, leaving them for Eldean to make a pie. Eldean's blackberry pie was something Jack treasured more than pure gold. The pie had a tender crust and a filling of only sweetened berries. The result was a fluid filling*—messy, but delicious! Faces stained with purple easily identified who "got into the pie."

4 cups wild Pacific blackberries, looked over and cleaned using very little water

1½ to 2 cups granulated sugar

pastry for 2-crust pie (recipe page 311)

1. Preheat oven to 400 degrees. Roll out half of pastry and place in 9-inch pie pan. Combine berries and sugar in bowl, gently mixing together and place in pastry-lined pie pan.

2. Roll out pastry for top, place on pie. Seal and crimp edges, and cut decorative slits in top to vent. Place directly on pie sheet (as described in glossary), or with cookie sheet on the rack under pie, and bake for 45-50 minutes or until golden brown.

*Eldean's daughter, Sydney, often added 2-3 tablespoons flour to pie mixture for a thicker filling.

OCEAN SHORES, COPALIS BEACH, AND PACIFIC BEACH

Brisk winds carrying the smell of the ocean and waves splashing on the sand bring a lyrical tranquillity to the 25 miles of Pacific beaches extending north of Grays Harbor. Resort communities dot the coastline. The largest, Ocean Shores, began in the 1950s and boasts a golf course as well as a variety of hotels and condominiums. Copalis Beach is the oldest of the resort towns. Here, cottages and motels are available for visitors who wish to walk the beaches or dig for clams. Pacific Beach has the most scenic setting, tucked in at the stern of a deep cove, where the sand is upstaged by some dramatic rocks.

These beaches are home to the famous **razor clams**, the tasty mollusk with a sporting chance against eager shovel diggers. These creatures can dig as fast as 9 inches per minute to a depth of 3 feet. The chase is fun, and with experience and endurance avid clam diggers enjoy catching these speeding bi-valves.

Sautéed Razor Clams with Cilantro Cocktail Sauce

SERVINGS: 4

Many proclaim these to be the best eating clams in the world! Like other mollusks, razor clams should be cooked briefly.

12-16 razor clams

½ cup all-purpose flour

½ teaspoon salt

⅛ teaspoon freshly ground pepper

2 tablespoons butter or margarine

3 tablespoons vegetable oil

1. Make cocktail sauce first and refrigerate.

2. Prepare clams.*

3. Combine flour, salt, and pepper. Dust clams with seasoned flour and set aside.

4. Heat butter and oil in a large skillet over medium heat. Increase heat to high, add clams and sauté briefly—about 1-2 minutes on each side. Serve with sauce.

TO MAKE SAUCE

Combine all ingredients in bowl, cover and chill.

CILANTRO COCKTAIL SAUCE

1 cup ketchup

2 tablespoons fresh lime juice

1½ tablespoons prepared horseradish

2 tablespoons minced cilantro

*TO PREPARE CLAMS:
Gently pull the clam from the shell, cutting the muscles if necessary. With scissors, cut away all dark areas, including tip of neck and stomach. Cut neck (digger) in half so clam will lie flat. Rinse thoroughly under running tap water to remove all sand. Place on paper towel to dry.

QUINAULT

Quinault, a tiny Indian village, lies deep in the rain forest where the woods, dense with lush green vegetation, are dominated by giant trees rising from a blanket of mosses and ferns. Douglas firs, supported by massive eight-foot trunks, soar to heights of 200 to 300 feet. Visitors who venture into the forests past snow banks, waterfalls, and towering firs, cedars, spruce, and hemlocks enter a natural enchanted shrine. Nearby Lake Quinault offers canoers a tranquil setting and a reminder of the time when only the Native American saw this splendor. The lake offers good **trout** and **steelhead** fishing, and wild **blackberries** are common in the forests.

Blackberry Sorbet

SERVINGS: 4

This tastes like fresh-picked berries from the vine.

4½ cups blackberries, fresh or frozen and thawed

water

¾ cup granulated sugar

1 teaspoon fresh lemon juice

1. In a food processor or blender, puree berries. Strain mixture by stirring and pressing puree through strainer into a bowl to remove seeds. Place 2 tablespoons of puree with enough water to make ⅓ cup juice.

2. In a medium saucepan, combine sugar, ⅓ cup fruit juice, and lemon juice, and cook over medium heat until sugar is dissolved, stirring constantly. Add rest of fruit puree and stir to combine. Take off heat and cool. Chill in refrigerator.

3. Freeze chilled mixture in ice cream maker, following manufacturer's directions. If you do not have an ice cream maker, pour mixture into shallow pan and place in freezer, stirring every 20 minutes for 1 hour and 20 minutes or until sorbet is creamy and starting to harden. Cover and freeze 3 hours or overnight.

FORKS

Misty rain and scented forests bring an earthy fragrance to the air in Forks. This community, the center of the logging business in the Olympic Peninsula, takes pride in its long history with the industry, which is reflected in the town's Timber Museum. Fourth of July is celebrated here with a boisterous three-day festival including fireworks, timber-related contests, and a parade with bands, floats, and logging trucks displaying Douglas fir logs the size of railroad cars.

Mushroom hunting is superb in the forests near Forks from the common **chanterelle** to the more exotic **xerocomus**. The nearby Bogochiel River is legendary for good **steelhead** fishing, and professional guides are available for winter steelhead runs. Many wild **blackberries** are found in and near Forks.

Broiled Steelhead Filets with Sesame Seed Butter

SERVINGS: 6

Steelhead are sea trout, born in the river, traveling to the sea for adolescence, and returning to the river to spawn. If steelhead is unavailable, use salmon in this recipe.

Steelhead filet, about 2-3 pounds

¼ cup butter or margarine

juice of one lemon

juice of one orange

1 tablespoon soy sauce

2 tablespoons sesame seeds

salt and freshly ground pepper

lemon wedges

1. After removing bones, place filet on broiler pan.

2. Preheat broiler. Melt butter in saucepan, add lemon and orange juice, then add soy sauce and heat for 5 minutes. Pour ½ mixture over filet, flesh side up, and sprinkle with sesame seeds and salt and pepper.

3. Broil, basting with remaining butter mixture. Broil until fish is opaque throughout, about 7-10 minutes. Serve with lemon wedges.

Chanterelles in Puff Pastry Shells

SERVINGS: 6 SHELLS

These pastry shells with wild mushroom filling take the spotlight for an elegant lunch, or support any meat or poultry dish for dinner. Both the shells and sauce can be made ahead and reheated at serving time.

6 frozen puff pastry shells

½ pound chanterelles

1 tablespoon vegetable oil (optional)

½ teaspoon salt

6 tablespoons plus 2 teaspoons butter or margarine, divided

1½ cups chicken stock (recipe page 313) or broth

1 cup heavy or light cream (for light cream, see page 322)

6 tablespoons all-purpose flour

1 teaspoon dried thyme

¼ teaspoon black pepper, freshly ground

minced chives for garnish

*TO DRY SAUTÉ:
Slice chanterelles and place in skillet on high heat, with no oil. Sprinkle with salt to help bring out the juices. Stir constantly until mushrooms begin to give off liquid. Cook them in their own juices until moisture evaporates.

1. Preheat oven to 400 degrees. Defrost frozen puff pastry shells and bake according to directions on package. When puff pastry shells are baked, take from oven and remove tops with fork. (Shells may be baked, then reheated.)

2. Meanwhile, clean chanterelles by brushing with dry mushroom brush (or tooth brush) or with dry paper towel. If necessary, rinse quickly under running water, but do not soak in water. (The following method of dry sautéing works well with fresh-picked wild mushrooms, bringing out the flavor and eliminating any rubbery texture. If store-bought or drier mushrooms are used, place the optional 1 tablespoon oil in skillet before starting to sauté mushrooms.) Dry sauté.* Turn down heat, add 2 teaspoons butter, and continue cooking over low heat until tender. Remove from heat and set aside.

3. Make sauce by combining chicken stock and cream in a small saucepan and heating slowly over low heat. Melt 6 tablespoons reserved butter in a separate saucepan over medium heat, add flour and stir until well combined, about 3 minutes. Take off heat, add warmed stock and cream, and stir with whisk until smooth. Place pan back on burner over medium high heat, stirring until thickened. Add thyme, pepper, and cooked chanterelles to sauce. (If sauce thickens too much, add more stock.)

4. Evenly divide sauce into the 6 shells and sprinkle with minced chives. Add shell tops if desired. Serves 6 with one shell each, or 3 people with 2 shells each.

Wild Blackberry Mousse

SERVINGS: 6

Serve in glass goblets rimmed with fresh blackberries.

5 cups fresh blackberries, or frozen and thawed

½ cup plus 2 tablespoons granulated sugar, divided

1 packet unflavored gelatin (about 2 teaspoons)

2 tablespoons water

1 cup heavy (whipping) cream

1 teaspoon vanilla

blackberries for garnish, optional

1. Cook berries and ½ cup sugar in saucepan over medium heat, stirring frequently. Cook for 15 minutes or until mixture is juicy. Place in food processor or blender and puree. Strain into bowl to remove seeds, stirring and pushing down on mixture in strainer.

2. Sprinkle gelatin over 2 tablespoons water in small saucepan and let stand off heat until softened, about 5 minutes. Place over low heat and stir mixture until melted.

3. Incorporate gelatin mixture into warm blackberry puree. (If puree has cooled considerably, warm slightly.) Refrigerate until cold, but not set, stirring occasionally, about 30-45 minutes.

4. Whip cream until soft peaks form, add reserved 2 tablespoons sugar and vanilla, and beat a few seconds until just incorporated. Fold whipped cream into berry mixture and spoon mousse into 6 stemmed goblets or dessert dishes. Cover with plastic wrap and chill 2 hours or overnight. Garnish with berries, if desired.

SOUTHWEST WASHINGTON

Crimson cranberry bogs ripple with the ocean breezes. Unpolluted bays hold oysters, and clams hide in beaches of sand and rock. Salmon glide through rough ocean waters. Inland, orchards yield fruits and nuts, and treasured huckleberries grow on mountain slopes. Open spaces offer land for chicken and dairy farms.

Yelm
Centralia
Chehalis
Kelso
Longview
Woodland
Vancouver
Camas
Washougal
Cathlamet
Skamokawa
Ilwaco
Long Beach
Seaview
Oysterville
Nahcotta
Ocean Park
South Bend
Raymond
Tokeland
Grayland
Westport

YELM

Yelm is a small rural community nestled near the Nisqually River. Native Americans originally called it Chelm, meaning "heat waves rising from the earth." They believed the Great Spirit sent these waves to make the earth bountiful and productive. Today, hens on farms near Yelm, along with those near Seattle and Rochester, are the largest producers of **eggs** in the state. There are about five million laying hens in the state of Washington, and each hen lays approximately 240 eggs annually; this adds up to over a billion eggs a year. Could the heat waves help?

Brunch Hot Deviled Eggs

SERVINGS: 6

These can be made the day ahead, then assembled and heated in the morning for a welcome addition to any brunch.

12 large eggs, hard-cooked*

3½ cups milk

⅓ cup butter or margarine

½ cup all-purpose flour

salt and white pepper to taste

¼ cup freshly grated Parmesan cheese

¼ cup grated Swiss or Gruyere cheese

1 teaspoon Dijon or Dijon-style mustard

additional freshly grated Parmesan cheese

1. Shell cooled hard-cooked eggs and cut in half lengthwise. Remove egg yolks, mash, and set aside.

2. Heat milk in a small saucepan over low heat. Make sauce by melting butter in separate medium saucepan over low heat, adding flour and blending together for 3 minutes. Take off heat, add heated milk all at once, return to heat, and stir until thickened and smooth, about 5 minutes. Add salt and pepper to taste. Take out ½ cup, cool, and set aside.

3. To the remaining sauce, add the cheeses and blend and cook over low heat until smooth. Combine the reserved ½ cup sauce with mashed egg yolks and Dijon mustard, and stuff egg whites.

4. Place eggs, stuffed side up, into a medium, broiler-safe buttered casserole or individual broiler-safe au gratin dishes. (Dish may be covered and refrigerated at this point, then the eggs brought to room temperature, the sauce heated, and poured over eggs.) Cover eggs with cheese sauce and sprinkle with additional grated Parmesan cheese. Brown under broiler, watching carefully. Serve hot.

*TO HARD-COOK EGGS:

Place eggs in single layer in a large saucepan. Add enough tap water to come at least 1 inch above eggs. Cover and quickly bring just to boiling. Turn off heat. If necessary, remove pan from burner to prevent further boiling. Let eggs stand, covered, in the hot water 15–17 minutes for large eggs.

Immediately run cold water over eggs or put them in ice water until completely cooled. To remove shell, crackle it by tapping gently all over. Roll egg between hands to loosen shell, then peel, starting at the large end. Hold egg under running cold water or dip in bowl of water to help ease off the shell.

CENTRALIA AND CHEHALIS

Set in the middle of the Cowlitz Plains in southwestern Washington are the twin towns of Centralia and Chehalis. Centralia, founded by a freed slave in 1852, was first called Centerville, and Chehalis was named Sandersville in 1858 when a post office opened. Some historic buildings in the area reflect the life of early residents; most notable is the Claquato Methodist Church, the oldest church still standing in Washington state. This small white wooden chapel still sits on its original site, where services were first held in 1858. Other historic structures in the area include the Borst Mansion (1857), the Olympic Club (1888), and historic Fort Borst.

South of these towns are the sporting pleasures of the Cowlitz River. Here Mayfield and Mossyrock dams form reservoirs with swimming beaches, boat launches, and surrounding picnic areas.

Many dairy farms grace the rolling Cowlitz Plains, providing **milk** for processing at the local Darigold plant, and the largest concentration of **chicken** growers in the state is located in surrounding Lewis County.

Hot Grilled Chicken Salad with Greens and Spicy Peanut Dressing

SERVINGS: 6

In this salad, greens are napped with a spicy dressing and topped with grilled chicken.

DRESSING

⅔ cup creamy peanut butter

2 cloves garlic, minced

4 tablespoons granulated sugar

½ cup soy sauce

½ cup rice vinegar

1 teaspoon ground ginger

½ teaspoon dry crushed
red pepper (more for very hot
dressing)

SALAD

Romaine lettuce, cleaned,
dried, and torn into pieces
(about 6-8 cups)

spinach, cleaned, dried, and
torn into pieces (about 6-8 cups)

3 scallions, sliced

½ red pepper, thinly sliced

12 pea pods, cut in julienne strips

1 cup red cabbage, thinly sliced

⅓ cup water chestnuts,
sliced and drained

olive oil

3 whole chicken breasts,
boned and skinned

salt and pepper to taste

cayenne pepper

½ cup dry roasted peanuts,
coarsely chopped

1. Make dressing first: combine all ingredients in a food processor or blender and blend until smooth. Set aside.

2. To make salad: combine torn lettuce and spinach leaves in a large bowl, add scallions, red pepper, pea pods, red cabbage, and water chestnuts. Set aside.

3. Prepare grill. (Either indoor stove-top grill or outdoor barbecue grill may be used.) Brush olive oil over chicken breasts and season with salt, pepper, and a light sprinkling of cayenne pepper. Cook chicken pieces over hot grill about 4-5 minutes on each side or until done. Slice cooked chicken in strips crosswise. Toss salad with dressing to coat, place on individual plates, and top with chicken slices and peanuts.

37

"Down Home" and "Downtown" Chicken Pot Pies
SERVINGS: 4-5 DOWNHOME PIES; 4 DOWNTOWN PIES

The "down home" pies are chock-full of chicken pieces and garden vegetables then topped with buttermilk biscuits, while the "down town" pies are brimming with chicken breast pieces, shiitake mushrooms, and julienne carrots with a covering of puff pastry rounds. Turkey may replace the chicken in these pies.

DOWN HOME CHICKEN POT PIES

4 tablespoons butter or margarine, divided

½ medium onion, diced

1 carrot, diced

1 rib celery, diced

1 cup fresh cooked or frozen peas

1 cup fresh cooked or frozen whole kernel corn

1½ cups boneless cooked chicken, cut up and without skin

1½ cups chicken stock (recipe page 313) or canned broth

½ cup milk

4 tablespoons all-purpose flour

freshly ground pepper to taste

1 chicken-flavored bouillon cube for salt seasoning

BISCUITS

1 cup all-purpose flour

¼ teaspoon salt

1 teaspoon baking powder

½ teaspoon sugar

¼ teaspoon baking soda

3 tablespoons butter or margarine

⅓ cup buttermilk

melted butter to brush on tops

4 or 5 individual deep dish casserole dishes

1. Preheat oven to 400 degrees. Melt 1 tablespoon butter in saucepan over medium heat, add diced onion, carrot, and celery, and sauté until tender, stirring frequently. Add peas, corn, and chicken pieces, and combine. Set aside off heat.

2. Heat chicken stock and milk in saucepan over medium heat, or in a microwave-safe container in microwave oven until warm. Melt reserved 3 tablespoons butter in saucepan over medium heat, add flour; cook about 3 minutes, stirring frequently. Take off heat, add warm stock/milk mixture all at once. Return to heat and stir constantly until thickened. Add pepper and bouillon cube to taste. Add cooked vegetable mixture and set aside while making biscuits.

3. To make biscuits, mix together flour, salt, baking powder, sugar, and baking soda in bowl. Cut in butter until mixture forms coarse meal. Stir in buttermilk. Roll out to ½-inch thickness and, with 2½ inch biscuit-cutter, cut into 4 or 5 biscuits.

4. To assemble: place sauce in 4 or 5 individual deep-dish casserole dishes. If sauce has cooled, reheat in saucepan before placing in casserole dishes. Put biscuits on top, brush with melted butter, and bake 15-20 minutes or until biscuits are brown.

DOWNTOWN CHICKEN POT PIES

1 unbaked frozen puff pastry sheet from 17½ ounce package, thawed according to manufacturer's directions

1 egg and 1 tablespoon water mixed together to make egg wash

4 tablespoons butter or margarine, divided

¼ pound fresh shiitake mushrooms, cleaned and coarsely chopped*

2½ cups chicken stock (recipe page 313) or canned broth

1 cup carrots, julienne

4 tablespoons all-purpose flour

1 (14 and ½ ounce) can pearl onions, drained

1½ to 2 cups cut up cooked chicken breasts^^

freshly ground pepper

salt, if needed

1 tablespoon port wine, optional

4 individual deep dish casserole dishes

Regular mushrooms may be used instead of shiitakes. When cleaning mushrooms, use mushroom brush, clean toothbrush or paper towels. Do not soak; water should be used sparingly.

**Boneless, skinless chicken breasts may be cooked quickly in a microwave oven for use in this recipe.*
Cover breasts with waxed paper and microwave on high for approximately 5 minutes, or until juices run clear. Let stand 5 minutes before cutting.

1. Preheat oven to 350 degrees. Cut puff pastry into four "rounds" to fit individual casserole dishes. Cut hole, the size of a dime, in the middle of each pastry piece. Brush pastry pieces with egg wash. Decorate with extra cut-out designs if desired, brushing with egg wash. Place "rounds" on cookie sheet and bake 15 minutes. Set aside while making filling.

2. Melt 1 tablespoon butter in a medium skillet, add chopped mushrooms, and sauté over medium heat until tender, stirring frequently. Set aside.

3. Bring chicken stock to boil in large saucepan, add carrots and cook (blanch) for 2 minutes or until tender. Remove pan from heat and with slotted spoon remove carrots and place on plate. Reserve broth.

4. In a separate large saucepan over medium heat, melt remaining 3 tablespoons butter, add flour and cook 3 minutes, stirring frequently. Take pan off heat, add reserved broth (which should still be warm; if not, reheat) all at once, return to heat and stir constantly until thickened. Add cooked mushrooms and carrots, drained onions and chicken. Grate fresh pepper over, taste to see if salt is needed. Add port, if desired.

5. Evenly pour warm sauce mixture into 4 casserole dishes. (If sauce has been left to cool, rewarm before placing in casserole dishes.) Top with baked puff pastry "rounds" and bake, uncovered, in 350 degree oven for 15 minutes.

Orange and Mocha Scented Frozen Chocolate Milk

SERVINGS: 4-6

Use 1 percent milk in this light and full-flavored dessert. This recipe is an adaptation of Frozen Hot Chocolate by Alice Medrich from her book Chocolate and the Art of Low-Fat Desserts.

¾ cup granulated sugar

½ cup unsweetened cocoa powder (preferably Dutch processed)

2¼ cups 1 percent milk, divided

3 tablespoons freshly brewed espresso (or 3 tablespoons boiling water with 1½ teaspoons instant espresso)

⅛ teaspoon ground cinnamon

1½ teaspoons grated orange zest (peel)

1. Place sugar and cocoa in medium saucepan and mix together, add 1 cup milk, stirring until smooth. Add remaining 1 cup milk (reserving ¼ cup), espresso, and cinnamon, and combine and heat mixture over low heat until sugar is dissolved, stirring frequently.

2. Pour mixture into ice cube tray or trays, with cube dividers inserted, and cover. Freeze eight hours or overnight.

3. Remove trays from freezer and empty cubes into food processor with steel blade inserted. Add remaining ¼ cup milk. (It will help to break up the cubes some with a fork before processing.) Process until smooth. Add grated orange zest and process quickly, just until incorporated. Serve immediately in individual serving dishes.

KELSO AND LONGVIEW

Where the Columbia takes a sharp bend toward the Pacific Ocean in southwest Washington it is joined by the Cowlitz River. Nearby, on the banks of the Cowlitz, a Scotsman, Peter Crawford, first envisioned a community. The vision became a reality about 1850 and Crawford named the town Kelso in honor of his birthplace in Scotland. Today, Kelso residents remember their Scottish heritage and celebrate with the Highlander Festival each September.

Years ago, a small town called Monticello stood on the banks of the Columbia across from Kelso, but the raging floods of 1866 and 1867 ruthlessly washed away its stores and houses. In the early 1900s, the Long-Bell Lumber Company needed a deep-water port on the Columbia, and built the city of Longview near the site of old Monticello. The company built Longview with a large dike to make certain this town would stay put. Lumbering remains Longview's main industry, and the Weyerhaeuser mill there is the largest lumber mill ever built.

In late February and early March, thousands of fishermen flock to the banks of the Cowlitz River around Kelso to capture **smelt**, usually scooping them up in hand-held nets. The large run of these small fish supports Kelso's claim that it is the "Smelt Capital of the World." Nearby, the Columbia River offers **salmon** and **sturgeon** fishing. **Steelhead** and **trout** abound in smaller rivers and creeks.

Individual Salmon Wellingtons with Dijon Cream Sauce

SERVINGS: 6

Duxelles (diced and sautéed mushrooms) top the salmon in these Wellingtons. However, a recipe for a cream cheese and dill filling is included for variety and ease of preparation.

Duxelles (recipe page 312)
or cream cheese filling
(recipe follows)

6 salmon filets,
about 5 ounces each

2 bay leaves

2 tablespoons pickling spice

2 tablespoons butter or margarine

1 cup dry white wine

1 tablespoon lemon juice

½ teaspoon salt

pepper

1 package (10-ounce)
frozen puff pastry shells

1 egg mixed with
one tablespoon water

DIJON CREAM SAUCE

1 cup crème fraîche or sour cream
(crème fraîche recipe, page 312)

1 tablespoon Dijon or
Dijon-style mustard

CREAM CHEESE FILLING
(for Salmon Wellingtons)

½ cup regular or
light cream cheese (4 ounces),
room temperature

2 garlic cloves, minced

2 tablespoons minced fresh dill
or ¾ teaspoon dried

1. Make cream cheese filling or duxelles (recipe page 312) and set aside.

2. To prepare salmon: take out as many bones as possible from filets. Combine bay leaves, pickling spice, butter, white wine, lemon juice, salt, and pepper in large saucepan or skillet and bring just to boil over medium high heat. Reduce heat. Liquid should be simmering. Add salmon filets. Cover pan and simmer over low heat for 8-10 minutes or until filets are opaque throughout.

3. Remove filets from poaching liquid, cool slightly, and remove skin and any remaining pickling spices from each piece; set aside.

4. Roll out thawed pastry shells on floured surface to approximately 8-inch circles. Spread 1 tablespoon duxelles (or cream cheese filling) on top of each salmon filet. Wrap pastry circles around each filet. Decorative pieces of extra puff pastry may be placed on smooth top surface of each piece, if desired. (If made ahead, wrap each piece in plastic wrap and refrigerate.)

5. When ready to bake, preheat oven to 425 degrees. Place pastry-wrapped filets on cookie sheet, brush with egg-water mixture. Place in oven for approximately 15 minutes or until pastry is nicely browned. Make Dijon Cream Sauce and keep warm. Serve pastry-wrapped filets with sauce.

TO MAKE SAUCE
Combine crème fraîche or sour cream and mustard in a small saucepan and heat over low heat until warm.

TO MAKE FILLING
Beat cream cheese in bowl, add garlic, dill, and combine.

Oven-fried Breaded Smelt

SERVINGS: 6

This is an easy way to cook lots of smelt at the same time.

3 pounds smelt

3 tablespoons lemon juice

1 teaspoon salt

¼ teaspoon freshly ground pepper

¾ cup all-purpose flour

2 eggs, beaten with 1 tablespoon water, placed in flat dish

1½ cups freshly ground bread crumbs, placed in flat dish or on waxed paper

½ cup melted butter or margarine, divided

lemons for garnish

1. Preheat oven to 450 degrees. Rinse smelt thoroughly. On cutting board, cut off heads. With knife slit underneath side, stopping before tail. Remove viscera; slide knife under center bone and remove backbone with knife, or by pulling it out. Fold closed. Pat smelt dry with paper towel. Sprinkle with lemon juice and let stand for ten minutes.

2. Combine salt and pepper with flour, and roll smelt in mixture. Dip the floured fish into egg mixture, then roll in bread crumbs.

3. Pour ¼ cup melted butter into a large baking dish. Place smelt in baking dish and drizzle remaining ¼ cup butter on top. Bake, uncovered, for about 5 minutes or until lightly brown. Place smelt on platter and serve with lemon wedges.

WOODLAND

Named for its wooded setting, Woodland is the center of a broad community of smaller towns that includes Kalama, La Center, Amboy, and Ridgefield. In the spring of 1922, people in and around Woodland feared a dike would fail to hold back the rising waters that could flood the area's rich bottom land. When the dike held and crops could be planted, jubilant townsfolk began a celebration they called Planter's Day. This yearly event, Washington state's oldest continuous festival, is still observed and features many events, including a famous frog jumping contest. Some farming continues in the area; now, local farmers plant mainly carrots, corn, and berries.

Cream of Carrot Soup with Marsala

SERVINGS: 6

Serve this soup either hot or chilled as a first course to a special dinner or for a light supper.

2 cups peeled, sliced carrots

1 cup diced onion

1 cup diced celery

3 tablespoons long-grain rice

4 cups chicken stock
(recipe page 313) or broth

¾ teaspoon salt, or to taste

freshly ground pepper

⅛ teaspoon Cayenne pepper

1⅓ cups heavy or light cream
(for light cream, see page 322)

½ cup Marsala

1. In a large saucepan, combine vegetables, rice, and broth, and bring to boil over high heat. Reduce heat to low, cover saucepan, and simmer gently for 20 minutes, or until vegetables and rice are tender.

2. Place cooked mixture in food processor or blender and puree. Return pureed mixture to a large saucepan, add salt and peppers. Heat over low heat and stir in cream. (Place in bowl to refrigerate if serving cold or if cooling and reheating later.)

3. Heat over medium heat, or leave chilled. Just before serving add Marsala.

Ginger Carrot Soup

SERVINGS: 4

Fresh ginger gives this simple soup a bold taste.

2 cups carrots, sliced about ½ -inch thick

1 rib celery, sliced about ½ -inch thick

¼ cup coarsely chopped onion

2½ cups chicken stock (recipe page 313) or canned chicken broth

1 tablespoon freshly grated ginger (less, if preferred)

freshly ground pepper

salt, if needed

Garnish with sprigs of cilantro or Italian parsley or slices of the green part of scallions (optional)

1. Place carrots, celery, onion, and stock in medium saucepan. Bring to boil over medium heat. Reduce heat to low and simmer, covered, for thirty minutes.

2. Place entire mixture in food processor with steel blade inserted, and puree. Add ginger, pepper, and salt, if needed. (The amount of salt needed depends on the salt content in the chicken stock or broth.) This is a thick soup. If you wish to thin the mixture, add more broth and combine. Serve warm with garnish, if desired.

VANCOUVER

Like its counterpart in British Columbia, the city of Vancouver honors adventurer and explorer George Vancouver, who sailed these waters in 1792. The Vancouver in Washington began as a Hudson's Bay trading post in 1825. Today, the Fort Vancouver National Historic Site recalls the times of these early trappers and traders. The original trading post has been recreated with a blacksmith shop, bakery, other shops, and a museum displaying items of the era. Nearby stand the Vancouver Barracks, a military post where General Ulysses S. Grant once served, and Officers' Row, a cluster of 21 Victorian houses built for officers between 1849 and 1906.

Surrounding Clark County has a long history of agriculture; farming and orchard planting began with the Hudson's Bay establishment of Fort Vancouver over 150 years ago. One of the original trees planted by the Hudson's Bay Company still stands today and is aptly called, "The Old Apple Tree." Many **fruits, berries, nuts,** and **vegetables** are still grown by local farmers. Some farms grow both **walnuts** and **hazelnuts (filberts.)** Clark County boasts about half the state's filbert trees, annually producing 23 percent of the nation's crop. No matter how you crack them, filberts and hazelnuts are the same nut. Natives of Vancouver usually call them filberts.

Mother's Spiced Walnuts
MAKES ABOUT 2 CUPS

I remember these as special after-school treats. Or use spiced nuts in salads.

⅓ **cup light corn syrup**

⅓ **cup butter or margarine**

2 **tablespoons water**

1 **teaspoon cinnamon**

½ **teaspoon nutmeg, preferably freshly ground**

½ **teaspoon ground cloves**

⅛ **teaspoon salt**

½ **pound large walnut pieces**

1. Preheat oven to 250 degrees. Combine first 7 ingredients in medium saucepan over medium heat and bring to boil. Take off heat, add walnuts, and stir to coat.

2. Place walnuts on cookie sheet and bake 1 hour.

Fettuccine with Hazelnut Sauce

SERVINGS: 6-8

Hazelnuts add flavor and crunch to this Alfredo sauce.

water

salt

1 garlic clove, minced

2 teaspoons fresh minced parsley

½ teaspoon dried basil, or
1½ teaspoon minced fresh

2 tablespoons vermouth
(or dry white wine)

2 cups heavy or light cream
(for light cream, see page 322)

1 cup chopped hazelnuts, toasted
and skinned (for toasting nuts,
see page 323)

¼ teaspoon salt

freshly ground pepper to taste

1 cup freshly grated
Parmesan cheese

1 pound fettuccine, fresh or dried

additional grated
Parmesan cheese

additional chopped parsley and
toasted hazelnuts for top
(optional)

1. To cook pasta, start heating water in a large stock pot with about a tablespoon of salt.

2. Combine garlic, parsley, basil, and vermouth in a medium saucepan over medium heat and cook for 2 minutes. Add cream and cook over medium high heat until slightly thickened and reduced. Add hazelnuts, salt, pepper, and ½ cup of Parmesan cheese, and whisk until cheese is melted; add remaining ½ cup cheese and stir until melted. Keep warm.

3. When water is boiling, cook fettuccine as directed on package; drain thoroughly. Toss the sauce lightly with fettuccine and serve immediately. Additional freshly grated Parmesan cheese, chopped parsley, and hazelnuts may be sprinkled on top.

Old Apple Tree Apple Butter

MAKES ABOUT 6 CUPS

This old-fashioned goodness is superb on toast, or add a splash of vinegar and use as a meat, poultry, or game accompaniment.

4 pounds tart apples, washed, stemmed, and cored

2 cups apple cider

brown sugar

3 teaspoons ground cinnamon

1 teaspoon ground cloves

1 teaspoon ground allspice

juice and grated zest (peel) of one lemon

1. Coarsely chop apples without peeling. Cook apples and cider, covered, in a large heavy bottomed pan over medium heat until apples are soft, about 30 minutes. Press mixture through a food mill, or puree in food processor. Measure sauce by cups.

2. Return mixture to pan and add ½ cup brown sugar for each cup of applesauce. Cook over low heat until sugar dissolves. Add spices, juice, and zest, and continue to simmer over low heat, stirring every 10-20 minutes, for about 1½ hours, or until mixture is reduced by half to a thick smooth butter.

3. Ladle hot mixture into hot sterilized canning jars and vacuum seal by processing in a water bath canner for 10 minutes. (Refer to page 324 for water bath procedure.) Or, cool mixture, ladle into jars, cover, and refrigerate up to 3 months.

Hazelnut Caramel Bars
MAKES ABOUT 20 BARS

These bars, chock full of toasted hazelnuts, are perfect to serve for dessert at casual buffet-style get togethers.

COOKIE BASE

1 cup all-purpose flour

3 tablespoons granulated sugar

⅓ cup butter or margarine, well chilled

1 egg yolk, beaten

FILLING

2 cups whole hazelnuts, toasted and skinned (for toasting nuts, see page 323)

¼ cup butter or margarine

⅔ cup packed light brown sugar

¼ cup light corn syrup

¼ cup heavy cream or light cream (for light cream, see page 322)

¼ teaspoon salt

1 teaspoon vanilla

1. To make base: preheat oven to 300 degrees. In food processor, or bowl, combine flour and sugar. Cut butter into small pieces and add to flour and sugar. Process (or combine with pastry blender) until fine crumbs form. Add egg yolk and blend briefly. Do not over-mix. Dough should just hold together when pressed. Press into bottom of 8-inch square pan. Bake until pale gold, about 25 minutes. Remove pan and turn oven to 375 degrees.

2. To make filling: place toasted hazelnuts on baked cookie base and spread evenly. Combine butter, brown sugar, corn syrup, and cream in a medium saucepan, and bring to boil, stirring constantly over medium heat. Boil one minute, add salt and vanilla, and pour over hazelnuts. Bake for ten minutes. Remove from oven and set pan on wire rack to cool. Cut into bars with small sharp knife.

50

Walnut Torte with Chocolate Glaze

SERVINGS: 10

This impressive nut torte with an apricot filling and chocolate glaze is made in minutes with a food processor.

2 cups walnuts

¾ cup butter or margarine, room temperature

1 egg, lightly beaten

¼ teaspoon salt

¾ cup granulated sugar

1 cup all-purpose flour

1 teaspoon cinnamon

¼ teaspoon baking powder

1 tablespoon grated orange zest (peel)

¾ cup apricot jam

walnut halves, for garnish

whipping cream, for garnish (optional)

1. Preheat oven to 375 degrees. Butter a 9-inch springform pan and dust with flour.

2. Finely grind walnuts in food processor and add all other ingredients except jam. Process for 1 minute or until well blended. Divide dough in half.

3. Press one-half of mixture into the bottom of springform pan, spreading dough to the sides of pan, with floured hands. Spoon jam evenly over dough, leaving a ½-inch border. Form another layer of dough by breaking and flattening remaining dough into small, flat pieces, using floured hands, and placing pieces in an even layer on top of the preserves. Bake in oven for 35 minutes.

4. Make chocolate glaze. Pour and spread on top of warm torte as soon as it comes out of oven. Place walnut halves around edge of glaze. Cool. (May need to be refrigerated for glaze to set.)

5. Remove springform ring when glaze is set. Serve with whipped cream, if desired.

CHOCOLATE GLAZE

6 ounces semi-sweet chocolate (cut in pieces or use high-quality chocolate chips)

1 tablespoon prepared coffee

3 tablespoons butter or margarine

TO MAKE GLAZE

Melt chocolate in top of double boiler over simmering water or in microwave oven, stirring every 30 seconds until melted. Whisk in coffee and butter.

CAMAS AND WASHOUGAL

The towns of Camas and Washougal are set along the spectacular Columbia River Gorge, where steep cliffs rise on either side of the powerful river. Strong winds funnel through this ravine, creating a draft over the Columbia, ideal for windsurfers. Recently, the gorge has become known as the "windsurf capital of the world," bringing surfers from all over to play and compete. Rafting, sailing, swimming, and fishing attract more outdoor lovers to the area. Nearby Beacon Rock, rising 850 feet above the Columbia, provides a panoramic view of the gorge, Mt. Hood in Oregon, and Mt. Adams in Washington.

Camas and Washougal are located in Clark County, a region that produces ten to fifteen million pounds of Italian Prune **Plums** yearly. **Hazelnut (filbert)** trees also fill many local orchards. Nearby rivers and lakes provide excellent fishing for **steelhead.** Also close by is the Gifford Pinchot National Forest, a mecca for **huckleberry** pickers.

Plum and Hazelnut Conserve

YIELDS ABOUT 10 ONE-HALF-PINT JARS

Serve this conserve as an accompaniment to poultry and wild game, or try it with cream cheese on a toasted English muffin.

2 pounds prune plums (about 2½ cups chopped)

1 orange, including rind, cut in quarters

2 cups water

½ cup raisins

½ cup coarsely chopped hazelnuts, toasted and skinned (for toasting nuts, see page 323)

½ teaspoon cinnamon

½ teaspoon allspice

¼ teaspoon cloves

6 cups granulated sugar

1 box (1¾ ounces) powdered pectin

about 10 one-half-pint jars, sterilized

1. Halve and pit ripe plums, chop fine, and set aside. In food processor with steel blade inserted, chop orange fine and place in saucepan with water; simmer, covered for 20 minutes. Combine undrained orange mixture with plums.

2. In large saucepan or stock pot, measure 4½ cups orange-plum mixture and add raisins, hazelnuts, and spices. Measure sugar and set aside. Add pectin to fruit in saucepan. Place over high heat and stir until mixture comes to a hard boil. (It cannot be stirred down.) Immediately add all sugar and stir in. Bring to full rolling boil and boil hard for one minute, stirring constantly.

3. Remove from heat. Skim off foam with metal spoon, stir and skim for 5 minutes. Ladle into sterilized jars and vacuum seal by processing in a water bath canner for 10 minutes. Refer to page 324 for water bath procedure.

Chocolate Hazelnut Decadence with Rum Cream

SERVINGS: 8

The Whipped Rum Cream is a nice contrast to this dense chocolate torte.

1 cup hazelnuts, toasted and skinned (for toasting nuts, see page 323)

6 ounces good quality semi-sweet chocolate (cut in chunks)

½ cup butter

1 teaspoon vanilla

3 eggs, lightly beaten

¾ cup granulated sugar

1. Preheat oven to 300 degrees. Take out 8 nuts (or one for each serving) for garnish. Finely chop the rest of nuts in a food processor or by hand.

2. Melt chocolate and butter over low heat in small saucepan (or in microwave oven). Remove from heat and add vanilla; cool.

3. In another bowl, whisk together eggs and sugar until blended, do not overbeat. Fold in cooled chocolate mixture along with ground hazelnuts. Pour into lightly greased and floured 9-inch springform pan.

4. Bake for 45 minutes. Cool. Refrigerate for at least 2 hours or longer. Make Whipped Rum Cream. Unmold cake from springform pan and slice. Serve with Whipped Rum Cream. Place reserved toasted hazelnut on top of each piece.

WHIPPED RUM CREAM

¾ cup heavy (whipping) cream

2 tablespoons corn syrup

3 tablespoons dark rum

TO MAKE WHIPPED RUM CREAM

Whip cream in a bowl until stiff. Stir in corn syrup and rum and whisk to rethicken.

Huckleberry Cream Tart

SERVINGS: 6-8

Wild huckleberries are full of flavor and combine well with cream cheese.

TART SHELL

⅓ **cup butter**

¼ **cup granulated sugar**

1 **egg yolk**

1 **cup all-purpose flour**

FILLING

3 **cups huckleberries
(fresh or frozen)**

1 **cup granulated sugar mixed
with ¼ cup all-purpose flour**

1 **tablespoon lemon juice**

1 **(3-ounce) package
cream cheese, regular or light**

½ **cup confectioners' sugar**

½ **teaspoon vanilla**

½ **cup heavy (whipping) cream**

1. Preheat oven to 375 degrees. Make tart shell by beating butter with ¼ cup sugar until light and fluffy. Add egg yolk and combine. Gradually beat in flour until just blended. Form dough into ball and press into bottom and sides of an ungreased 9-10 inch tart pan with removable bottom. Bake in oven for 10-12 minutes. Cool on rack.

2. Combine huckleberries, sugar-flour mixture, and lemon juice in a medium saucepan and cook over medium or medium-high heat just long enough to thicken, about 12-15 minutes, stirring frequently. (Turn down heat if mixture boils rapidly.) Berries should remain nearly whole. Let cool.

3. Beat the cream cheese, confectioners' sugar, and vanilla in a medium bowl until light. Whip the cream stiff in separate bowl and fold into cream cheese mixture. Spread evenly into baked tart shell and top with the cooled huckleberry mixture. Chill in refrigerator for 2 hours or longer before serving.

CATHLAMET AND SKAMOKAWA

Morning fog hugs the streams and the Columbia River in southwest Washington near Cathlamet and Skamokawa. Native Americans called this fog Skamokawa or "smoke over the river." The small town of Cathlamet is positioned high on a bluff above the Columbia, while the village of Skamokawa lies close to the river, with some of its buildings on pilings jutting out over the water. Near these towns, one can take a short ferry ride across the Columbia River and arrive in Oregon in minutes.

The banks of the Columbia River are ideal spots for fishermen to try their luck at catching **salmon** and **sturgeon**.

Sturgeon Filets with Cream and Capers
SERVINGS: 4

Firm, white-fleshed sturgeon is acclaimed by many to be one of the finest eating fish available.

1½ pounds sturgeon filet, cut in 4 serving pieces

about ⅓ cup all-purpose flour seasoned with ½ teaspoon salt and freshly ground pepper

1 tablespoon butter

1 tablespoon vegetable oil

½ cup sherry

½ cup heavy or light cream (for light cream, see page 322)

2 teaspoons capers

1. Dust fish pieces with seasoned flour. Heat butter and oil in a large skillet over medium high heat. Place filets in skillet and cook 4-6 minutes per side, depending on thickness.

2. When cooked (opaque throughout) take filets from skillet and keep warm on heated platter with foil tent. Pour off oil from pan and add sherry and cream. Cook sauce over medium heat until it is reduced by about one-third. Add capers. Place filets on plates and cover with sauce.

COWLITZ COUNTY HISTORICAL MUSEUM

COLUMBIA RIVER STURGEON AND ROYAL CHINOOK SALMON.

COURTESY IRENE MARTIN

ILWACO

Ilwaco is a fishing village, the home of many charter, sport, and commercial fishing boats that work the mouth of the Columbia River and the ocean. Here, where the Columbia meets the Pacific Ocean, scores of vessels were wrecked by treacherous waters, and the site was once called the "graveyard of ships." Now, river-mouth jetties help control the mighty Columbia and calm the waters for boats.

Many Chinook and Coho **salmon** swim the waters off the mouth of the Columbia. **Albacore tuna** migrate along the coast from July through October and are caught within a few miles of Ilwaco. **Sturgeon** and **bottom fish** are also available.

Autumn ushers in the Cranberry Harvest Festival held the third weekend of October in Ilwaco. This is the time of year when nearby cranberry bogs are flooded and harvested, providing **cranberries** for market and processing.

Smoked Salmon and Pesto Appetizer Cheesecake
SERVINGS: 16

Smoked salmon, pesto, and cream cheese are a triumphal trio anytime and make this appetizer cheesecake a winner.

2 teaspoons butter or margarine, room temperature

¼ cup fine dry breadcrumbs

½ cup plus 2 tablespoons grated Parmesan cheese, divided

2 (8-ounce) packages regular or light cream cheese, room temperature

1 cup ricotta cheese

2 tablespoons finely minced onion

¾ teaspoon salt

¼ teaspoon cayenne pepper

⅛ teaspoon white pepper

3 dashes Tabasco sauce

3 eggs

5 or 6 ounces smoked salmon, flaked and checked through to remove any bones

¾ cup basil pesto, recipe below or use commercial

¼ cup pine nuts

crackers

fresh basil leaves, optional

1. Preheat oven to 325 degrees. Rub butter or margarine over bottom and up 1 inch on sides of a 9-inch spring-form pan. Mix breadcrumbs with 2 tablespoons grated Parmesan cheese and coat buttered area of pan with crumb mixture.

2. Beat cream cheese, ricotta, remaining ½ cup Parmesan cheese, minced onion, salt, peppers, and Tabasco in large bowl until light. Add eggs, one at a time, beating after each addition. Gently stir in flaked salmon.

3. Spoon one-half of cheesecake mixture into prepared pan. Spoon pesto carefully over, leaving 1-inch edge. Spoon remaining salmon cheesecake mixture over and gently smooth top. Sprinkle with pine nuts.

4. Bake 40-45 minutes or until center is just firm. Place on rack and cool. Cover and refrigerate 4 hours or longer. Loosen cheesecake by running a small sharp knife around sides. Release sides of pan and place cheesecake on platter. Surround with crackers and garnish with fresh basil leaves.

PESTO SAUCE

3 cups fresh basil leaves

3 cloves peeled garlic

½ cup toasted pine nuts (see page 323 for toasting nuts)

½ cup freshly grated Parmesan cheese

¼ teaspoon each salt, pepper

6 tablespoons olive oil

TO MAKE PESTO SAUCE

Combine basil leaves, garlic, pine nuts, Parmesan cheese, salt, pepper, and olive oil in a food processor and puree all ingredients. Leftover pesto may be refrigerated up to 5 days and used on cooked pasta or as a seasoning on vegetables or fish.

Grilled Fresh Tuna Marinated with Soy and Orange

SERVINGS: 4

Grilled fresh tuna is a treat. I always look forward to the summer runs.

4 fresh albacore tuna steaks, about 1 inch thick

⅓ cup sesame or olive oil

2 tablespoons orange juice

1 tablespoon soy sauce

1 tablespoon diced onion

1 clove garlic, minced

1 tablespoon grated orange zest (peel)

freshly ground pepper

fresh orange wedges

1. Prepare grill or broiler, if necessary. (Stove-top grill, barbecue grill, or broiler may be used.) Rinse tuna steaks in cold water and pat dry. Combine oil, orange juice, soy sauce, diced onion, garlic, grated orange zest, and pepper in large dish. Marinate tuna in mixture for 15-20 minutes, turning once.

2. Remove tuna from marinade and place on heated grill, barbecue, or under broiler. Baste with marinade while cooking. Grill or broil about 5-6 minutes on each side, or until fish is opaque throughout.

3. When steaks are cooking make Orange Butter Sauce to drizzle over steaks or pass separately. Serve steaks with fresh orange wedges.

ORANGE BUTTER SAUCE

2 tablespoons butter or margarine

1 tablespoon orange juice

1 teaspoon chopped chives

TO MAKE ORANGE BUTTER SAUCE

Melt butter in small saucepan, add orange juice and chives, and combine.

Cranberry Pork Chops

SERVINGS: 6

Tart cranberries incorporated into a Dijon cream sauce add a taste dimension to the mild pork.

2 teaspoons oil

6 center-cut pork chops, 1 to 1½ -inches thick

½ teaspoon salt

pepper

½ cup orange juice, plus 1 tablespoon, divided

½ cup heavy or light cream (for light cream see page 322)

½ cup fresh cranberries (or frozen and thawed), chopped

¼ cup cognac or brandy*

2 teaspoons Dijon or Dijon-style mustard

1 tablespoon cornstarch

cranberries for garnish, about 30

*Chicken stock may be used instead of the cognac or brandy.

1. Heat oil in a large non-stick skillet over medium heat and brown chops on both sides. Season chops with salt and pepper. Add 1 tablespoon orange juice, cover pan, reduce heat, and cook for 20-25 minutes or until chops are done.

2. Transfer chops to a platter and keep warm in an oven heated to lowest temperature. Whisk together reserved ½ cup orange juice, cream, chopped cranberries, cognac or brandy, mustard, and cornstarch in a small bowl. Add to warm skillet and cook over medium heat until thickened, stirring frequently.

3. Remove chops from oven and pour sauce over, garnishing with fresh cranberries.

LONG BEACH AND SEAVIEW

The quiet of winter in the town of Long Beach gives way to crowds, excitement, and entertainment when the summer months arrive. The sand, sea, and sun bring many visitors, and two local festivals draw thousands. In July, a sand sculpturing contest attracts artists who sculpt castles and dramatic art forms on the beach with sand, water, and their own creative energy. Crowds come to watch the art in motion, taking photographs that give the only permanence to these creations. August brings more than 100,000 spectators to the Long Beach peninsula for the largest kite festival in North America. Kites of all colors and forms soar in the sharp ocean winds along the 28-mile-long beach.

The community of Seaview stands on the site where a summer hotel was built in 1871. The owner named the hotel Seaview, a name adopted by the town that later grew up around it. Though the hotel is gone, many houses dating back to the 1880s and the Shelburne Inn built in 1896 remain in this picturesque seaside community.

Four percent of the nation's **cranberries** come from bogs near Long Beach and Seaview. **Claming** and **fishing** are recreational pleasures all along the peninsula.

Long Beach Cranberry Chutney
YIELDS ABOUT 2 CUPS

Serve as an adjunct to turkey, chicken, pork, game, or even with hot dogs.

1 cup fresh cranberries
(or frozen, and partially thawed)

1 medium onion, quartered

1 medium green pepper,
quartered

1 medium tart apple,
cored, and quartered

½ cup granulated sugar

½ cup apple cider vinegar

¾ teaspoon salt

1. Put cranberries, onion, green pepper, and apple in food processor and chop coarsely. (If some large pieces remain, chop them by hand so as not to grind the mixture too finely.)

2. In a large saucepan, combine cranberry mixture with sugar, vinegar, and salt. Bring to boil, reduce heat, and simmer, covered, for 10 minutes. Cool and refrigerate. If keeping for more than 2-3 weeks, process for canning by ladling into hot, sterile canning jars and process in water bath canner for 10 minutes. Refer to page 324 for water bath procedure.

Brandied Cranberries
YIELDS ABOUT 3 CUPS

Not only can these versatile spiked berries be used as an accompaniment to turkey, chicken, or game, they are equally delicious on vanilla ice cream.
These will keep up to 6 months refrigerated.

12 ounces fresh cranberries

1½ cups granulated sugar

1 teaspoon grated
orange zest (peel)

½ cup brandy

1. Preheat oven to 350 degrees. Place berries in large pan so berries are not more than one berry deep. Pour sugar and sprinkle grated orange zest over berries and seal with aluminum foil, leaving a small air vent. Bake in oven for 30 minutes or until berries begin to pop. Take out of oven, remove foil. Cool for 5 minutes.

2. Stir and place berries in a bowl and stir again. Pour brandy over and let set for 15 minutes. Place in covered jar and allow to steep for two weeks in refrigerator. These berries keep up to six months in refrigerator. Serve cool or at room temperature.

Cornmeal-crusted Razor Clams with Roasted Tomato and Pepper Salsa

SERVINGS: 4

The charred tomato and red pepper give a nice smoky flavor to the salsa.

12-16 razor clams

¾ cup cornmeal

¾ teaspoon salt

2 tablespoons butter or margarine

3 tablespoons vegetable oil

ROASTED TOMATO AND PEPPER SALSA

1 red pepper, seeded and cut in ½-inch wedges

½ medium onion, sliced in ½-inch wedges

2 cloves of garlic, peeled but left whole

1-2 jalapeño peppers,* cut in half lengthwise (use gloves when preparing)

2 teaspoons vegetable oil

1 medium unpeeled tomato, cut in 1-inch wedges, seeded

½ teaspoon salt

1 teaspoon cumin

½ teaspoon chili powder

2 teaspoons chopped cilantro

*Use 1 jalapeño pepper for mild salsa and 2 for a hot salsa.

1. Make Roasted Tomato and Pepper Salsa and set aside. Prepare razor clams (refer to page 27). Mix cornmeal and salt together. Dip razor clams in cornmeal mixture and place on waxed paper until all clams are coated.

2. Heat butter and oil in large skillet over medium heat. Increase heat to high, add clams, and sauté briefly, about 1-2 minutes on each side. Serve with salsa.

TO MAKE SALSA

1. Preheat oven to 400 degrees. Place red pepper, onion, garlic, and jalapeño pepper in roasting pan with no rack. Brush with vegetable oil. Roast in oven for 12 minutes.

2. Add tomato and roast 5 minutes longer, or until vegetables are tender and slightly charred. Remove from oven; place mixture in food processor with steel blade inserted. Add salt, cumin, and chili powder. Process until almost smooth, or to desired consistency. Place in bowl and add cilantro.

Cranberry Mousse in Hazelnut Butter Crust

SERVINGS: 6-8

A light cranberry mousse is set in a crisp nut crust for a texture and flavor contrast in this dessert.

CRUST

1 cup all-purpose flour

2 tablespoons confectioners' sugar

5 tablespoons butter or margarine

¼ cup toasted and skinned hazelnuts, finely chopped (see page 323 for toasting nuts)

FILLING

½ cup granulated sugar

¼ cup all-purpose flour

1 envelope unflavored gelatin

½ teaspoon salt

2 cups cranberry juice cocktail

1 envelope meringue mix (½ of 1.2 ounce packet) plus ⅓ cup sugar and ⅓ cup water*

½ cup heavy (whipping) cream

additional whipped cream for garnish

fresh or brandied cranberries (recipe page 63) for garnish, optional

1. Preheat oven to 425 degrees. To make crust: blend together flour, confectioners' sugar and butter until crumbly. Add hazelnuts and mix together. Place in the bottom of a 9-inch springform pan, pat evenly. Prick well with fork. Bake in oven for 7 minutes or until lightly browned. Cool.

2. To make filling: combine ½ cup sugar, flour, gelatin, and salt in a medium saucepan. Add cranberry juice, stir to blend. Place over medium-high heat, stirring constantly, until thickened and bubbly. Cool, chill in refrigerator until mixture mounds when spooned, about an hour. Check every 15 minutes.

3. Prepare meringue mix as directed on package by combining mix with ⅓ cup sugar and water, and beat with mixer until soft peaks form. Fold into cranberry mixture. Whip ½ cup cream and fold into cranberry mixture.

4. Pile cream mixture on top of crust, chill several hours in refrigerator until set. With knife, cut around the sides of pan, then release sides of springform pan. Garnish with dollops of whipped cream and fresh or brandied cranberries, if desired.

Raw egg whites should be avoided because of concern of Salmonella, so meringue powder is incorporated into the filling instead of the usual 3 beaten egg whites. Meringue mix can be found at many supermarkets in the baking section.

OYSTERVILLE, NAHCOTTA, AND OCEAN PARK

Oysterville and Nahcotta, two oystering towns on the eastern side of the Long Beach Peninsula, face beautiful, unspoiled Willapa Bay. Oysterville, settled first, grew rapidly to house the people who worked the oyster beds. The native Olympia oysters became delicacies, bringing a dollar apiece in San Francisco during the gold rush days of the 1800s. Oysters were like gold, and Oysterville like a gold-mining town—boisterous, lively, and wealthy. But the "gold" was over-harvested and pollutants destroyed many beds. Oysterville was nearly deserted until the importation of a Japanese oyster, the Pacific, in the early 1900s. These imported mollusks helped the oyster industry and Oysterville survive.

Nahcotta, settled in the late 1800s and named after a local Indian chief, was similar to neighboring Oysterville in that business was mainly oystering. In 1909, disaster struck when a fire reduced the town to ashes. The oystering business somehow survived and the small town was gradually rebuilt. Today, the local Northwest Oyster Farm Plant shows visitors how oysters are planted and harvested.

Ocean Park was originally established as a Methodist Church resort in 1887. No longer church owned, today it is a small seaside community. Turn-of-the-century cottages and historical buildings bring charm to this tiny resort town.

Of the **oysters** found and farmed here in Willapa Bay, **Pacific** oysters flourish and the prized **Olympias** are becoming more available. Many oysters find their way into cans in Nahcotta. A specialty is the alderwood smoked oysters that are vacuum-packed.

Grilled Bacon-wrapped Oysters

SERVINGS: 2 FOR MAIN COURSE, 4 AS APPETIZERS

These are great appetizers, or 2 brochettes make a serving for dinner.

16 oysters, scrubbed and shucked

¼ cup lemon juice

2 dashes Tabasco sauce

salt

freshly ground pepper

5 strips bacon, cut in thirds, plus ⅓ of another strip (16 pieces in all)

8 mushroom caps

melted butter or margarine, about 1 tablespoon

4 skewers

1. Preheat broiler or barbecue grill. Sprinkle the oysters with lemon juice that has been mixed with Tabasco sauce. Sprinkle with salt and pepper. Wrap a third of a strip of bacon around each oyster.

2. Using four skewers, arrange on each: a mushroom cap, four bacon-wrapped oysters, and another mushroom. Brush mushrooms with melted butter and broil under broiler or over charcoal grill until bacon is cooked and oysters curl around the edges, turning after one side is cooked. Cook about 4-5 minutes on first side and 2-4 minutes on second side. Serve.

Alderwood Smoked Oysters and Cream Cheese Spread

SERVINGS: 4

Dedicated oyster-haters have liked this spread.

1 (3-ounce) package regular or light cream cheese, softened

4 ounces smoked oysters, chopped (preferably vacuum packed)

1 tablespoon dry sherry (or cream)

2 tablespoons mayonnaise, regular or light

1 teaspoon minced onion

finely chopped chives

Beat cream cheese in bowl until light, combine with rest of ingredients except chives. Chill until serving time and top with chives. Serve with crisp crackers.

SOUTH BEND, RAYMOND, AND TOKELAND

On the southern bend of the Willapa River lies the town South Bend. It began as a sawmill community, but today business tends more to oystering. The summer season opens with the annual Oyster Stampede on Memorial Day weekend, which commemorates the legendary yearly "stampede" of oysters to their new resting grounds. South Bend is the county seat of Pacific County and houses an impressive courthouse nicknamed by some "A Gilded Palace of Reckless Extravagance." Stately on the outside, the inside is richly decorated with an ornamental art glass dome, 29 feet in diameter, hanging over the rotunda. This opulent dome brings light and elegance to the interior.

Nearby Raymond is located at the mouth of the Willapa River, which winds its way through the downtown area before emptying into Willapa Bay. Lumbering was the main industry in town until a large local mill recently closed.

North of Raymond is Tokeland, a sport fishing village with the vast Pacific Ocean on one side and scenic Willapa Bay on the other. Boaters fish in the Pacific and land lovers surf-fish or look for crabs near shore. Located on the Pacific flyway migratory path, Tokeland is inviting to avid bird watchers.

These three towns rim Willapa Bay, an inlet with over 20,000 acres of privately owned oyster beds from which are harvested the bulk of the West Coast **oyster** crop. **Dungeness crabs** and several kinds of **fish** are also at home in these waters.

Sautéed Willapa Bay Oysters

SERVINGS: 4

The breading stays on these oysters after they have been placed in the freezer for a half hour. Serve with sour dough bread and Terri's Cabbage Salad, page 104.

2 eggs

¾ cup milk

3 dashes Tabasco sauce

2 cups fine cracker crumbs, (saltines)

2 cups fresh oysters, shucked, cleaned, and patted dry

3 tablespoons butter or margarine

2 tablespoons vegetable oil

lemon wedges

1. In bowl, beat eggs, add milk and Tabasco sauce. In another bowl, place cracker crumbs. Dip patted-dry oysters in egg mixture, then coat well with cracker crumbs. Place on waxed-paper-lined cookie sheet. When all oysters are prepared, place sheet in freezer for one-half hour.

2. Heat butter and oil in a large skillet over medium high heat. Turn heat to high, add prepared oysters, and cook for 1½ to 2½ minutes on each side, depending on size of oyster. Do not crowd when cooking. Serve with lemon wedges.

Baked Oysters in Garlic Butter and Blue Cheese

SERVINGS: 4

Here, sharp blue cheese contrasts with mild oysters.

12 oysters

4 tablespoons butter or margarine

1 large clove garlic, minced

1 tablespoon lemon juice

dash of Tabasco sauce

salt and freshly ground pepper, to taste

½ cup white bread crumbs

2 tablespoons freshly grated Parmesan cheese

2 tablespoons minced parsley

¼ cup blue cheese, crumbled

1. Scrub oyster shells carefully and pry open. Separate oyster carefully from shell and replace on half shell.

2. Preheat oven to 425 degrees. Combine butter and garlic in small saucepan and heat over low heat until butter is melted. Remove from heat and stir in lemon juice, Tabasco sauce, and salt and pepper.

3. In small bowl combine bread crumbs, Parmesan cheese, and minced parsley.

4. Place oysters in shallow baking pan lined with crumpled foil. Crumble blue cheese over oysters. Spoon bread-crumb mixture evenly on tops. Drizzle with butter mixture. Bake 10-20 minutes, or until done.

GRAYLAND

Captain Robert Gray visited a large inlet off the coast of Washington in the late 1700s. He sailed away, but years later his name was still remembered in the region. The harbor became known as Grays Harbor and the small community as Grayland.

In the 1930s local Finnish immigrants imported cranberry plants from Cape Cod, and so began a thriving industry for the area. Now, acres of rippling carpets of purple and green vines produce record crops of the tart berries each year. Near Grayland, over 90 percent of the **cranberries** are machine dry picked and sold fresh, frozen, or dried. A few farmers flood their bogs and the berries are then beaten from the vine by a machine. These berries are sold canned or as juice.

Cranberry Oatmeal Muffins

MAKES 8 MUFFINS

Dried cranberries enhance the flavor of these moist muffins. The recipe can easily be doubled.

1 cup quick-cooking rolled oats

1 cup buttermilk

⅓ cup vegetable oil

½ cup brown sugar, packed

1 egg

1 cup all-purpose flour

1 teaspoon baking powder

1 teaspoon baking soda

½ teaspoon salt

½ cup dried cranberries

½ teaspoon orange flavoring or 1 tablespoon grated orange zest (peel)

extra rolled oats

1. Preheat oven to 375 degrees. Mix together the oats and buttermilk and let stand 5 minutes. To mixture, add oil, brown sugar, egg, and combine.

2. In another bowl, mix together the flour, baking powder, baking soda, and salt. Stir flour mixture into batter and fold in cranberries and orange flavoring or zest. Grease or spray muffin tins with vegetable spray.

3. Fill tins three-fourths full and sprinkle tops of muffins with extra rolled oats. Bake for 20-25 minutes or until centers are cooked and tops are lightly browned. Remove from oven and cool 10 minutes on rack. Remove from tins.

Cranberry Orange Glazed Ham

SERVINGS: 15

Serve for New Year's or Easter.

1 (12 to 14-pound)
ready-to-eat ham, bone-in

Whole cloves

1 cup packed brown sugar,
divided

1 cup cranberry juice cocktail

¼ cup honey

3 tablespoons cider vinegar

2 tablespoons Dijon or
Dijon-style mustard

2 oranges, sliced

about 12 whole cranberries,
fresh or frozen and thawed

1. Preheat over to 325 degrees. Trim fat from ham, leaving a thin layer. Score fat remaining on ham in diamond designs and stud with cloves. Place ham, fat side up, on rack in shallow roasting pan. Coat exposed portion with ½ cup brown sugar. Bake, uncovered, for 2½ hours.

2. Combine remaining ½ cup sugar, cranberry juice, honey, cider vinegar, and mustard in a medium saucepan over medium-high heat, mix well, and bring to boil. Boil 3 minutes, stirring constantly.

3. Remove ham from oven. Place orange slices on ham, securing in center with wooden picks, leaving tips of picks exposed. Pour hot cranberry mixture over ham and return to oven. Bake an additional ½ hour or until internal temperature reaches 140 degrees, basting occasionally.

4. Remove roasting pan from the oven and place ham on warm serving platter. Place a fresh cranberry on each exposed pick in the middle of orange slices before serving. Skim fat from juices in pan, and pour the juices into a sauceboat and serve along with the ham.

WESTPORT

Westport is the self-proclaimed salmon sport-fishing capital of the world. Offshore sport fishing for salmon boomed in the late 1950s and early 1960s, turning the small fishing village into a port with an amazingly large assortment of charter and commercial crafts and a town filled with motels, charter offices, and restaurants. Salmon fishing fluctuates from year to year now, and tuna and bottom fishing have become increasingly important to the town. During some seasons, sharp restrictions are issued to shorten the salmon season. When there is a salmon season, derbies are held daily. Excitement mounts as boats arrive back at port with their catch, fishermen vying to see who caught the largest prize of the day. King and Silver **salmon** are prime catches along with a variety of **bottom fish.** A walk along the wharf brings glimpses of the day's catch and the opportunity to buy commercially caught **Dungeness crabs.**

Barbecued Westport Salmon with Lemon Butter Sauce

SERVINGS: 6-8

Whether caught at Westport or found fresh in the market, salmon reigns supreme.
It is cooked and sauced simply in this recipe.

1 whole salmon (3-6 pounds) with head removed, butterflied (This can be done at a fish market.)

4 tablespoons butter or margarine, softened

1 teaspoon salt

1 tablespoon brown sugar

LEMON BUTTER SAUCE

⅓ cup melted butter

1 tablespoon lemon juice

1. Start coals in barbecue grill. Take out as many bones as possible from salmon. Combine softened butter, salt, and brown sugar. Rub flesh side of fish with mixture.

2. Place salmon, skin side down, in a tray of heavy-duty aluminum foil with sides crimped up to at least one inch. When coals are hot and covered with ash, lay foil tray of salmon on the grill over coals. Cover barbecue, making certain that vents are open or prepare a foil tent so the smoke can circulate around the fish.

3. Cook about 15-25 minutes, or until center of fish reaches 140 degrees, or the flesh is opaque throughout. Make lemon-butter sauce by combining melted butter and juice and serve with the salmon.

Dungeness Crab Cakes with Red Pepper Sauce

SERVINGS: 4

I first tasted this combination at a favorite restaurant and liked the taste counterpoint that the spicy sauce gave the delicate fresh crabcakes. At home, I created a similar combination.

½ pound Dungeness crabmeat

1 tablespoon olive oil

¼ cup finely chopped onion

¼ cup finely diced celery

2 cups fresh white bread crumbs, crusts removed

1 egg, slightly beaten

3 tablespoons mayonnaise, regular or light

1 tablespoon chopped parsley

1 tablespoon dry sherry

4-5 drops Tabasco sauce

Panko crumbs* or dry bread crumbs for coating

2 tablespoons butter or margarine

1 tablespoon vegetable oil

1. Make Red Pepper Sauce.

2. Check over crabmeat to see that all shells are removed. Heat olive oil in a large saucepan over medium heat and sauté onion and celery. Remove from heat and add cooked vegetables to crab meat along with soft bread crumbs, egg, mayonnaise, parsley, sherry, and Tabasco sauce.

3. Form into about 8 patties and coat with crumbs. Cover and refrigerate 20 minutes or longer. (Pepper sauce may be made at this time, if not already prepared. Directions follow.)

4. Heat butter and oil in large skillet and cook crab cakes over medium-high heat until golden brown on each side, about 3-5 minutes a side. Serve with warm Red Pepper Sauce.

Panko crumbs are Japanese breading crumbs found in many supermarkets. If unavailable, use dry bread crumbs.

RED PEPPER SAUCE

1 tomato

2 tablespoons butter

1 red pepper, chopped

1 clove garlic, minced

2 tablespoons cider vinegar

3 tablespoons brown sugar

1 teaspoon chili powder

TO MAKE RED PEPPER SAUCE

1. Bring water to boil in saucepan, put tomato in water for 10 seconds, then cool under cold tap water. Peel, seed, and chop.

2. Melt butter in saucepan, add chopped tomato, red pepper, and garlic. Bring to boil, reduce heat, and simmer for 20 minutes, uncovered. Add and stir in vinegar, brown sugar, and chili powder. Simmer 15 minutes. (If made ahead, reheat before serving with crab cakes.)

NORTH PUGET SOUND
&
SAN JUAN ISLANDS

Dairy farms fill rich pasture land. Crops of berries and vegetables cover verdant valleys. Seaside, the ocean offers up mussels, clams, crabs, and varieties of fish.

Lynden

Ferndale

Bellingham

Eastsound

Friday Harbor

Lopez

Anacortes

Sedro Woolley

Mount Vernon

La Conner

Coupeville

Marysville

LYNDEN

Lynden's Dutch heritage means that even today this "little bit of Holland" in the Northwest is full of old-world charm. Streets are bordered with plots of colorful tulips, and many local merchants wear white caps and wooden shoes. Shops offer products from Holland, and a four-story windmill stands in the center of town. Here, all lawns are neatly manicured, the houses sparkle, and streets are scrubbed to perfection. Even the air smells clean.

Lynden is perched above the fertile Nooksack River Valley, with some of the richest farmland in the country. Dairying is by far the largest industry in the valley. This region leads the state in milk production with four hundred highly efficient dairy farms in Whatcom County. These farms send more than a billion pounds of **milk** to market every year, enough to keep **dairy products** on the tables of over a million and a half Americans.

Berries are the second largest crop; locally grown **raspberries, strawberries,** and **blueberries** are sold fresh and frozen, and a few farms produce their own jams and berry products to sell nationally. Vegetables also grow in the fertile valley, mainly **corn** and **seed potatoes. Chickens** are raised on some farms, and a **hazelnut (filbert)** orchard is nearby.

Chicken Breasts Filled with Ricotta and Spinach

SERVINGS: 4

These are popular items at a nearby deli. I decided to make a recipe for home use.

4 large chicken breast halves, with bone and skin

2 tablespoons butter or margarine, divided

1 scallion, finely chopped

1 clove garlic, minced

1½ cups chopped fresh spinach

¾ cup ricotta cheese

1 tablespoon minced parsley

3-4 dashes Tabasco sauce

3 tablespoons freshly grated Parmesan cheese

1 egg white

freshly ground pepper

½ teaspoon salt

1. Preheat oven to 375 degrees. Leaving skin attached, debone chicken breasts. Gently loosen skin from long side of each breast piece, leaving skin attached at curved side. Set aside.

2. In a medium skillet, melt 1 tablespoon butter over medium heat, add scallion and garlic and cook 2 minutes, stirring frequently. Add spinach and cook until wilted, about 2 minutes. Remove from heat and add ricotta, parsley, Tabasco, Parmesan cheese, egg white, pepper, and salt, combining well.

3. Stuff ¼ of the stuffing under skin of each breast piece and press to spread evenly. Place on baking pan. Melt remaining 1 tablespoon butter and brush over breasts. Sprinkle with salt and grate pepper over. Bake 45-50 minutes or until cooked throughout, basting occasionally.

Olie Bollen

YIELD: ABOUT 25 PUFFS

These old-world Dutch treats are served in many homes in Lynden today, using milk and butter from the nearby dairy farms. This recipe is an adapted version of one from The Heritage Cook Book *(Meredith Corporation).*

3¼ cups all-purpose flour, divided

2 packages dry yeast

1 cup milk

⅓ cup granulated sugar

¼ cup butter

1 teaspoon salt

1 teaspoon vanilla

2 eggs

3 egg yolks

¾ teaspoon nutmeg (or mace)

¾ cup raisins

1½ teaspoons grated lemon zest (peel)

oil for frying

SUGAR CINNAMON TOPPING

½ cup sugar mixed with 1 teaspoon ground cinnamon

1. In large bowl of mixer, combine yeast and 2 cups of the flour, and set aside.

2. In a medium saucepan, combine milk, ⅓ cup sugar, butter, and salt and heat over medium heat until mixture reaches 115 degrees, stirring constantly. Stir in vanilla. Add to flour mixture and whisk together.

3. Add eggs and egg yolks to mixture and beat with electric mixer at low speed for ½ minute. Scrape sides of bowl and beat at high speed for 3 minutes.

4. Stir in the remaining 1¼ cups flour, nutmeg, raisins, and lemon zest with wooden spoon. Cover, let rise until double in bulk, about one hour.

5. Heat oil, about 2-3 inches deep in deep-fat fryer or large heavy saucepan, to 375 degrees. Drop batter by rounded teaspoonfuls into hot fat, fry about 2-3 minutes, turning to brown all sides.

6. Drain on paper towels. Roll in cinnamon-sugar mixture while warm.

Strawberries in Raspberry Sauce with Orange Cream

SERVINGS: 6-8

*When the berries are at their peak, this simple dessert makes the most of their beauty and taste.
The orange cream is passed separately for those who wish to have a light dessert,
without a topping.*

ORANGE CREAM*

1 (8-ounce) package cream cheese, regular or light

⅓ cup granulated sugar

2 tablespoons cream or milk

1½ teaspoons grated orange zest (peel)

1 teaspoon vanilla

2 tablespoons orange juice

BERRIES

1 pint fresh raspberries

¼ cup confectioners' sugar

1 tablespoon orange juice

2½ pints fresh strawberries, hulled

1. Beat together cream cheese, granulated sugar, cream, orange zest, vanilla, and 2 tablespoons orange juice in a medium bowl until smooth. (This may be made ahead and refrigerated, then brought to room temperature, adding more orange juice if too thick.)

2. Puree raspberries in food processor or blender. Strain into bowl; remove seeds by pressing through sieve and stir in confectioners' sugar and 1 tablespoon orange juice. Place strawberries in dessert dishes or parfait glasses and cover with raspberry sauce. Pass orange cream separately.

*The orange cream is also delicious as a dipping sauce for whole strawberries.

Dutch Chocolate Ice Cream with Toasted Hazelnuts and Chocolate Chunks

SERVINGS: 6-8

This is a dark, rich, and smooth ice cream. If hazelnuts are not available, use toasted pecans.

1 cup half-and-half

½ cup unsweetened cocoa, preferably Dutch

3 eggs

½ cup granulated sugar

1½ cups heavy (whipping) cream, divided

1½ teaspoons vanilla

⅛ teaspoon cinnamon

2 ounces sweet dark chocolate, chopped

½ cup toasted hazelnuts (see page 323 for toasting nuts)

1. Place water in bottom of double boiler, about 1½ inches deep, so it will not touch top part. Bring just to boil over medium heat, reduce heat so water is hot but not boiling. In top of double boiler, combine half-and-half with cocoa. Place top over bottom of double boiler and whisk frequently until mixture is smooth and thick. Take off heat.

2. In a medium bowl, whisk eggs with sugar and 2 tablespoons whipping cream. Take 2 tablespoons of chocolate mixture and add to egg mixture and stir together. Combine all egg mixture with chocolate mixture in top of double boiler over hot water and return to medium low heat. Whisk mixture frequently for about 15-20 minutes until it reaches 160 degrees.

3. Remove from heat, stir in vanilla, cinnamon, and remaining cream. Place in a medium bowl and chill in refrigerator for 3 hours or longer. Place chopped chocolate in refrigerator to chill.

4. Pour mixture into chilled ice cream maker and when ice cream becomes slushy, fold in nuts and chilled chocolate pieces. Use ice cream maker according to manufacturer's directions. Makes about 1½ quarts.

FERNDALE

Rich soil lured early settlers to farm near Ferndale. Evidence of early farm life is seen at the historic Hovander Homestead, originally built in 1903. Today, this preserved farm and its surrounding sixty acres are open to the public. Visitors can view a Victorian home, enter a huge red barn, pet farm animals, and picnic along the restful waters of the Nooksack River.

Produce from this area included **raspberries, strawberries, corn, carrots, green peas, green beans,** and **potatoes.** Approximately 4,000 acres in Western Washington are devoted to growing red raspberries, and many of these farms are near Ferndale. **Chickens** are also raised by many farmers.

Chicken with Port, Crème Fraîche, and Mushroom Sauce

SERVINGS: 4-6

Crème Fraîche is easily made, or available in many supermarkets.

3 tablespoons butter or margarine, divided

1½ cups cleaned, sliced mushrooms*

salt

6 large chicken breast halves, boned and skinned

all-purpose flour

2 cups chicken stock (page 313) or canned reduced-sodium broth

1 cup Port

1 cup Crème Fraîche, commercial or homemade, recipe page 312

¼ teaspoon freshly ground pepper

*To clean mushrooms use mushroom brush, clean toothbrush, or paper towels. Do not soak; use water only sparingly.

1. Melt 1 tablespoon butter in a large skillet and sauté mushrooms over medium heat until tender, stirring with wooden spoon. Season mushrooms with salt and remove from skillet and set aside.

2. Dust breasts lightly with flour. Heat remaining 2 tablespoons butter in skillet and sauté breasts over medium heat until browned and cooked through, about 5 minutes on each side. Remove from skillet and keep warm in oven which has been heated, then turned off, or on warmed platter with foil vented over.

3. Add chicken stock to pan, bring to boil over high heat and reduce by one-half, stirring constantly. Add Port and reduce again by one-half. Reduce heat, stir in Crème Fraîche to Port mixture and boil and reduce again over medium heat until sauce is slightly thickened, about 5-10 minutes. Add reserved mushrooms and pepper. Serve chicken breasts with sauce.

81

Grilled Green Beans

SERVINGS: 4

Two ways of grilling green beans are offered here. The open-grill procedure does not take long on the grill so the beans may be grilled after the meat, poultry, or fish has been cooked. However, you will need to parboil the beans first. The covered-grill method will take about 20–25 minutes on the grill. They may be grilled and kept warm on the side of the grill while the meat, poultry, or fish is being grilled.

1 pound fresh green beans, trimmed and washed

2 quarts boiling water in large kettle or stockpot (for open-grill method)

¾ teaspoon salt, preferably sea salt or Kosher salt

melted butter or olive oil

1 tablespoon minced parsley

metal tray, with openings, to place on grill (for open-grill method)

aluminum foil pan (for covered- grill method)

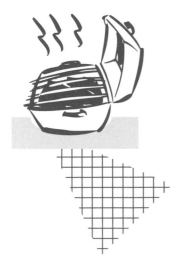

OPEN-GRILL METHOD

1. Parboil beans by dropping beans into large pot of boiling water. Bring water back to boil and cook, uncovered, about 4-5 minutes or until beans are tender but still slightly crunchy. Drain and place under cold running tap water or immerse in a pot of cold water. Drain again and pat dry with paper towel. The beans may be used immediately or covered and placed in refrigerator until ready to grill.

2. Place metal tray on hot grill. Add beans and stir and cook until heated through and slightly grilled. Add salt. Take off grill. Place in serving dish and top with melted butter and parsley if desired.

COVERED-GRILL METHOD

1. Place uncooked beans in an aluminum foil pan on hot grill. Drizzle with enough olive oil to coat, about 2 tablespoons. Add salt and toss to coat.

2. Place or close cover over grill with vents open. Grill over high heat, tossing occasionally, for about 20 minutes or until beans are tender but still crisp. Sprinkle with parsley.

Raspberry Tiramisu

SERVINGS: 8-12

Tiramisu, meaning "pick me up" in Italian, has become a favorite dessert in the States. Mascarpone cheese is available in many supermarkets or specialty food shops; if unavailable, use cream cheese.

4 egg yolks

¼ cup plus 1 tablespoon granulated sugar, divided

4 tablespoons Marsala wine

2 (8-ounce) containers mascarpone cheese (2 cups)

½ cup confectioners' sugar

1 teaspoon vanilla

1 teaspoon almond flavoring

1 cup heavy (whipping) cream

½ cup espresso, freshly brewed*

½ cup dark rum

¼ cup Kahlua liqueur

6-10 ounces (about 30) ladyfingers, split. (These are sponge cookies available frozen or fresh in the bakery section.)

2 cups raspberries (fresh, or frozen and thawed)

unsweetened cocoa powder

* If an espresso machine is unavailable, use powdered espresso and boiling water to make ½ cup.

1. Combine egg yolks with ¼ cup granulated sugar in top of double boiler, whisk 1 minute. Place over bottom of double boiler with simmering (not boiling) water. Cook over medium or low heat and when mixture becomes warm add Marsala. Whisk mixture constantly until it becomes slightly thickened and reaches 160 degrees. Remove from heat and continue whisking until slightly cooled and set aside.

2. Beat mascarpone cheese in a medium bowl until smooth. Add confectioners' sugar, vanilla, and almond flavoring and blend together.

3. In another medium bowl, whip cream until soft peaks form. Blend whipped cream into mascarpone cheese mixture. Whisk again until stiff peaks form.

4. Combine espresso, remaining 1 tablespoon granulated sugar, rum, and Kahlua in small bowl.

5. To assemble: place half of the ladyfingers in a 9x13-inch flat pan. Drizzle with ½ espresso mixture. Spread ½ mascarpone mixture in pan, then all the egg mixture. Cover with remaining ladyfingers, drizzle with rest of espresso mixture, and sprinkle with raspberries. Spread remaining mascarpone cheese mixture over. Sift cocoa powder evenly over top. Cover with plastic wrap and refrigerate for at least 5 hours and up to 3 days.

BELLINGHAM

Bellingham lies between the bay shores on the west and a forested and farmland backdrop to the east. Attracted by the pastoral beauty, many people settled here in the 19th century. Today, some of their Victorian homes, maintained throughout the years, display a rich historic legacy.

Old Fairhaven, a district in south Bellingham, is a restored community typical of the late 1800s. Many of Fairhaven's original red-brick buildings still stand, now housing coffee shops, art galleries, specialty shops, and restaurants—all within a 4- or 5-square block neighborhood.

To the east of Bellingham lie many **dairy farms.** Additionally, several farmland acres yield **potatoes, green peas, green beans, sweet corn, cucumbers, raspberries, strawberries,** and **blueberries.** Nearby **poultry** farms raise Washington chickens. To the west, fishermen snag **rock cod, true cod,** and other varieties. **Oysters** and other **shellfish** flourish along Chuckanuck Drive to the south.

Chicken Breasts Stuffed with Cream Cheese, Crab, Mushrooms, and Sherry

SERVINGS: 4 WITH 2 BREASTS; 8 WITH 1 BREAST EACH

This dish can be made ahead, refrigerated, then baked before serving.

3 tablespoons butter or margarine, divided

2 cups chopped mushrooms, divided

salt and freshly ground pepper

3 ounces softened cream cheese, regular or light

½ cup crab meat

2 tablespoons sherry

1 teaspoon dried thyme, divided

8 large chicken breast halves, skinned and boned

3 tablespoons all-purpose flour

½ cup chicken stock (recipe page 313) or canned broth

½ cup milk

½ cup dry white wine

1 cup grated Swiss cheese

2 tablespoons minced parsley

1. Preheat oven to 325 degrees, unless baking later. Melt 1 tablespoon butter in a medium skillet over medium heat, add ½ cup chopped mushrooms and cook until tender. Season with salt and pepper, remove from heat and combine with cream cheese, crab, sherry, ½ teaspoon thyme and set aside.

2. Pound 8 chicken breast halves until ¼ inch thick. (Covering the breasts with waxed paper before pounding is helpful.) Season lightly with salt and pepper. Spoon mushroom mixture onto chicken pieces. Roll pieces around filling and place, seam down, in lightly greased baking dish large enough to hold all rolls. Set aside.

3. Melt remaining 2 tablespoons butter in skillet over medium heat and sauté remaining 1 and ½ cups mushrooms until juices evaporate. Stir in flour and reserved ½ teaspoon thyme; blend in stock, milk, and wine. Cook, stirring, until sauce thickens, and season with salt and pepper. Pour sauce over rolled chicken pieces. (Dish may be refrigerated at this time, then taken out about ½ hour before baking.)

4. Sprinkle with cheese. Bake, uncovered, for 1½ hours. Sprinkle with parsley and serve.

WASHINGTON STATE HISTORICAL SOCIETY

Grilled Chicken Marinated in Yogurt and Ginger

SERVINGS: 4

This chicken is moist and tender whether grilled or baked. Apple or pear chutney makes a good accompaniment.

1 fryer, cut up (without neck and giblets), skin removed if desired

salt and pepper

1⅓ tablespoons freshly grated ginger or 1½ teaspoons ground ginger

2 cups plain yogurt

½ teaspoon cloves

1 teaspoon cinnamon

⅛ teaspoon ground nutmeg

1 tablespoon lime juice

2 tablespoons brown sugar

1. Place chicken in 9x13 non-metallic baking dish, sprinkle with salt and pepper and 1½ teaspoons freshly grated ginger or ½ teaspoon ground ginger. Combine remaining ginger with rest of ingredients in a medium bowl. Pour mixture over chicken, cover and refrigerate at least 2 hours, preferably overnight. Chicken may then be grilled or baked.

2. To grill: prepare grill. When coals are hot or grill ready, place chicken pieces on well-oiled rack, about 5 inches above heat. Cook, turning and brushing with marinade for about 45 minutes or until chicken is done. Discard unused marinade.

3. To bake: preheat oven to 350 degrees. Bake chicken with marinade for 45-50 minutes. To serve, lift chicken from pan onto serving platter. Discard marinade.

Buttermilk Corncakes

SERVINGS: 6

Serve these for breakfast with maple syrup, or for lunch or dinner topped with sour cream and chives.

¾ cup all-purpose flour

⅔ cup yellow cornmeal

1 tablespoon granulated sugar

¼ teaspoon salt

¼ teaspoon baking powder

¼ teaspoon baking soda

2¼ cups buttermilk

2 eggs

3 tablespoons butter or margarine, melted

⅓ cup canned creamed corn

⅔ cup coarsely chopped corn kernels (fresh, frozen, or canned may be used)

2-4 tablespoons vegetable oil for frying

maple syrup, or sour cream and chives for topping

1. Mix the flour, cornmeal, sugar, salt, baking powder, and baking soda in a medium bowl and set aside. In a large bowl, whisk together the buttermilk, eggs, and melted butter. With wooden spoon, stir in creamed corn and corn kernels. Add the dry ingredients to corn mixture and stir just to blend.

2. Heat 1 tablespoon oil in large nonstick skillet over medium-high heat and pour in batter to form corncakes, about 2½ inches in diameter. Cook about 2 or 3 minutes on one side, turn and cook other side about 2 minutes.

3. Cook remaining corncakes, adding remaining oil when needed. Serve with maple syrup or sour cream and chives.

Spinach, Raspberries, and Seared-scallop Salad with Raspberry Vinaigrette

SERVINGS: 4

Serve this wonderful combination on a summer evening, after picking ripe raspberries.

RASPBERRY VINAIGRETTE

¼ cup raspberry vinegar

2 tablespoons balsamic vinegar

¾ cup vegetable oil

1 tablespoon poppy seeds

¼ cup pureed, sieved raspberries*

salt and pepper to taste

TO MAKE VINAIGRETTE

Whisk together the vinegars, add oil in slow steady stream, and combine. Add poppy seeds, pureed raspberries, and salt and pepper to taste, combine.

*Puree about ½ cup or more raspberries in food processor and press through sieve to remove seeds to make about ¼ cup puree.

SALAD

5 cups torn spinach leaves

½ cup sliced celery

1 cup honeydew melon balls or chunks (other melons may be substituted)

1 cup fresh raspberries

2 teaspoons butter or margarine

1 teaspoon oil

8-10 ounces scallops; may need to be cut in bite-size pieces

½ tablespoon raspberry vinegar

½ cup slivered almonds, toasted (see page 323 for toasting nuts)

TO MAKE SALAD

Toss spinach with celery, melon balls, and raspberries in serving bowl and set aside. Heat butter and oil in large skillet, add scallops, and sauté until done, about 2-3 minutes on each side. Lightly season with salt and pepper and sprinkle with drops of raspberry vinegar. Add warm scallops to salad and drizzle enough dressing to coat and gently toss again. Sprinkle with toasted almonds.

Glazed Chocolate Kahlua Cheesecake with Caramel Kahlua Sauce

SERVINGS: 14

Serve small pieces in a pool of sauce.

CRUST

1½ **cups ground chocolate wafers**

¼ **cup melted butter or margarine**

FILLING

32 **ounces (4 8-ounce packages) cream cheese, regular or light**

1 **cup granulated sugar**

4 **eggs**

¼ **cup sour cream, regular or light**

¼ **cup heavy (whipping) cream**

6 **ounces semi-sweet chocolate, melted and cooled**

⅓ **cup Kahlua**

l. Preheat oven to 325 degrees. Mix cookie crumbs and melted butter in a small bowl. Place mixture in ungreased 9 or 10-inch springform pan and press down. To prevent water from seeping into cheesecake when baking, cover pan underneath and up over sides with a sheet of foil. Set springform pan in large roasting pan.

2. In mixing bowl, beat cream cheese until smooth, add sugar gradually until it is dissolved, about 2 to 3 minutes. Blend in eggs one at a time. Fold in sour cream, cream, melted chocolate, and Kahlua.

3. Pour mixture over crust into springform pan. Bring water to boil in kettle. Set roasting pan on rack in middle of oven. Pour enough boiling water in roasting pan to come up half way on the sides of the springform pan. Bake 1 hour and 5 minutes, or until cake is set (center of cheesecake will still slightly jiggle). Turn off heat and leave door slightly ajar (using a long-handled spoon) for 1 hour. Remove springform pan from roasting pan and set on rack to cool. Cover and refrigerate 5 hours or longer.

4. Remove sides of springform pan from chilled cheesecake and place on wire rack with waxed paper underneath. Pour glaze over cheesecake covering it completely.

GLAZE

8 ounces semi-sweet chocolate, chopped or chips

1 cup heavy (whipping) cream

2 tablespoons granulated sugar

3 tablespoons corn syrup

1½ tablespoons Kahlua

TO MAKE GLAZE

Combine chocolate, cream, sugar, and corn syrup in top of double boiler, and cook over simmering water until chocolate is about melted. Or, combine in glass bowl and heat in microwave on high for about 2 minutes, stirring every 30 seconds. Remove from heat and stir until smooth. Add Kahlua and combine.

Optional: Place excess glaze in a small bowl and chill 1 hour. Whip and fill pastry bag with whipped mixture and pipe rosettes around the top edge of cheesecake. Refrigerate cheesecake. To serve, place separate slices of cheesecake in pool of sauce, or serve cheesecake with sauce passed separately. Caramel Kahlua Sauce recipe follows.

CARAMEL KAHLUA SAUCE

1 cup granulated sugar

⅓ cup water

1 cup heavy (whipping) cream

2 teaspoons Kahlua

TO MAKE SAUCE

1. Whisk together sugar and water in a heavy medium saucepan. Place saucepan over medium heat and cook until sugar dissolves, without stirring. (The pan may be swirled to mix sugar and water, but do not stir.)

2. After sugar is dissolved, continue cooking over medium heat without stirring until syrup turns golden in color, about 10-12 minutes.

3. Remove pan from heat and whisk in cream. (It will bubble vigorously; just keep whisking.) If cream does not completely incorporate, return pan to heat and continue whisking. Add Kahlua.

4. Let syrup cool and thicken.

EASTSOUND

Waters of an inlet off Orcas Island penetrate deeply into the middle of the island, nearly bisecting it. At the point where the gentle waves finally meet land lies a small community named Eastsound. Here, colorful little shops and art galleries offer hand-crafted items, many created by local artists who are attracted to this island's quiet rural beauty. Orcas Island is the largest of the San Juan Islands, and most of its 36,000 acres are lush, green, and hilly. Mount Constitution in Moran Park, the highest spot on the island, offers spectacular views of Mt. Baker, Mt. Rainier, the Cascades, the Olympics, and Canadian mountains.

Some great spots for fishing in the waters alongside Orcas Island bring **salmon, cod, rock fish,** and **halibut** to the lines of fishermen. **Dungeness crabs, butter clams, geoduck clams,** and **shrimp** are also prevalent.

Poached Salmon Filets in Champagne with Champagne Sauce

SERVINGS: 4

Celebrate with this special dish.

¾ **cup brut champagne**

1 **tablespoon butter**

2 **bay leaves**

2 **teaspoons pickling spice**

2 **slices lemon, with rind**

4 **salmon filets (6-7 ounces each) preferably king salmon. (Remove as many bones as possible.)**

salt and freshly ground pepper

CHAMPAGNE SAUCE

¼ **cup brut champagne**

1 **cup heavy or light cream (for light cream, see page 322)**

Sprigs of fresh dill for garnish, optional

To poach fish: in large heavy saucepan or skillet with cover, add champagne, butter, bay leaves, pickling spice, and lemon slices. Bring to boil, add salmon filets, reduce heat, and simmer over low heat, covered, for 12 minutes or until salmon is opaque throughout. (Champagne sauce may be made at this time.) Season filets with salt and pepper. Remove from pan and take off skin and any remaining pickling spices from fish. Nap filets with sauce and serve. Place fresh dill sprig on top of each filet.

TO MAKE SAUCE

Make sauce by heating champagne over medium-high heat in a small saucepan and reducing by one-third. Add cream and reduce again by about one-third or until slightly thickened.

FRIDAY HARBOR

Friday Harbor, on the island of San Juan, is the largest city and the commercial center of the 172 San Juan Islands. This picturesque harbor is a merry mix of fishing village, antique shops, art galleries, and a marina bustling with many boats, large and small, luxurious and humble. Tourists flock here in the summer, especially in July when the annual jazz festival opens.

Off the coast, fishing is excellent for **salmon, cod,** and **halibut,** as well as shellfish such as **Dungeness crabs, clams,** and **shrimp.** Farmers grow **strawberries** and **raspberries,** and some **beef cattle** are raised on the island of San Juan.

Hot Dungeness Crab and Shrimp Sandwiches

SERVINGS: 6

Crab and shrimp are piled high on sourdough bread, and baked with cheese on top, in these open-faced seafood sandwiches.

2 cups flaked Dungeness crab meat (checked over so no shells remain)

1 cup cooked baby shrimp

3 ounces cream cheese, regular or light, at room temperature

⅓ cup mayonnaise, regular or light

¼ cup diced red pepper

¼ cup diced green pepper

6 slices lightly toasted sourdough bread

2 cups grated cheddar cheese

1. Preheat oven to 400 degrees. Combine all ingredients except bread and cheddar cheese in a medium bowl. Place toasted sourdough bread on cookie sheet. Evenly divide seafood mixture on top of bread slices. Top with grated cheese.

2. Bake on a cookie sheet for 10 to 12 minutes. Cut each slice of bread in half before serving these open-faced sandwiches.

Grilled Roast Beef and Sautéed Onion Sandwiches

SERVINGS: 4

The blue cheese and horseradish sauce adds a "zip" to these sandwiches.

3 tablespoons butter or margarine, divided

1 medium onion, peeled and sliced thinly

½ cup crumbled blue cheese

2 tablespoons mayonnaise, regular or light

1 tablespoon prepared horseradish

1 pound cooked roast beef, thinly sliced

freshly ground black pepper

8 slices sourdough bread

1. Melt 2 tablespoons butter in large saucepan, add onion slices and cook, covered, over medium heat until tender. Open lid and stir occasionally. Remove onions from pan, spoon onto plate, and reserve.

2. Combine blue cheese, mayonnaise, and horseradish in a small bowl. Evenly divide and spread mixture on one side of 4 bread slices.

3. Place remaining 4 bread slices on cutting board and top with sliced beef and cooked onions. Season with freshly ground black pepper. Complete each sandwich by adding a cheese-coated bread slice, placing the cheese side over the onions.

4. Melt remaining 1 tablespoon butter in skillet over medium high heat and grill sandwiches about 2 minutes on each side, or until lightly browned. Serve.

LOPEZ

Quiet, peaceful Lopez Island has little commercial development, not many resort spots, and only the small village of Lopez to supply local residents and a few visitors. People craving a bustling night life avoid Lopez, but those who seek tranquillity love this isle. Lush scenery and level terrain make Lopez a haven for bicyclists. Quiet bed and breakfasts, secluded cabins and a place to enjoy beauty and serenity attract others. **Sheep** and **cattle** graze in meadows, and old orchards laden with **apples** and other fruits reflect the importance of agriculture on this island. Beaches are rich with **Dungeness crab, clams**, and **shrimp** and fishers leave from Fisherman's Bay to snag **salmon** and other varieties.

Dungeness Crab Stuffed Mushroom Caps

SERVINGS: 12 AS APPETIZERS

For a change, select extra large mushrooms and serve these as a main course for a light supper.

24 large mushrooms, stems removed

½ pound Dungeness crabmeat (checked thoroughly for shell pieces)

½ cup finely diced onion

2 small ribs celery, finely diced

2 cloves garlic, minced

½ red pepper, finely diced

½ green pepper, finely diced

1 egg, slightly beaten

3 tablespoons melted butter or margarine

1 tablespoon chopped parsley

crushed Ritz crackers or other butter crackers, as needed

Parmesan cheese, freshly grated

1. Clean mushrooms by using a mushroom brush or clean toothbrush or paper towels. Do not soak.

2. Preheat oven to 375 degrees. Place mushrooms in a single layer on a baking dish. Combine other ingredients, except cracker crumbs and Parmesan cheese, in a medium bowl. Add enough cracker crumbs to mixture as needed to make a moist stuffing.

3. Stuff mushrooms with filling, sprinkle Parmesan cheese on top, and bake, uncovered, until tops are brown, about 12-15 minutes. (Mushrooms are done when they yield slightly to the touch.)

ANACORTES

Visitors come to Anacortes to catch a ferry or head their boat for a cruise through the San Juan Islands and beyond. Fishing is the main business in Anacortes, where people work as commercial fishers or builders of fishing boats. This port town is also home base for numerous boating, fishing, and scuba diving charter services.

Nearly a century ago many Croatians settled in Anacortes, and today their descendants preserve old-world traditions. The Croatian Cultural Center honors this heritage, sponsoring the talented and lively Vela Luke Croatian Dancers, who perform at many local festivals.

The Washington coast waters off Anacortes provide fishers with **rockfish, salmon, halibut,** and **cod.**

Sautéed Rockfish (Snapper) with Fresh Tomato Salsa

SERVINGS: 4

A tomato salsa adds spice and color to the sautéed fish.

SALSA

2 medium tomatoes

2 Serrano chili peppers

½ finely chopped onion

¼ cup chopped fresh cilantro (or substitute parsley)

2 cloves garlic, minced

½ teaspoon salt

½ teaspoon lime juice

FISH

1½ pounds rockfish (snapper) filets, cut in serving pieces

salt, freshly ground black pepper and cayenne pepper

flour

1½ tablespoons oil

1. To make salsa: place tomatoes in boiling water for 10 seconds, then under cold tap water, and slip off skins. Seed and chop finely. (To seed tomatoes, cut crosswise and squeeze or scoop out seeds.)

2. Using rubber or disposable gloves, remove seeds and stem from peppers under cold running water. Finely chop and place in medium bowl with tomatoes. Mix in rest of ingredients and combine as long as 2 hours before serving.

3. To prepare fish: take out as many bones as possible from filets. Sprinkle filets with salt, pepper, and cayenne, and dust rockfish with flour on both sides. Heat oil in a large skillet and swirl around. Over medium high heat, place filet pieces in skillet and cook about 6 minutes on each side or until fish is opaque throughout. Spoon salsa over warm fish filets and serve. Pass any extra salsa.

SEDRO WOOLLEY

Loggers who came to the Skagit Valley to cut cedar trees renamed a small community "Sedro," from the Spanish word *cedro* (cedar). It replaced the uninspiring and downright embarrassing original name of "Bug" given by one of the first settlers. After a few years, the community of Sedro merged with nearby Woolley, creating this town. Today, eye-catching outdoor murals on business district buildings depict the history of logging in the area. This early industry has been mostly replaced by agriculture, as small farms now cover much of the valley's early forested lands. **Raspberries, blueberries,** and **strawberries** compete with such vegetables as **cabbage, cauliflower, corn, broccoli, cucumbers, carrots, green peas,** and **spinach** in the fields. Small **dairy farms** are also in the valley.

Raspberry Streusel Coffee Cake

SERVINGS: 6

This always reminds me of a bed and breakfast where I had a similar coffee cake, along with quiche and fresh fruit.

½ **cup butter or margarine**

½ **cup granulated sugar**

2 **eggs**

1 **teaspoon almond flavoring**

1½ **cups all-purpose flour**

1½ **teaspoons baking powder**

½ **teaspoon baking soda**

¼ **teaspoon salt**

¾ **cup buttermilk**

1 **cup raspberries, fresh or frozen and thawed, well drained**

STREUSEL TOPPING

⅓ **cup brown sugar**

⅓ **cup all-purpose flour**

3 **tablespoons butter**

½ **cup sliced almonds**

1. Preheat oven to 350 degrees. Grease and flour a 9-inch round cake pan or 9-inch springform pan. Cream butter and sugar in a large bowl until light, add eggs, and beat well. Stir in almond flavoring.

2. Combine flour, baking powder, baking soda, and salt in separate bowl. Add flour mixture alternately with buttermilk to batter, beating after each addition, beginning and ending with flour mixture. Carefully fold in raspberries. (Raspberries should be dry.)

3. Make streusel topping by combining brown sugar, flour, and butter to a crumbly mixture in small bowl, then add almonds.

4. Pour coffee cake mixture into prepared pan and sprinkle with streusel topping. Bake in oven for 45-55 minutes or until cake tester inserted in center of cake is clean when drawn out. Cool on rack for 10 minutes. If using springform pan, remove sides.

WASHINGTON STATE HISTORICAL SOCIETY

Skagit Valley Harvest Soup

SERVINGS: 6-8

A cornucopia of vegetables makes this soup special.

2 tablespoons butter or margarine

1 medium onion, chopped

4 celery ribs, chopped

1 large leek, sliced
(leek needs to be well cleaned)

2 large carrots, diced

1 large potato, peeled and diced

1 tablespoon fresh basil, chopped

1 bay leaf

½ teaspoon dried thyme or
1½ teaspoons fresh

3 tablespoons all-purpose flour

5 cups chicken stock
(recipe page 313) or broth

2 large tomatoes

1 cup peas, fresh or frozen

1 cup chopped fresh spinach

½ medium cabbage, shredded

4 tablespoons parsley, chopped

1 teaspoon salt, or to taste

freshly ground pepper to taste

freshly grated Parmesan cheese

1. Melt butter in large stockpot over medium heat and add onion, celery, leek, carrots, potato, basil, bay leaf, and thyme. Cook, stirring frequently, for 5 minutes or until vegetables are slightly softened. Stir in flour. Gradually add stock, stirring constantly.

2. Bring to boil, reduce heat, cover, and simmer gently for 30 minutes. Peel tomatoes by plunging in boiling water in medium saucepan for 10 seconds, then rinsing under cold water. Slip off skins and chop.

3. Add tomatoes, peas, spinach, cabbage, and parsley to soup, and simmer for 10-15 minutes longer, uncovered. Add salt and pepper to taste. Serve with Parmesan cheese sprinkled on top.

Mary Lynn's Romaine Salad with Strawberries and Toasted Almonds

SERVINGS: 4

Use only fresh berries in this delicious summer salad.

RED WINE VINAIGRETTE

⅓ cup red wine vinegar

⅓ cup vegetable oil

⅓ cup granulated sugar

1 minced clove of garlic

salt and pepper to taste

SALAD

vegetable or olive oil spray

3 ounces sliced almonds

2 teaspoons melted butter

1 teaspoon granulated sugar

1 head romaine lettuce, cleaned and dry

¾ cup chopped scallions

1 can (8 ounce) mandarin oranges, well drained

10-12 fresh strawberries, stemmed and cut in fourths

1. Make dressing: combine thoroughly vinegar, oil, sugar, and garlic in food processor or shake thoroughly in jar with lid. Add salt and pepper to taste and set aside.

2. Preheat oven to 300 degrees. Spray cookie sheet with vegetable or olive oil spray. Sprinkle almonds on top. Drizzle butter over and sprinkle with sugar. Toast in oven for 8-10 minutes or until lightly browned. Remove from oven and set aside to cool.

3. Slice romaine lettuce diagonally into about ½-inch slices. Cut slices into large bite-size pieces and place in salad bowl. Add chopped scallions, orange segments, and strawberries. Toss with dressing to coat. Sprinkle with toasted almonds.

MOUNT VERNON

West of Mount Vernon, more than a thousand acres turn brilliant hues of purple, yellow, pink, and blue when the tulips, daffodils, and irises bloom in the springtime. Mild winters, rich soil, plentiful rain, and the expertise of early Dutch settlers enabled the Skagit Valley to become a major bulb and fresh flower region of the world. This profusion of color is celebrated each spring at the Tulip Festival, headquartered in the town of Mount Vernon.

Other farmers in the area produce approximately 40 percent of all the fresh **green peas** in the United States as well as vegetables such as **cabbage, cauliflower, broccoli, cucumbers, carrots, spinach,** and **corn.** Local residents boast that the rich Skagit Valley soil makes their **strawberries, raspberries,** and **blueberries** of superior quality. Many **dairy farms** supply milk for the state and the local Washington Cheese Factory. Nearby **poultry farms** send fryers to market. **Apple** orchards throughout Skagit and neighboring Whatcom County yield Jonagolds, Gravensteins, Melroses, and Liberties along with many other varieties.

Braised Fresh Peas with Lettuce, Parsley, and Mint

SERVINGS: 4-6

Pea pods are added to the peas when cooking to intensify their flavor.

8 large lettuce leaves (Boston)

3 tablespoons butter or margarine

½ to ¾ pound shelled peas

4 empty pea pods, cut diagonally into strips

¼ cup water

½ teaspoon salt

⅛ teaspoon granulated sugar

1 tablespoon parsley

scant ⅛ teaspoon nutmeg, preferably freshly grated

6 fresh mint leaves, minced

1. Cut lettuce leaves into ¼-inch strips.

2. In large saucepan, over medium heat, melt butter, add lettuce strips, peas, and pea pods. Stir and add water, salt, sugar, parsley, and nutmeg. Bring to gentle boil, reduce heat, cover pan and simmer until peas are tender. (Cooking time will vary according to how tender the fresh peas are—somewhere between 10-20 minutes.) Drain, remove pea pods, add fresh mint leaves, and serve.

Vegetables au Gratin
SERVINGS: 8

Here, a colorful array of vegetables is topped with a cream sauce. The water used to cook the vegetables is incorporated into the sauce to add flavor.

2 cups water

1½ teaspoons salt, divided

2 cups peeled and sliced carrots

2 cups cauliflower pieces (flowerets)

2 cups broccoli pieces (flowerets)

2 cups trimmed whole green beans

2 tablespoons butter or margarine

2 tablespoons all-purpose flour

½ cup heavy cream, light cream, or half-and-half (for light cream, see page 322)

⅛ teaspoon pepper, freshly ground

1 cup freshly grated Parmesan cheese

1. Heat water with ¾ teaspoon salt over medium high heat in large saucepan. Bring water to boil and add carrots, cauliflower, broccoli, and green beans. Reduce heat to low, cover pan, and cook for 20 minutes. Drain vegetables, reserving liquid. Place vegetables in baking dish (one that can be placed under broiler).

2. Heat butter in a medium saucepan over low heat until melted, blend in flour, and continue cooking and stirring for about 3 minutes. Remove from heat, add cream, and ½ cup of reserved vegetable liquid. Return to heat, bring to boil, stirring constantly, and boil 1 minute. Add reserved ¾ teaspoon salt and pepper. Pour cream sauce over vegetables. (Dish may be refrigerated at this point, then brought to room temperature.)

3. Sprinkle with Parmesan cheese, place under broiler for 3-5 minutes, watching carefully, until lightly browned. Serve.

WASHINGTON STATE HISTORICAL SOCIETY

Terri's Cabbage Salad

SERVINGS: 4

Toasted almonds and sesame seeds add crunch to this cabbage salad.

DRESSING

½ **cup vegetable oil**

3 **tablespoons rice vinegar
(or white wine vinegar)**

2 **tablespoons granulated sugar**

½ **teaspoon salt**

½ **teaspoon pepper**

2 **scallions, chopped**

SALAD

½ **head of cabbage, thinly sliced**

½ **(.3 ounce) package dry ramen
noodles, crumbled (ramen, with
seasoning packet removed)**

2 **tablespoons sesame seeds,
toasted**

2 **tablespoons sliced almonds,
toasted**

1. Make dressing by placing all ingredients in jar with lid and shaking vigorously to combine.

2. In salad bowl combine sliced cabbage and crumbled noodles. Add dressing to coat. Sprinkle with toasted sesame seeds and toasted almonds and toss again. (For toasting nuts, see page 323 in glossary.)

Country Chicken and Parsley Dumplings

SERVINGS: 4

This old-time favorite of tender chicken pieces braising in a flavorful broth and topped with dumplings is as good today as it was years ago.

**1 chicken (3 to 3½ pounds)
cut up, without giblets and neck**

freshly ground pepper

½ teaspoon salt

**1½ tablespoons vegetable oil
(more if needed)**

**4 medium carrots, peeled and
cut in 1-inch pieces**

2 celery ribs, cut in 1-inch pieces

1 medium onion, cut in eighths

1¼ cups milk, divided

**3 cups chicken stock
(recipe page 313)
or canned broth**

1 large or 2 medium bay leaves

3 tablespoons all-purpose flour

1. Remove as much skin as possible from chicken pieces, if desired. Salt and pepper each piece, rubbing into chicken.

2. In large Dutch oven or heavy kettle, heat oil over medium heat. Raise heat to medium high, add chicken a few pieces at a time so as not to crowd, and cook, turning until browned on all sides. When finished, take out chicken pieces and wipe pan dry with paper towel.

3. Return chicken to pan along with carrots, celery, onion, 1 cup milk, chicken stock, and bay leaf. Bring mixture to boil, reduce heat, cover, and simmer for one hour.

4. Make dumplings: recipe on following page.

5. When chicken and vegetables have cooked for 1 hour, transfer them to a heated platter and keep warm with foil tent in oven that has been heated, then turned off. Skim any fat from top of broth, bring back to boil, then reduce to simmer. Drop the dumpling dough from a wet tablespoon onto the simmering broth. Cover and simmer until the dumplings are puffed and cooked through, about 20-25 minutes. When cooked, arrange dumplings on platter surrounding the chicken and vegetables and continue to keep warm.

6. Combine 3 tablespoons flour with reserved ¼ cup milk by whisking together or shaking vigorously in a covered jar until smooth. Add 3 tablespoons warm broth to flour mixture and shake or whisk until smooth. Gradually stir mixture into broth in pan, bring to boil stirring constantly until slightly thickened. Ladle some sauce over chicken and dumplings, saving the rest to pass separately in small bowl. Sprinkle with chopped parsley. Serve. (Recipe continues on next page.)

(Country Chicken and Parsley Dumplings continued)

DUMPLINGS

1 cup all-purpose flour

2 teaspoons baking powder

½ teaspoon salt

⅛ teaspoon ground nutmeg, preferably freshly ground

1 tablespoon minced parsley

2 tablespoons chilled shortening

⅓ cup milk

chopped parsley, for garnish

TO MAKE DUMPLINGS

In a medium bowl, combine with fork 1 cup flour, baking powder, salt, nutmeg, and minced parsley. Cut in shortening with pastry blender (or with two knives) until mixture resembles coarse meal. Add milk, all at once, and mix lightly just until dough holds together. Set aside until needed.

Easy Apple Raisin Chutney
MAKES ABOUT 1⅓ CUPS

Homemade chutneys are superior to most commercial brands; however, they often take hours to prepare. This quick recipe is great to have on hand when time is short.

2 large tart cooking apples, peeled, cored, and finely diced

½ cup raisins

½ cup brown sugar

⅓ cup apple cider vinegar

¼ cup diced onion

¼ cup water

1 teaspoon tumeric

¼ teaspoon salt

½ teaspoon ground ginger

¼ teaspoon cinnamon

⅛ teaspoon ground cloves

1. Combine all ingredients in a medium microwave-safe bowl and cook on high, covered, for 10 minutes, stirring once. Uncover and cook 5 more minutes on high.

2. Cool and refrigerate, covered, up to 3 weeks.

La CONNER

The quaint fishing village of La Conner clings to the Swinomish Channel, making it easy for boats to tie up close by. Those that moor in port now are sailing, fishing, and sightseeing boats. But when the town flourished in the 1800s, the boats that came to port were river boats and sternwheelers, exporting lumber and the bountiful harvest from the Skagit Valley.

La Conner's main street looks much like it did during its heyday, and the town is filled with many old Victorian houses. Today, throngs of visitors come to this village by the channel to see the picturesque setting. They stay in old inns, browse through antique and collectors' shops, watch the boats, fish, and tour the countryside to see the flowers. East of La Conner, in the spring, many fields turn to yellow, red, and lavender when the vibrant-colored tulips, daffodils, and irises are in bloom.

The local fishing fleet and shellfish harvesters bring in **salmon, rockfish, Dungeness crabs, oysters,** and **clams.** In winter, fishermen jig for **smelt** when these small fish migrate through the Swinomish Channel. At other places in Washington people net smelt, but fishers on the Swinomish River jig for them. Long lines with multiple hooks are lowered in the water and jerked quickly to attract and catch the smelt. This prompts the local saying that "any jerk can snag a smelt in La Conner." The town celebrates the return of the smelt with a derby held every February. Farmers east of La Conner grow **berries, peas,** and other **vegetables.**

Fettuccine with Vegetables and Ricotta Sauce

SERVINGS: 6

Serve as a vegetarian main dish or as an adjunct to baked or grilled chicken or meat.

1 cup part-skim-milk ricotta cheese (no-fat ricotta cheese is not recommended)

3 dashes Tabasco sauce

1½ to 2 tablespoons olive oil

1 carrot, cut in julienne pieces

1 cup broccoli,
cut in small bite-sized pieces

1 cup cauliflower,
cut in small bite-sized pieces

½ cup peas
(fresh, or frozen and thawed)

1 small zucchini,
cut in julienne pieces

¼ red pepper, thinly sliced

3 cloves garlic, finely chopped

½ teaspoon salt, or to taste

freshly ground pepper

¾ pound fettuccine

2 tablespoons freshly grated
Parmesan cheese,
more for top if desired

2 tablespoons minced fresh basil
or 2 teaspoons dry

1. Place ricotta cheese and dashes of Tabasco sauce in food processor with steel blade inserted and process for about 45 seconds, or mix together in a small bowl, to a smooth consistency. Set aside.

2. Start heating water in large stock pot to cook fettuccine.

3. Heat olive oil in large skillet over medium heat and add all vegetables including garlic, and season with salt and pepper. Sauté for about 5 minutes, stirring constantly. (Vegetables should be tender but crisp.) Reduce heat, add ricotta mixture, and stir to coat vegetables. Turn off heat and keep warm.

4. Cook fettuccine in large pot of salted boiling water according to directions on package or until tender but still firm. Drain. Place pasta in large bowl and add vegetable sauce and toss. Stir in Parmesan cheese and chopped basil. Sprinkle with additional cheese and freshly grated pepper.

Broiled Smelt with Lemon Butter Sauce

SERVINGS: 4-6

Try this during the smelt season when these small fish are found in streams and local fish markets.

20 smelt

½ cup melted butter or margarine (more if needed), divided

1 cup fine dry bread crumbs, seasoned with salt and pepper

2 tablespoons chives, chopped

2 tablespoons lemon juice

1. Rinse smelt and place on cutting board. Cut off heads; with knife, slit belly (underneath side). Remove viscera, slide knife under bone and remove center bone with knife or by pulling backbone out with hand. Lay flat.

2. Coat smelt in ¼ cup of melted butter, then with bread crumbs. Place smelt flat, skin side up, on buttered pan and broil about 2 minutes or until smelt are cooked. Meanwhile, combine reserved ¼ cup melted butter with chives and lemon juice in a small bowl. Drizzle lemon-butter sauce over cooked smelt and serve.

COUPEVILLE

One of the oldest communities in the state, Coupeville, on Whidbey Island, has changed little throughout the years. The original village along the water's edge still retains its 19th-century ambiance with preserved old buildings, including an 1874 meat market, an 1892 bank, and a hotel built in 1890. Well-maintained Victorian residences surround the old town.

Whidbey is still rural, with peaceful pasture land, berry farms, and secluded beaches. Farming brought early settlers to the island around 1850, and much of the land is still devoted to agriculture. The island's most famous crop is **loganberries,** which make their way into pies, jams, and other treats such as the island's celebrated Whidbeys Liqueur. The renowned and succulent **Penn Cove mussels** come from nearby waters. These mild, plump mollusks are Northwest delicacies.

Steamed Penn Cove Mussels with White Wine, Thyme, and Cream

SERVINGS: 4-6

This is one my favorite ways to eat mussels.

3 pounds mussels

3 tablespoons olive oil

¼ cup chopped onion

4 large cloves garlic, minced

½ teaspoon dried thyme

1 cup dry white wine

**½ cup heavy or light cream
(for light cream see page 322)**

2 tablespoons finely chopped parsley

1. Scrub mussels well in several changes of water, pull off beards with fingers, or use pliers. Rinse mussels again. Drain.

2. Heat olive oil in large saucepan and sauté onion and garlic until tender. Add thyme and wine and bring to boil. Add mussels, cover, and steam 4-5 minutes or until mussels have opened. Transfer mussels to plate or large bowl and cover to keep warm. (Discard any mussels that did not open.)

3. Strain broth through double thickness of cheesecloth into clean bowl and return to saucepan. Add cream to broth and heat briefly. Ladle broth over clams and sprinkle with parsley.

Loganberry Cheesecake with Whidbey's Liqueur Sauce
SERVINGS: 10

If loganberries are unavailable, try raspberries. In place of Whidbey's Liqueur use Framboise or Crème de Cassis.

CRUST

2 cups vanilla wafer crumbs

½ cup melted butter or margarine

FILLING

8 ounces white chocolate, cut in small pieces

4 (8-ounce) packages cream cheese, regular or light, at room temperature

¾ cup granulated sugar

4 eggs

2 tablespoons flour

1½ teaspoons vanilla

2 cups loganberries

WHIDBEY'S LIQUEUR SAUCE

1 cup loganberries

3 tablespoons Whidbey's Liqueur

¼ cup sifted confectioners' sugar

1. Preheat oven to 250 degrees. To make crust: combine vanilla wafers and melted butter in bowl. Press into bottom of 10-inch ungreased springform pan.

2. To make filling: melt white chocolate in top of double boiler over gently simmering water over medium heat. Stir occasionally with wooden spoon or wire whisk. Set aside.

3. In large mixing bowl, beat cream cheese until light. Add sugar and beat until fluffy and sugar is dissolved, about 2-3 minutes. Beat in eggs, one at a time, and continue beating until smooth. Add flour and vanilla and combine well. (If using electric mixer, remove bowl from mixer before adding chocolate.) Add melted chocolate very gradually and whisk until smooth.

4. Place loganberries on top of crust. (Be certain berries are dry.) Pour filling over berries and bake for 1½ hours or until top is firm. Place cheesecake on rack to cool. Refrigerate, covered loosely, overnight. Remove side of pan and let stand 20 minutes before serving with sauce.

5. Drizzle sauce over each piece, or place a slice of cheesecake in a pool of sauce.

TO MAKE SAUCE

Puree 1 cup loganberries in food processor, push mixture through sieve into bowl to remove seeds. Combine with liqueur and sugar.

MARYSVILLE

Marysville's Strawberry Festival and colorful parade are part of the community's biggest celebration, drawing as many as 30,000 people to town each June. Visitors come to have fun and celebrate the harvest of the area's most famous crop. Fertile flat delta land at the mouth of the nearby Snohomish River provides prime soil for growing not only luscious **strawberries,** but also **blueberries** and **raspberries**. These berries are sold locally and are also nationally distributed.

SUSAN PARISH COLLECTION

Old-fashioned Strawberry Shortcake at its Best

SERVINGS: 6

Serve in large individual bowls and enjoy!

1½ to 2 quarts fresh strawberries

½ cup granulated sugar

2 tablespoons Grand Marnier (or orange juice)

½ teaspoon vanilla

Extra sugar for sprinkling on top

1 cup heavy (whipping) cream

SHORTCAKE

2¼ cups all-purpose flour

6 tablespoons granulated sugar

1½ teaspoons baking powder

¾ teaspoon baking soda

⅛ teaspoon salt

1½ teaspoons grated orange zest (peel)

½ cup chilled butter or margarine, cut in pieces

¾ cup buttermilk

1. Rinse berries and let dry. Hull and set aside 6 large ones. In food processor or blender, puree half of remaining berries with sugar, Grand Marnier and vanilla. Slice remaining berries and stir into puree. Cover and let stand 20 minutes, or make ahead and refrigerate for no more than six hours. If refrigerated, let warm to room temperature before serving.

2. To make shortcakes: preheat oven to 400 degrees. Combine flour, sugar, baking powder, baking soda, salt, and orange zest together in large bowl. Cut in chilled butter with pastry blender (or forks) until mixture resembles coarse crumbs. Add buttermilk, tossing with fork, until mixture can be gathered into a ball.

3. Roll dough out on a floured surface to about 1-inch thickness. The dough may then be cut into 6 rounds with large cookie cutter, or cut into squares. Sprinkle with sugar, place on lightly greased cookie sheet, and bake for 20-23 minutes or until done. (These may be made ahead and reheated for a few minutes in a 250 degree oven.) Cool shortcakes slightly; split them.

4. Whip cream. Spoon strawberries over bottoms, replace tops, and spoon more berries over. Serve with whipped cream and reserved whole berries. This dessert is best served in large individual bowls.

PUGET SOUND

Waters of the sound abound with fish. Fields of berries, fruits, and vegetables fill valleys, grow on plateau lands, thrive on islands, and surround the base of snow-topped mountain peaks.

Everett
Snohomish
Monroe
Edmonds
Poulsbo
Seattle
Mercer Island
Bellevue
Kirkland
Redmond
Issaquah
Woodinville
Bainbridge Island
Renton
Kent
Auburn
North Bend
Snoqualmie
Fall City
Carnation
Duvall
Bremerton
Port Orchard
Vashon
Tacoma
Puyallup
Sumner
Gig Harbor
Olympia

EVERETT

Everett, at the edge of Gardner Bay, boasts a bustling waterfront and the second largest marina on the West Coast, harboring boats of all shapes and sizes. The Marina Village, a renovated portion of the waterfront district, resembles an 1890s community. There, visitors can browse and buy at quaint shops. To the west is the chance to fish in Puget Sound; to the east is the fertile Snohomish valley, where thousands of acres offer an array of vegetables, fruits, and dairy products.

In the bountiful valley, **milk production** ranks first in agricultural products, and **poultry**, including both **egg** production and **fryers**, ranks second. Fruit and vegetable farms supply **apples, beans, beets, blueberries, broccoli, cabbage, carrots, cauliflower, corn, cucumbers, lettuce, peas, potatoes, pumpkins, raspberries, rhubarb, squash, strawberries,** and **zucchini.** Commercial and sport fishermen bringing **English sole** and other varieties of **fish** from the waters of Puget Sound.

Buttermilk, Sour Cream Pancakes with Blueberry Syrup

SERVINGS: 4-6

These light, tender pancakes are my husband's favorite breakfast.
When blueberries are unavailable, use maple syrup.

2 cups all-purpose flour

2 teaspoons granulated sugar

¾ teaspoon salt

2 teaspoons baking powder

1 teaspoon baking soda

2 cups buttermilk

1 cup sour cream, regular or light

2 eggs

BLUEBERRY SYRUP

2½ cups blueberries

½ cup granulated sugar

1 tablespoon corn syrup

⅓ cup water

½ teaspoon lemon juice

dash cinnamon

1. Make blueberry syrup.

2. In large bowl combine flour, sugar, salt, baking powder, and baking soda. In another medium bowl, combine buttermilk, sour cream, and eggs, and mix together. Add buttermilk mixture to flour mixture and combine.

3. Let rest 10 minutes before baking on lightly greased hot griddle. Ladle batter onto griddle to make 5-inch pancakes. Cook until golden on both sides.

TO MAKE SYRUP

1. Combine berries, sugar, corn syrup, water, and lemon juice in a medium saucepan and cook over medium-high heat.

2. Bring to boil, reduce heat, and gently boil, stirring occasionally, until berries pop and syrup is slightly thickened, about 20 minutes. Stir in cinnamon and set aside to cool. Serve at room temperature.

Sole with Mushrooms, Cheese, and Wine Sauce

SERVINGS: 6

This delicate dish is to be made ahead, then assembled and cooked just before serving.

2 pounds sole filets

½ cup dry white wine

2 tablespoons lemon juice, divided

salt

white pepper

4 tablespoons butter or margarine, divided

2 tablespoons all-purpose flour

½ cup half-and-half or milk

⅛ teaspoon nutmeg, preferably freshly ground

½ pound sliced mushrooms*

1 cup grated Swiss cheese

freshly ground nutmeg

*Clean mushrooms with mushroom brush, clean toothbrush, or paper towels. Do not soak in water.

1. Preheat oven to 400 degrees. Arrange filets in shallow baking dish. Pour into the pan the wine and 1 tablespoon lemon juice; sprinkle fish with salt and pepper. Cover and bake for 10 minutes. Gently remove filets from pan and place in another baking pan. Drain off liquid and measure 1 cup. (If there is not enough juice, add water to make 1 cup.) Cover and refrigerate fish.

2. Make sauce by melting 2 tablespoons butter in medium saucepan over medium heat and stirring in flour. Cook for 3 minutes. Meanwhile, heat half-and-half in small saucepan until warm. Combine cream with reserved fish liquid. Take butter mixture off heat, and add cream mixture, all at once. Return to heat and stir constantly over medium heat until thickened. Add nutmeg. Season with salt and pepper. Cover sauce with waxed paper and chill.

3. When ready to serve, take fish and sauce from refrigerator, about ½ hour before continuing cooking. Preheat oven to 400 degrees. Melt remaining 2 tablespoons butter in large skillet over medium heat, adding 1 tablespoon reserved lemon juice and mushrooms. Sauté mushrooms until tender, season with salt and pepper. Spoon mushrooms over fish, then cover with sauce evenly. Sprinkle with grated cheese.

4. Bake, uncovered, for about 7 minutes or until sauce is bubbling and cheese is browned. Watch carefully. Sprinkle with fresh ground nutmeg and serve.

Spicy Chicken and Noodles with Eric's Peanut Sauce

SERVINGS 4

Chicken and noodles with a spicy flair!

12 ounces linguine or spaghetti

1 egg white

1 tablespoon cornstarch

2 boneless, skinless chicken breasts, sliced into strips

4 tablespoons vegetable oil

1 tablespoon dry
red pepper flakes

½ red pepper, cut in thin strips

4 scallions thinly sliced, divided

1 cup dry-roasted peanuts, divided

1. Make Peanut Sauce; set aside.

2. Cook pasta in stock pot in boiling water (with salt) until tender, but still firm, according to directions on package. Drain and place in large serving bowl. Stir peanut sauce again and add to noodles. Cover with vented foil to keep warm.

3. Meanwhile, whisk together egg white and cornstarch in bowl and add chicken strips to coat. Heat oil in wok or skillet over high heat. Add 1 tablespoon red pepper flakes and stir-fry for 10 seconds; add chicken strips and stir-fry for about 2 minutes; add red pepper strips and continue cooking until chicken is cooked, about 5 minutes. Add chicken strips and peppers to noodles, then add half the scallions and half the peanuts. Mix together. Sprinkle remaining scallions and peanuts on top. Serve.

PEANUT SAUCE

⅓ cup hot water

⅓ cup smooth peanut butter

2 teaspoons soy sauce

2 teaspoons rice or
white wine vinegar

2 cloves garlic, minced

1 teaspoon granulated sugar

¼ teaspoon dry red
pepper flakes

TO MAKE PEANUT SAUCE

Blend together hot water and peanut butter in a small bowl. Stir in soy sauce, vinegar, garlic, sugar, and ¼ teaspoon red pepper flakes.

Cannelloni Stuffed with Chicken

SERVINGS: 4

Béchamel (white) sauce and ground chicken bring variety to this cannelloni.

4 tablespoons butter or margarine

4 tablespoons all-purpose flour

2 cups milk, heated to warm

1 teaspoon salt, divided

½ teaspoon white pepper, divided

⅛ teaspoon nutmeg, preferably freshly grated

4 tablespoons olive oil, divided

3 tablespoons minced onion

3 tablespoons finely chopped celery

2 tablespoons finely chopped carrots

2 tablespoons minced parsley

2 cups ground chicken

¼ teaspoon oregano

¼ teaspoon basil

¾ cup dry white wine

12 cannelloni squares (or use fresh lasagna pasta pieces cut in 4-inch squares, or wide lasagna noodles, cooked and cut in 4-inch lengths.)

freshly grated Parmesan cheese

1. Make white sauce: in saucepan melt butter, stir in flour, and cook over medium heat for 3 minutes or until bubbly. Take pan off heat, add 2 cups heated milk, and return pan to heat. Stir constantly until sauce is smooth and thickened. Reduce heat to low and season sauce with ¼ teaspoon salt, ¼ teaspoon white pepper, and nutmeg. Take off heat and set aside.

2. In skillet, heat 2 tablespoons olive oil and sauté minced onion, celery, carrots, and parsley about 5-7 minutes or until vegetables are tender. Set aside. Heat remaining 2 tablespoons olive oil in another skillet and sauté ground chicken until cooked and no longer pink. Add cooked chicken to cooked vegetable mixture along with remaining ¾ teaspoon salt, oregano, basil, remaining ¼ teaspoon white pepper, and wine. Simmer mixture until wine is reduced to about 2 tablespoons. Stir in ½ cup white sauce and set aside.

3. Preheat oven to 400 degrees. Cook pasta squares in boiling salted water as directed on pasta package. Drain and rinse in cool water. Dry each pasta piece and divide filling among the pasta squares, using about ¼ cup in each square. Roll up jelly-roll style and place seam-side down in buttered baking dish. Pour remaining white sauce over pasta, and top with grated Parmesan cheese. (May be refrigerated at this point, then brought out for 30 minutes before baking.)

4. Bake, uncovered, at 400 degrees for 15-20 minutes. Take from oven and let settle for 10-15 minutes before serving.

Cucumber and Rice Vinegar Salad

SERVINGS: 4-6

This refreshing and simple salad works well with many menus.

2 cucumbers, peeled

½ - ¾ teaspoon salt

½ cup rice vinegar

1½ tablespoons granulated sugar

1. Slice cucumbers very thin with potato peeler. Place slices in layers in a medium bowl; lightly salt each layer. Put plate on top and weight (anything heavy). Cover and refrigerate for 2 hours. Drain.

2. Combine vinegar and sugar, pour over cucumbers, and refrigerate one hour longer. Serve drained on lettuce leaves, or in individual bowls along with the vinegar mixture.

SNOHOMISH

In a valley of meandering rivers and fertile farmland lies Snohomish, a town famous for its charming old Victorian houses and shops filled with treasured antiques. Antique shops are so prevalent in this community that it calls itself the "Antique Capital of the Northwest." Looking skyward from Snohomish, one can often see colorful hot air balloons from nearby Harvey Airfield floating gracefully over the countryside.

Dairy cattle graze in the Snohomish Valley, where fresh vegetables and fruits also flourish. Harvest time brings large crops of **peas** and **corn.** Other vegetables grown are **beets, broccoli, cabbage, carrots, cucumbers, green beans, potatoes,** and **onion.** Local fruits are **apples, blueberries, raspberries, strawberries, rhubarb,** and **Italian plums.** This is also a great place to get **pumpkins** in the fall.

Kari's Grilled Polenta with Fresh Corn and Red Peppers

SERVINGS: 6

Kari usually serves this with grilled chicken, a Caesar salad, and french bread.

2 cups whole milk

½ cup cornmeal

¾ cup chopped red pepper

¾ cup fresh corn kernels (canned or frozen may be substituted)

1 cup Parmesan cheese, freshly grated

4 dashes Tabasco sauce

½ teaspoon salt

freshly ground pepper

vegetable spray

extra grated Parmesan cheese for top

10-inch quiche pan or 10-inch pie pan

1. Bring milk to boil in a high-sided saucepan over medium-high heat. Add cornmeal and constantly beat until very thick and mixture pulls away from the sides of pan. Take off heat. Add red pepper, corn, Parmesan cheese, dashes of Tabasco sauce, and salt and pepper.

2. Prepare quiche pan or 10-inch pie pan by placing plastic wrap on bottom which extends over sides. Spray wrap with vegetable spray and pour mixture into quiche pan or large pie pan, covering with extended plastic wrap. Refrigerate 1 hour or longer until firm to touch.

3. Take from refrigerator, remove plastic wrap. Cut in wedges, place on lightly buttered cookie sheet, and broil until lightly browned (about 3-4 minutes). Turn and brown other side, watching carefully. Sprinkle lightly with Parmesan cheese and serve.

Cindy's Pasta Salad
with Peas, Cherry Tomatoes, and Peppers

SERVINGS: 8

If penne noodles are unavailable, use another type of pasta in this colorful salad.

⅓ cup white wine vinegar

2 tablespoons water

2 teaspoons salt

½ teaspoon granulated sugar

2 teaspoons minced fresh
tarragon or ½ teaspoon dried

1 large clove garlic,
minced and mashed to a
paste with ½ teaspoon salt*

pepper, freshly ground

½ cup olive oil

1 pound medium penne or
rigatoni (or other pasta)

boiling water and about
1 tablespoon salt for pasta

½ pound green peas,
fresh or frozen,
cooked until just tender

4 cups cherry tomatoes,
cut in halves

1 yellow pepper, sliced

1 orange pepper, sliced

½ cup shredded fresh basil leaves

1. In large bowl or food processor, whisk together vinegar, water, 2 teaspoons salt, sugar, tarragon, garlic-salt paste, and pepper. Add oil in small stream, whisking constantly until well combined.

2. Cook pasta in salted, boiling water in large kettle, as directed on package. Drain and cool under cool water. Place in colander to drain completely. In bowl, toss pasta with dressing, add peas, tomatoes, peppers, and basil and toss salad again. Serve.

*TO MASH MINCED GARLIC AND SALT:

Place salt on cutting board with minced garlic over. With paring knife blade, mash together, pressing blade back and forth over garlic and salt.

MONROE

In the early 1900s, many people came to Monroe to log. When the trees were gone, the folks turned to farming and raising horses. Now, many local horse training and breeding centers bring people from around the world to buy and breed their horses here. Farmers raise some **cattle** and the nearby U-Pick farms offer **strawberries, raspberries, blueberries, peas, garlic, beans, cucumbers, cauliflower, broccoli, cabbage, carrots, zucchini, corn,** and **potatoes.** The Evergreen State Fair is held in Monroe each August, with the best display of fresh produce often coming from the fair's home town.

SPECIAL COLLECTIONS, UNIV. OF WASHINGTON LIBRARIES, CURTIS PHOTO, NEG. #39202

Roasted Vegetable and Melted Mozzarella Sandwich

SERVINGS: 4 OPEN-FACE SANDWICHES

A number of restaurants are now serving roasted vegetable sandwiches.
Try these open-faced sandwiches at home.

1 large carrot, peeled

½ large onion

2 medium red potatoes

1 sweet potato, peeled

¼ red pepper

½ zucchini

2 tablespoons olive oil

2-3 cloves garlic,
peeled and slivered

salt and freshly ground pepper

1 tablespoon minced fresh thyme
or 1 teaspoon dry thyme

1 tablespoon minced fresh basil
or 1 teaspoon dry basil

1½ cups grated Mozzarella cheese

mayonnaise, regular or light

4 slices warm toasted
sourdough bread

2 tablespoons minced
fresh parsley

1. Preheat oven to 425 degrees. Dice carrot, onion, red potatoes, sweet potato, red pepper, and zucchini into ¼-inch pieces.

2. Pour olive oil in large roasting pan and place in oven until oil is smoking hot, about 3-4 minutes. Remove pan from oven and add diced vegetables, garlic, salt, pepper, thyme, and basil. Cook, uncovered, until vegetables are tender and brown, about 20 minutes. Stir once during cooking.

3. Take pan from oven and sprinkle grated cheese on top of vegetables. Return to oven to melt cheese, about 2 minutes.

4. Lightly coat mayonnaise on warm toasted bread. With spatula, remove about ¼ of vegetable-cheese mixture from pan and place on top of bread slice. Repeat until all bread slices are covered. Sprinkle with minced parsley.

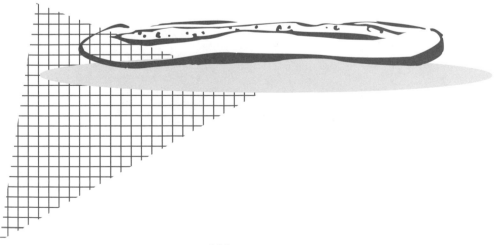

Strawberry Frozen Torte

SERVINGS: 8

This impressive frozen torte has a beautiful pink color.

5 cups strawberries

1½ cups granulated sugar

⅓ cup water

1 teaspoon light corn syrup

4 egg whites

2 tablespoons framboise or framboise syrup (optional)

2 cups heavy (whipping) cream

13-14 split ladyfingers (enough to line an 11-inch springform pan)

strawberries for garnish

1. Puree strawberries in food processor, take out 2 cups, and combine with sugar, water, and corn syrup in small saucepan. Bring to boil and cook over high heat until temperature reaches soft ball stage (238 degrees) on candy thermometer. Skim off foam at top.

2. Beat egg whites in separate bowl until stiff peaks form; gradually beat in hot syrup. Continue beating at high speed for 8 minutes, or until meringue mixture cools to room temperature.

3. Fold in remaining strawberry puree and framboise. In another bowl, whip cream until stiff, fold into meringue.

4. Butter the sides of a 10½ or 11-inch spring-form pan and line with split lady fingers. Pour in the strawberry mixture. Cover and freeze at least 8 hours or up to a week. Remove sides of spring-form pan, garnish with fresh strawberries, and cut in wedges.

EDMONDS

Edmonds is a picturesque waterfront community where ferries dock and depart regularly. Street corners and lamp posts are bright with beds and baskets of flowers, and views of Puget Sound and the Olympic Mountains are visible from many streets and shops. There are several waterfront parks here, including an underwater marine park for scuba divers. A public fishing pier offers anglers an opportunity to catch **salmon, sole,** and sometimes even **squid.**

Fried Calamari (Squid) in Beer Batter

SERVINGS: 4

Serve as appetizers, or for supper with jicama, carrot, and cabbage slaw and sourdough bread.

2 pounds cleaned squid, sliced into rings

BEER BATTER

1 cup all-purpose flour

2 teaspoons baking powder

½ teaspoon salt

2 tablespoons vegetable or peanut oil

1 cup beer, room temperature

oil for frying

lemon wedges

1. Rinse calamari rings and pat dry with paper towel. Mix flour, baking powder, and salt in a medium bowl, add oil and beer and stir well. Let stand for 20-30 minutes.

2. Pour enough oil in a deep large skillet or electric fry pan to come to 1 to 1½ inches deep. Turn heat on high and heat oil to hot (350-380) degrees.

3. Coat dry slices of squid with beer batter. (At this point the coated slices look quite messy, but the end result will look fine.) Placed coated slices in hot oil and cook until lightly golden, about 2-3 minutes. These may need to be done in batches. Remove from oil with tongs or slotted spoon and drain on paper towels. Serve with lemon wedges.

POULSBO

For the first half of its existence, Poulsbo could easily have been mistaken for a small town on a fjord in Norway. Signs were in Norwegian, the people dressed in native costumes and most people spoke Norwegian. Early settlers were predominately Norwegian; however, others soon arrived from Sweden, Finland, and Denmark. In those early years, the community had no roads to the outside and transportation was limited mainly to boats. Settlers lived by fishing and farming, sometimes taking produce to the Pike Place Market in Seattle by steamboat. Today, highways connect Poulsbo with the outside world and English is spoken, but local businesses still display Scandinavian murals, the bakeries and restaurants serve Norwegian food, and some shopkeepers dress in authentic old-world costume. Poulsbo fishermen continue to sail from Liberty Bay to fish in surrounding Puget Sound for **cod, salmon,** and other **seafood.**

Lemon Baked Cod with Roasted Red Pepper Sauce

SERVINGS: 4-5

This traditional Norwegian dish is updated with a spicy red pepper sauce.
Melted butter may be used in place of sauce.

5 tablespoons all-purpose flour

½ teaspoon salt

⅛ teaspoon pepper

3 tablespoons butter or margarine

3 tablespoons lemon juice

**1½ pounds cod filets,
cut in serving pieces
(bones removed)**

1. Make Roasted Red Pepper Sauce. Set aside while preparing fish.

2. To prepare fish: preheat oven to 450 degrees. Combine flour, salt, and pepper, and place in shallow bowl or on waxed paper. Melt butter and place in shallow dish, add lemon juice, and combine. Dip fish in butter and lemon mixture; then coat each side in flour mixture.

3. Place in baking dish and pour any remaining butter mixture over fish. Bake 10-12 minutes or until fish is opaque throughout. Top with Roasted Red Pepper Sauce.

ROASTED RED PEPPER SAUCE

1 red pepper

2 scallions, chopped

**1 tablespoon sour cream,
regular or light**

1 tablespoon chopped parsley

**2 teaspoons Dijon or
Dijon-style mustard**

**1 tablespoon fresh chopped dill or
1 teaspoon dry**

TO MAKE SAUCE

1. Roast pepper by cutting off stem, halving lengthwise, removing seeds, and flattening slightly by pressing with hand. Place skin side up on oiled, heavy baking sheet or pan and place about 3-4 inches under broiler. Broil until skin is blistered and blackened, watching carefully. Place in paper bag to cool.

2. When cooled, remove skins. Puree pepper in food processor or blender and transfer to a medium bowl. Add rest of sauce ingredients and combine.

SEATTLE

Seattle is an emerald recently polished, now glistening. Her history is brief; her growth, dramatic. The city's beginnings date back only to 1851, when Arthur Denny and his group sailed up from Portland and were met by rain, a gray wilderness, and a few Duwamish Indians. Briefly settling at Alki Point, the party soon moved to a more protected spot near present-day Pioneer Square. "Duwamps" was the first name given this settlement before pioneer Doc Maynard had the good sense to suggest the more euphonious "Seattle," a name honoring the group's good friend, Chief Sealth.

Today, Seattle is the Northwest's financial, cultural, industrial, trade, and tourist center, serving over a million and a half people in the greater metropolitan area. A variety of events and conditions bolstered Seattle's growth. City fathers saw promise, not disaster, after the engulfing fire of 1889, and rebuilt the town even better than it was before. During the Alaskan Gold Rush of 1897, prospectors bought their supplies here, stimulating the building of new stores. Shipping flourished in Elliott Bay's deep harbor. The world fairs of 1909 and 1962 focused international attention on the city. The rise of the Boeing Company, and, more recently, Microsoft, stimulated economic development. Nearby rich natural resources fed growth of every kind, and the great natural beauty of the site attracted thousands.

Views of mountains and water can be seen everywhere in Seattle. To the west are the Olympics and Puget Sound, to the east lie the Cascade mountains and Lake Washington, to the south looms majestic Mount Rainier, and within the city are a number of lovely small lakes. Scenes on the lakes vary with the seasons yet entertain year round: sailboats swiftly moving across the water quickened by billowing spinnakers; lighted Christmas ships parading and bringing Yuletide music to thousands of listeners; boats with fishers during the salmon runs; speedboats with water-skiers skimming the waves; and in the fall, boats of all sizes chugging across Lake Washington to dock near the University of Washington, so boaters can take a short walk to the stadium to see the hometown Huskies play football.

Seattle's cerebellum is down around Fourth and Union streets, but its pulsating heart is at the Pike Place Market. The show goes on every day: in one ring farmers and fish mongers hawk their produce, in another, crafts-men display their wares, and in still another, improvisational musicians play and sing for those who have the time to listen. Energy and vitality abound amid the panoramic views of Puget Sound and the mountains beyond.

In the spring, local farmers bring in greens as diverse as **endive, water-cress, spinach, edible pea vines, lettuce, arugula, Savoy cabbage, Chinese mustard greens,** and **baby bok choy.** Farm tables are brim-full in the sum-mer with Washington-grown **berries** and vegetables including **peas, beans, cucumbers, zucchinis, corn, sweet onions, Chinese snow peas,** and **toma-toes** of red, yellow, and green. Varieties of **squash** and **pumpkins** decorate the tables in the autumn along with **apples, cabbage, collard greens, kale,** and **brussels sprouts.** In the winter, farmers come to sell honey, jams and jellies as well as winter crops of **potatoes, beets, turnips,** and **parsnips.** Four fish markets sell common and exotic specimens of all shapes and varieties. Near-by Puget Sound offers **salmon, octopus,** and a wide variety of **bottom fish.** The Northwest has the enviable reputation of having a plethora of fresh good foods to eat; most of these vegetables, fruits, herbs, wild mushrooms, seafood, poultry, and meat can be found at the lively Pike Place Market.

SPECIAL COLLECTIONS, UNIV. OF WASHINGTON LIBRARIES, NEG. #12305

Pike Place Market Seafood Bounty

SERVINGS: 4-6

It's fun to visit the Market and buy some fresh seafood to bring home to add to a simmering broth. The broth can be made a day or two earlier and refrigerated.

¼ cup olive oil

1 red pepper,
seeded and finely chopped

1 green pepper,
seeded and finely chopped

2 medium onions or one large,
chopped

3 cloves garlic, minced

½ cup finely chopped celery

½ cup chopped parsley, divided

2½ cups dry white wine

2 cups clam broth or bottled clam
juice, or fish stock

¼ cup tomato paste

1 cup water

2 bay leaves

1 tablespoon dried basil
(or 3 tablespoons fresh, chopped)

1 teaspoon dried thyme

1 teaspoon salt

freshly ground pepper to taste

1 cooked Dungeness crab,
cleaned and cracked

1 pound salmon filets,
skinned, boned, and cut in chunks

12 mussels or clams in shell,
well scrubbed
(mussels must be debearded)

½ pound scallops
(if large, cut in bite-sized pieces)

1. Heat oil in a large kettle, add peppers, onion, garlic, celery, and 2 tablespoons of the parsley. Cook over medium heat, stirring often until vegetables are soft. Add wine, broth, tomato paste, water, bay leaves, basil, and thyme. Season with salt and freshly ground pepper. Cover and simmer 15 minutes. (Broth may be refrigerated at this point and reheated when seafood is ready.)

2. Take the crab meat from the body and legs, discarding shells (or leave crab meat in legs for eater to individually shell). Bring broth to boil, reduce heat to low so broth is just simmering. Add all the prepared seafood, cover, and simmer until clams or mussels open, about 8-10 minutes. Discard bay leaves and any clams or mussels that do not open. Ladle some broth and seafood into large soup bowls. Sprinkle with remaining parsley.

Other firm-fleshed fish and shellfish can be used, depending on availability.

Saki Salmon

SERVINGS: 4

*The influence of Asian foods in northwest cooking
is reflected in this recipe. Directions for baking in a conventional and
microwave oven are offered. This recipe adapts well to microwave cooking,
for the fish is kept moist and the glaze gives needed color to the fish.*

**4 salmon filets
(about 6 ounces each)**

¾ cup saki (Japanese wine)

2 tablespoons granulated sugar

¼ cup soy sauce

**1½ tablespoons freshly grated
ginger (1½ teaspoons ground)**

1 teaspoon vegetable oil

**1 lemon grass stalk,* sliced
(or peeled lemon zest
from ½ of lemon)**

**2 teaspoons toasted sesame seeds
(see page 323 for toasting nuts)**

**Long, narrow stalks
containing lemon oil,
sometimes used in
flavoring Asian
soups and sauces.*

1. Remove bones from filets. In glass baking dish just large enough to hold filets, combine saki, sugar, soy sauce, ginger, vegetable oil, lemon grass (or lemon zest) and stir together. Add filets, flesh side down, and marinate, covered, in refrigerator for 30 minutes.

2. (If using conventional oven, preheat oven to 350 degrees.) Pour marinade into small saucepan and bring to boil over medium-high heat. Continue cooking, stirring frequently with wooden spoon, for 8 minutes or until mixture reduces by about one-third. Turn filets flesh side up in baking dish and brush with one-half of the reduced mixture (glaze). Discard lemon grass slices.

3. For microwave: Cover dish tightly with plastic wrap, and bake on high for 4 minutes. Remove from microwave oven, brush on remaining glaze. Cover again with plastic wrap and cook on high for 4 more minutes. Remove from microwave; let fish sit for 2 minutes before removing plastic wrap covering. Pour any extra glaze over filets, and serve. Sprinkle with sesame seeds.

For conventional oven: Bake uncovered 10 minutes at 350 degrees. Remove from oven. Brush with remaining glaze. Bake 5-10 minutes longer or until filets are opaque throughout. Sprinkle with sesame seeds.

Vegetable Medley Salad

SERVINGS: 4

These fresh vegetables and herbs are found at the Pike Place Market as well as most markets throughout the state. The recipe can easily be doubled.

water, 1 teaspoon salt added

½ cup diced peeled carrots
(about ½-inch dice)

½ cup diced red potatoes,
skins left on (about ½-inch dice)

½ cup green beans,
cut in ½-inch pieces

½ cup fresh corn kernels
(canned may be substituted)

½ cup diced celery
(about ½-inch dice)

½ cup chopped radicchio,
Belgium endive, iceberg or
red oakleaf lettuce

¼ cup diced red pepper

¼ cup diced Walla Walla Sweet
Onions (or red onion)

1 clove garlic, minced

¼ cup minced chives

¼ cup finely chopped parsley

VINAIGRETTE

2 cloves garlic

2 tablespoons Dijon
or Dijon-style mustard

1 tablespoon dried oregano

pinch dry rosemary

¼ cup rice vinegar,
or white wine vinegar

1 teaspoon salt

freshly ground pepper

¼ cup olive oil

⅓ cup vegetable oil

1 tablespoon capers (optional)

1. Make vinaigrette and set aside.

2. Bring about 4 quarts of water to boil in a large stock pot. Add salt, carrots, potatoes, green beans, and fresh corn. (If using canned corn, add later). Boil (blanch) 2 minutes. Drain and place under cold running water or into a bowl of ice water. Drain again and blot dry with paper towel.

3. In large bowl, combine celery, radicchio, red pepper, onion, garlic, chives, and parsley. (Add canned corn at this time.) Add cooked vegetables and toss to coat with vinaigrette. This salad may be made ahead, covered, and refrigerated until serving time.

TO MAKE VINAIGRETTE

1. In food processor with steel blade inserted, combine garlic, mustard, oregano, rosemary, vinegar, salt, and pepper.

2. Gradually add oils and process until mixture is thickened. Remove bowl from food processor, add capers. Set aside or refrigerate.

Seasonal Salad Greens with Balsamic Vinaigrette and Baked Chèvre Cheese

SERVINGS: 6

Balsamic vinegar has a deep, rich, brown color with a balanced sour and sweet taste.

1½ quarts (6 cups) mixed greens, such as endive, spinach, red lettuce, arugula, watercress, escarole, chicory, and radicchio

2 cloves garlic, minced

3 tablespoons Balsamic vinegar

1 tablespoon Dijon or Dijon-style mustard

¼ teaspoon dried thyme

¼ teaspoon dried basil or 1 teaspoon fresh, chopped

1 teaspoon granulated sugar

½ teaspoon salt

freshly ground pepper

½ cup olive oil

4 scallions

4 tablespoons minced parsley

3 ounces soft chèvre cheese, (other soft goat cheese or softened cream cheese may be substituted) rolled in 12 balls and flattened into disks

¾ to 1 cup bread crumbs

1. Clean and dry greens and crisp in refrigerator for 2 hours or longer.

2. Preheat oven to 350 degrees. Combine garlic, vinegar, mustard, thyme, basil, sugar, salt, and pepper in food processor or small bowl. Add olive oil in a thin stream and combine until emulsified (thickened). Add scallions and parsley to mixed greens in a large bowl and coat with dressing.

3. Coat the chèvre cheese in bread crumbs. Place on lightly greased baking sheet and bake for 10 minutes or until lightly toasted. Serve salad greens on individual plates and top with 2 baked cheese disks.

Càffe Latté Frozen Mousse

SERVINGS: 6-8

Coffee beans do not grow anywhere near Seattle, but the city imports and sells enough for it to be called the "coffee capital of the country." Espresso carts and shops reside on nearly every block. The càffe latté, the most popular drink, spurred the name "Latté Land" for the Seattle area.

¾ **cup fresh hot espresso***

8 ounces cream cheese, regular or light, at room temperature and cut in cubes

2 tablespoons Kahlua

2 cups heavy (whipping) cream

½ **cup granulated sugar**

ground cinnamon for tops

*If espresso machine is not available, use instant espresso (amount according to manufacturer's directions) with ¾ cup boiling water.

1. Pour hot espresso over cream cheese in a medium bowl and blend until cream cheese is melted. Stir in liqueur and set aside.

2. Partially whip cream, add sugar, and beat until cream holds shape. Fold in espresso mixture and pour into a quart mold, or individual demitasse cups or serving dishes.

3. Freeze without stirring. Remove from freezer 10 minutes before serving, and unmold if a mold is used. Serve sprinkled lightly with cinnamon.

MERCER ISLAND

Early Indians avoided Mercer Island, fearing its "sunken forests"—the huge chunks of the island that had broken off and dropped to the bottom of Lake Washington. Eventually, in the late 1800s, pioneers courageously settled on the wooded island. The island stayed intact and many more flocked to this patch of peaceful greenery in the middle of Lake Washington. In the 1900s, dairy farmers delivered milk to Seattle by rowboat from the island, loggers cut Douglas fir and cedar trees, and truck gardening was a viable industry. With the completion of the floating bridge in 1940 which joined Mercer Island to Seattle, the rural flavor of the island faded as roads were paved, stores constructed, and thousands of homes built to house the many who commuted to Seattle. Truck farms have vanished and now the only produce grown is found in private gardens.

Grand Prize-winning Brandy Eggnog Pie

SERVINGS: 6

Although this book usually highlights local products, for Mercer Island I included my recipe for Brandy Eggnog Pie, the 1986 Grand Prize Winner in a Mercer Island Reporter's *recipe contest. This pie is easy to make, a help during the busy holiday season.*

CHOCOLATE CRUMB CRUST

¼ cup butter, melted

1½ cups chocolate wafer or hydrox cookies, finely ground

FILLING

1 package (10-ounce) regular-sized marshmallows

¾ cup commercial eggnog

1 cup heavy (whipping) cream

4 tablespoons brandy

additional whipped cream for top

freshly grated nutmeg

1. Combine melted butter and crumbs together in a small bowl. Place in 9-inch pie plate and press evenly and firmly in place, covering bottom and sides. Chill in refrigerator one hour or longer.

2. Heat marshmallows and eggnog in a medium saucepan over low heat until mixture is smooth, stirring frequently. (Or heat in microwave oven on high, covered, for about 2 minutes, stirring once. Remove from microwave and stir until smooth.) Chill in refrigerator about 45-55 minutes, stirring every 10 minutes. Chill until thickened, but still able to stir.

3. Whip cream and fold into eggnog mixture along with the brandy. Pour into prepared chocolate crumb crust and refrigerate several hours. Decorate with additional whipped cream and grated nutmeg.

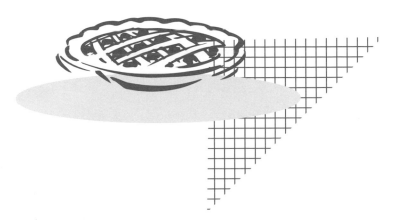

BELLEVUE

In the 1920s and 1930s, only a ferry connected the Bellevue area with Seattle, making it a lovely spot for summer cottages, small farms, and orchards. Decades later, two floating bridges joined the area to Seattle, and Bellevue's population exploded into the fourth largest city in Washington. Today, it has a high-rise city center, and businesses and industries that attract commuters from surrounding areas including Seattle. A lovely park built beside bustling Bellevue Square provides beauty and a spot to "stop and smell the roses" in the center of this busy city.

Bellevue annually hosts one of the largest outdoor arts and crafts shows in the country, held on the last weekend of July when the sun always shines—well, almost always. The exceptions were in 1970 and again in 1993, when some pesky raindrops interfered.

Strawberry fields covered the area before the suburban sprawl overtook them. Today, two local **blueberry** farms provide plump, ripe berries in July and August.

Kris's Blueberry Pie

SERVINGS: 6

My daughter, Kris, always requests this pie for her birthday. The berries are cooked briefly in the microwave to retain their flavor before adding to the conventionally baked pie crust.

5 cups blueberries, fresh or frozen

¾ cup granulated sugar

½ teaspoon cinnamon

3 tablespoons cornstarch

¼ teaspoon grated lemon zest (peel)

1 teaspoon water

baked pie crust
(recipe page 310)

CRUMB TOPPING

½ cup brown sugar, packed

½ cup butter or margarine

1 cup all-purpose flour

½ cup rolled oats,
regular or quick-cooking

½ teaspoon cinnamon

vanilla ice cream, optional

1. Preheat conventional oven to 400 degrees.

2. In a medium microwave-safe bowl, combine berries, sugar, cinnamon, cornstarch, lemon zest, and water. Cover and microwave on high for 6 minutes. Uncover, stir, and microwave another 4 minutes and stir. Continue cooking for 3-6 more minutes or until thickened, stirring after each minute. (Cooking time will vary with fresh or frozen berries.)

3. Place thickened mixture in baked pie shell. Combine crumb topping ingredients in a small bowl with fork or pastry blender. Crumble on top of pie and bake in conventional oven for 7-10 minutes or until lightly browned. Cool. Serve at room temperature or reheat in 250-degree oven until warm. Serve with ice cream if desired.

KIRKLAND

Located on the banks of Lake Washington, Kirkland has more than a mile of public shoreline dotted with public parks, boat landings, moorages, and trendy shops and restaurants. Local residents and visitors picnic, wind surf, swim, fish, sail, or listen to the summer evening concerts at the waterfront parks. Situated between two wetland wildlife habitats, residents often see Canadian geese, mallards, widgeons, loons, and blue herons flying overhead or stopping to visit and looking for a free lunch. The piers of the waterfront parks are popular places to catch **trout** and **bass**, and boaters fish Lake Washington for Chinook and Coho **salmon** during their runs.

Cheese Puffs with Smoked Salmon Filling

SERVINGS: 10 AS APPETIZERS

If you don't have time to make the puffs, use the filling to spread on crackers.

FILLING

6-7 ounces smoked salmon, bones removed

8 ounces softened cream cheese, regular or light

1 tablespoon lemon juice

1 tablespoon grated onion

2 tablespoons mayonnaise, regular or light

1 tablespoon horseradish

2 tablespoons chopped parsley

PUFFS*

1 cup water

½ cup butter or margarine, cut into small pieces

1 cup all-purpose flour, sifted

4 eggs

¾ cup grated cheddar cheese (use Cougar Gold, if available)

*The puffs have a preferred uniform appearance when piped through a pastry bag.

1. To make filling: place all ingredients in food processor or a medium bowl and blend until smooth.

2. To make puffs: preheat oven to 400 degrees. In a medium saucepan, combine water and butter and bring to a boil over medium heat, melting butter.

3. Remove from heat. Add all the flour at once and beat vigorously with a wooden spoon until mixture is smooth and begins to leave sides of pan and forms a ball. Return to medium heat and beat vigorously for 1 to 2 minutes. Remove from heat and add eggs, one at a time, beating well to incorporate until smooth and velvety. Add grated cheese. Pipe with a pastry bag with no tip attached (or use small teaspoon) onto baking parchment paper on cookie sheet, or a greased cookie sheet. Use about 1½ teaspoons of batter for each puff. (This will make approximately 50 puffs.)

4. Bake 10 minutes. Open oven door slightly and keep ajar, using a wooden spoon, and bake an additional 15 minutes. (This allows steam to escape from oven.) When baked, remove from oven and pierce each puff with a thin, sharp knife to let steam escape. Turn off oven; return puffs to oven for 30-45 minutes to dry out, leaving door ajar. Remove from oven and split and fill puffs with salmon filling. Puffs may be reheated briefly in a 350 degree oven to crisp before filling and serving.

REDMOND

First named Salmonberg for the spawning salmon coming up nearby Sammamish Slough, Redmond now honors its first postmaster, Luke McRedmond. Today, scenes near Redmond are both pastoral and industrial; horses still graze in the countryside, while electronic companies find this suburban community an ideal spot for their facilities. A 486-acre recreation area, Marymoor Park, offers fields for picnicking, tennis, horseback riding, softball, a children's farm, and a velodrome for serious cyclists.

From May through October, vendors sell a variety of produce, flowers, and crafts at the Redmond Saturday Market located right downtown, behind the Justice White House. A nearby U-pick farm offers mainly **strawberries.**

Sole with Strawberry Citrus Sauce

SERVINGS: 4

A colorful berry sauce tops these filets.

sole filets
**(20-24 ounces altogether)
Remove as many bones
as possible**

¾ **cup buttermilk**

½ - ¾ **cup all-purpose flour,
seasoned with ½ teaspoon salt
and freshly ground pepper**

1 tablespoon vegetable oil

1 tablespoon butter or margarine

STRAWBERRY CITRUS SAUCE

½ **cup fresh strawberries**

¾ **cup orange juice**

**1 teaspoon grated
orange zest (peel)**

1 tablespoon cornstarch

**1 tablespoon mayonnaise,
regular or light**

1. Make sauce and keep it warm.

2. Place buttermilk and seasoned flour in separate shallow dishes. Dip fish in buttermilk, coat with seasoned flour, and set aside.

3. Melt oil and butter in large skillet. Over medium heat, sauté filets, about 3 minutes on each side or until fish is opaque throughout. Place on serving plates and top with sauce.

TO MAKE SAUCE

Puree strawberries in food processor or blender and set aside. Combine orange juice, zest, and cornstarch in small saucepan and cook over low or medium heat until thick, stirring constantly. Stir in mayonnaise and pureed strawberries. Remove from heat; cover and keep warm in pan or in top of double boiler. (If sauce becomes too thick, add droplets of orange juice or water.)

ISSAQUAH

Early residents couldn't agree on what to name their town. At various times, people called it Squak, Olney, Englewood, and Gilman before the citizens finally decided on the Indian word "Issaquah" in 1890. "Gilman" is still the name of a boulevard and village shopping center, where old farmhouses and farm buildings have been brought together and transformed into tasteful shops, boutiques, and restaurants. Originally a town to house coal miners, today Issaquah is a suburb of Seattle with a small-town ambiance.

In the fall, spawning **salmon** swim up Issaquah Creek, and thousands of people come to celebrate their return at the annual Salmon Day Festival on the first weekend of October. Along with fish-watching, the Festival includes about 400 arts and crafts booths, entertainment, and a parade. Salmon can be seen throughout the year at the local fish hatchery.

Fettuccine with Smoked Salmon and Chèvre Cheese
SERVINGS: 4

With all ingredients on hand, this dish comes together in minutes.

**2 cups heavy or light cream
(for light cream see page 322)**

**6 ounces soft chèvre
(goat cheese) cheese,
cut in pieces**

**8 ounces smoked salmon,
flaked and all bones removed**

**½ teaspoon dry crushed
red pepper flakes**

1 pound fettuccini

salt

chopped chives

freshly ground pepper

1. Start heating water, with salt, in large pot for pasta. Heat cream in large saucepan over medium-high heat, until reduced by about one-third and slightly thickened. Add cheese pieces and blend in. When cheese has melted, stir in flaked smoked salmon and crushed red pepper. Take off heat, cover, and keep warm.

2. Meanwhile, cook pasta in boiling salted water until tender but still firm, according to package directions. Drain and place on serving dish. Cover with sauce. Top with chopped chives and freshly ground pepper.

WOODINVILLE

Once a small logging and farming town, Woodinville is rapidly growing, housing a population that commutes to Seattle, Bellevue, or nearby industrial parks, and comes home to "country living." The area's woodsy atmosphere, pastoral scenes, and homes with acreage for horses and bridle paths, along with views of mountains in the distance, attract many newcomers.

Fresh produce and U-pick farms offer **lettuce, peas, cauliflower, beets, strawberries, beans, cabbage, carrots, corn, cucumbers, zucchini, winter squash, pumpkins,** and **garlic.**

Zucchini, Queen Mary

SERVINGS: 6-8

This recipe is for the zucchini that "gets away" and resembles an ocean liner in size. Hence, the name "Zucchini, Queen Mary." The filled zucchini may be served as an accompaniment to grilled meat, fish, or poultry, or is a satisfying vegetarian main course.

1 zucchini, "Queen Mary" size (as long as 2 feet)

3 tablespoons olive oil

1 cup diced onion

⅔ cup diced red pepper

1 large tomato, seeded and diced

3 cloves garlic, minced

1½ cups bread crumbs

½ cup grated Parmesan cheese

1½ tablespoons fresh basil or ½ teaspoon dried

½ teaspoon salt

½ teaspoon dried thyme

freshly ground pepper, to taste

extra freshly grated Parmesan cheese

1. Preheat oven to 350 degrees. Cut zucchini lengthwise, scoop out pithy part, and discard. With spoon, scoop out flesh "ribbons" of zucchini, leaving ½-inch shell. Dice zucchini's cut-out flesh.

2. In large skillet, heat olive oil, add diced zucchini, onion, red pepper, tomato, and minced garlic. Cook over medium heat until vegetables are tender. Remove from heat and stir in bread crumbs, Parmesan cheese, basil, salt, thyme, and pepper. Stuff zucchini with vegetable mixture.

3. Place in large pan, loosely cover with foil, and bake one hour. Remove foil, top with additional Parmesan cheese, and bake 10 minutes longer or until tender. (Cooking time varies with size of zucchini.) Remove from oven and serve.

BAINBRIDGE ISLAND

Bainbridge Island's harbor community, Winslow, is a short distance from Seattle by boat. Commuters, tourists, and bicyclists all keep ferry boats busy connecting this community with the mainland.

In the late 19th century, Winslow was a shipbuilding center for tall-masted schooners, the area's major industry for many years. Now, tourists, small farms, fishing, and small industries keep some local residents busy while others ride the ferries to work. Ferryboat riders are treated to views of Mt. Rainier, the Olympics, Seattle's skyline, and an occasional killer whale rising powerfully out of the water.

Berry farms sell **strawberries, raspberries,** and **marionberries.** The Island Winery uses local berries and cool-climate grapes for their wines. Some local **vegetables** and **herbs** are sold commercially.

Marionberry Cobbler

SERVINGS: 6

It just isn't summer without tasting a berry cobbler. Other blackberries, including wild ones, may be used in this cobbler.

6 cups marionberries (or other blackberries)

⅓ cup plus ¼ cup granulated sugar, divided (more, if desired)

2 teaspoons lemon juice

2 teaspoons lemon zest (peel), minced

1½ cups all-purpose flour

½ teaspoon salt

2 teaspoons baking powder

¼ teaspoon baking soda

½ cup butter or margarine

1 cup sour cream, regular or light

vanilla ice cream or cream

1. Preheat oven to 400 degrees. Butter a 1½ or 2-quart baking dish. Combine berries, ⅓ cup sugar (more, if desired), lemon juice, and zest, and place in buttered baking dish.

2. In a medium bowl, combine flour, salt, baking powder, baking soda, and butter with pastry blender or forks to make a coarse-meal consistency. Add sour cream and combine.

3. Divide dough in six parts and form into patties. Place patties on top of berry mixture and sprinkle remaining ¼ cup sugar on top. Bake 40-45 minutes or until cobbler top is golden brown. Remove from oven and let stand before serving. Serve slightly warm, with a scoop of vanilla ice cream or pour cream over.

Bainbridge Berry Wine Cake

SERVINGS: 8

Sip some Bainbridge berry wine along with this not-too-sweet cake.

½ cup slivered almonds

1¾ cups all-purpose flour

1 teaspoon baking powder

½ teaspoon salt

¾ cup butter or margarine, room temperature

¾ cup granulated sugar

3 eggs

⅓ cup Bainbridge raspberry or strawberry wine

½ teaspoon almond extract

1 cup fresh raspberries or strawberries (strawberries should be cut in half)

powdered sugar

extra fresh raspberries or strawberries

1. Preheat oven to 325 degrees. Finely grind almonds and set aside. (May be done in food processor or blender.) Grease and flour 9-inch round cake pan.

2. Combine flour, baking powder, and salt in a small bowl and set aside. In large mixing bowl, cream butter until light, add sugar gradually, and beat until fluffy. Add eggs, one at a time, beating well after each addition. Stir in berry wine, almond extract, and ground almonds. Add dry ingredients, beating until just mixed.

3. Place 1 cup berries in prepared pan and pour batter over. Bake for 45-50 minutes or until cake tester comes out clean. Cool on rack for 10 minutes, remove from pan. To serve, dust top with powdered sugar and garnish with fresh berries, if desired.

RENTON, KENT, AND AUBURN

In the mid 1800s, white settlers began building cabins along the banks of the Cedar and Black rivers, which had been home to the Duwamish Indians for years. The fertile delta of the two rivers formed rich growing soil, the rivers held salmon, and wild berries grew profusely in the woods. Some years later, the Black River went dry and many Indians left the village. The town that grew on the banks was called Renton and eventually became dependent on industry—first coal mining and later lumbering and milling. In the 20th century, truck and rail-car manufacturing and Boeing's commercial airplane division transformed Renton into a thriving, industrialized city.

Kent and Auburn are located in a valley south of Renton. The Green River Valley's rich soil brought early settlers to farm. Once, the area was a major agricultural center, but now manufacturing dominates the economy. In the early days, farmers from the area brought their produce into Auburn for shipment down the Duwamish River to Seattle. Some small farms still use the fertile valley soil for growing vegetables, berries, and other fruits to sell locally or truck to Seattle.

Fruits grown on the farms include **raspberries, blueberries, strawberries, rhubarb, cherries, pears, apricots, prunes, grapes,** and **apples.** Vegetables include **beans, peas, beets, carrots, pumpkins, cucumbers, broccoli, Jubilee corn, cabbage, lettuce, cauliflower, peppers, potatoes,** and **tomatoes.**

Leafy Lettuce Salad with Blueberries, Walnuts, and Blueberry Cream Dressing

SERVINGS: 6

Serve in July or August when fresh blueberries are plump and ripe.

DRESSING

3 tablespoons blueberry vinegar

5 tablespoons sour cream, regular or light

2½ tablespoons mayonnaise, regular or light

¼ teaspoon salt

freshly ground pepper

⅛ teaspoon cinnamon

SALAD

3 cups torn red lettuce, cleaned and dry

3 cups torn Bibb lettuce, cleaned and dry

¾ cup fresh blueberries

½ cup walnut halves, toasted (see page 323 for toasting nuts)

TO MAKE DRESSING

Combine vinegar, sour cream, mayonnaise, salt, pepper, and cinnamon in a small bowl, and mix well.

TO MAKE SALAD

In salad bowl, toss dry lettuce leaves with blueberries; coat with blueberry dressing and toss again. Sprinkle with toasted walnut halves.

Caroline's Raspberry Yogurt Cream with Framboise

SERVINGS: 6

Caroline's collections of recipes include ones that are not only good but easy.
Teaching art history at Smith College keeps her busy, yet she still enjoys cooking and entertaining.

1 package (3⅛ ounce) raspberry-flavored gelatin

1 cup hot water

1 (10 ounce) package unthawed frozen raspberries

½ pint vanilla frozen yogurt

1 tablespoon framboise, optional

fresh raspberries for garnish

1. Dissolve gelatin in 1 cup hot water. Stir in raspberries; add yogurt and framboise and stir until it melts. (Frozen raspberries may need to be broken apart with a fork.)

2. Spoon into individual glass compote dishes and refrigerate until set. Top with fresh raspberries.

SNOQUALMIE VALLEY
North Bend, Snoqualmie,
Fall City, Carnation,
and Duvall

Snoqualmie Valley is surrounded by the forested foothills of the Cascade mountains. The Snoqualmie Indians once burned the woods periodically to hold back forest growth and keep open spaces for berries and edible roots. Later, the valley became farmland for early settlers who planted mainly hops, a crop that brought prosperity to the area until insect infestation and falling prices put an end to the industry in the late 1800s. Hop farms have now been replaced by vegetable, berry, and dairy farms.

Quiet rural communities of the valley include North Bend, Carnation, Snoqualmie, Fall City, and Duvall. Many visitors come to the area to view spectacular 268-foot high Snoqualmie Falls, climb rugged Mount Si, hike the many paths in the Cascades, ski at Snoqualmie Pass ski areas, or climb aboard an old steam train to enjoy a scenic ride.

A large **herb farm** featuring over 600 different herbs is located near Fall City. Truck and U-pick farms provide **blueberries, strawberries, garlic, shallots, corn,** and **pumpkins.** Near Carnation is a 900-acre working **dairy farm,** and the largest **sheep farm** in the valley.

WASHINGTON STATE HISTORICAL SOCIETY

Seven Herb Soup

SERVINGS: 6

This soup is made flavorful with fresh herbs (seven including the garlic). If not all these fresh herbs are available, use what your garden and the grocery store offer.

1½ tablespoons olive oil

¾ cup peeled and chopped onion

2 cloves garlic, minced

5 cups chicken stock
(recipe page 313)
or canned broth

½ pound spinach, cleaned and sliced

¼ cup each fresh chopped parsley, chervil, tarragon, sorrel, lovage, and lemon thyme

⅔ cup sour cream, regular or light

¼-½ teaspoon salt

freshly ground pepper

extra sour cream for garnish, as desired

1. Heat olive oil over medium heat in large saucepan, add onion, and cook for 2-3 minutes or until tender. Add garlic and continue cooking for 5 minutes. Add stock, bring to boil, reduce heat to low, and simmer; add spinach. Simmer until spinach is cooked, about 5 minutes. Add all chopped herbs. Simmer for 3 minutes and remove from heat. Cool slightly.

2. Puree mixture in food processor or blender. Return to saucepan, add sour cream, and salt and pepper to taste. Serve warm, or chill in refrigerator for 4 hours or longer. Serve cold with dollop of sour cream on top.

Deep Dish Shepherd's Pie with Garlic Mashed Potatoes

SERVINGS: 4

Plan ahead to have leftover roast lamb to use in this shepherd's pie.

GARLIC MASHED POTATOES

1½ pounds Russet potatoes, peeled and cubed

5 cloves garlic, peeled

1 tablespoon butter or margarine

¼ cup milk

¼ teaspoon dried rosemary

salt and freshly ground pepper to taste

FILLING

1½ tablespoons butter or margarine

1 cup sliced mushrooms

¼ cup green pepper, finely chopped

¼ cup onion, finely chopped

2 cups coarsely chopped cooked lamb

1½ cups beef stock (recipe page 314) or canned broth

¼ teaspoon dry thyme

⅛ teaspoon ground nutmeg, preferably freshly grated

1 cup cooked, sliced carrots

3 tablespoons flour mixed with 3 tablespoons water

⅓ cup grated cheddar cheese

2 tablespoons minced parsley for garnish

1. To make mashed potatoes: place cubed potatoes and garlic in steamer basket over water in saucepan. Bring water to boil and steam potatoes and garlic for 30-35 minutes or until fork tender. Drain water, take out steamer basket and return potatoes and garlic to pan and mash well. Add butter and mix well. Warm milk (in small saucepan on top of stove or in small container in microwave oven), add to potatoes, along with rosemary, salt, and pepper, and combine. Set aside.

2. Preheat oven to 350 degrees. Make filling: melt butter in large saucepan over medium heat, add mushrooms, green pepper, and onion, and sauté until tender. Add lamb, stock, thyme, nutmeg, and carrots, and stir together over medium heat for 5 minutes.

3. Whisk flour/water mixture with 6 tablespoons of the warm broth in a small bowl. Slowly stir in flour mixture to saucepan. Bring mixture to boil over medium-high heat, stirring constantly. Reduce heat and simmer 15 minutes, stirring frequently.

4. Place mixture in 6-8 cup casserole dish. Carefully spoon, or pipe with pastry bag, mashed potatoes over sauce. Sprinkle with grated cheese and bake 30 minutes. Remove from oven, sprinkle with parsley, and serve.

Strawberry White Satin Tart

SERVINGS: 8

Strawberries top a white chocolate filling in this tart.

CRUST

1⅓ cups all-purpose flour

¼ cup granulated sugar

½ cup butter, chilled and cut in small pieces

1 egg yolk

FILLING

6 ounces white chocolate, chopped

½ cup heavy (whipping) cream

2 tablespoons butter or margarine, room temperature

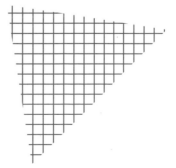

TOPPING

5 cups strawberries

½ cup currant jelly

whipped cream for garnish

1. To make crust: preheat oven to 300 degrees. In food processor (or with pastry blender) combine flour and sugar. Add butter pieces and process until fine crumbs form. Add egg yolk and process just until dough starts to hold together. Remove from bowl and with hands form a ball. Press over bottom and sides of 10- or 11-inch tart pan with removable sides. Bake for 30-35 minutes. Cool completely.

2. For filling, melt white chocolate slowly in top of double boiler over simmering water, stirring occasionally with wooden spoon, until smooth. Take off heat. Heat cream in separate pan but do not boil. Add to white chocolate along with butter and combine. Pour chocolate mixture in cooled tart crust and cool.

3. Cut stem-ends off strawberries so berries will lie flat on surface of pie. (Place cut berries on paper towel to completely dry.) Arrange strawberries in a single layer on filling; heat currant jelly over low heat in small saucepan and melt. Take jelly from heat and brush on each berry. Refrigerate. Before serving, pipe or spoon whipped cream on top.

BREMERTON AND PORT ORCHARD

A small ferry for pedestrians only connects Bremerton and Port Orchard, cities located on the east side of Puget Sound. Bremerton, the larger of the two, is home to the Puget Sound Navy Base and the Puget Sound Naval Shipyard, the city's largest industry. Port Orchard, by contrast, has had little industrial growth and retains a small-town ambiance. Strolling through Port Orchard's downtown area, one finds an antique mall, art galleries, coffee shops, covered sidewalks, and views of colorful sailboats in the harbor.

Port Orchard holds the fourth largest farmers' market in Washington state, operating every Saturday morning from May through October. The local Apple Day Festival in October is a time when fresh pressed cider is passed out, apple dishes of all kinds are available, and an apple expert is on hand to identify hundreds of varieties of the fruit. Flavorful apples have been grown in orchards near this port town for many years. In western Washington, apples tend mainly to be Gravensteins, Jonagolds, and other cooking varieties. In addition to **apples,** U-pick and truck farms in Kitsap County sell **berries, corn, beans, peas,** and other vegetables. Nearby are a number of **sheep** farms. Sport fishers cruise Puget Sound waters seeking a variety of **fish,** including **salmon.**

Grilled Salmon Filets with Fresh Blueberry Salsa

SERVINGS: 6

If berries are not in season, these basted salmon filets need only a squeeze of lemon.

6 salmon filets, skin removed
(about 6 ounces each)

4 tablespoons butter or margarine

2 tablespoons vermouth
(or lemon juice)

2 tablespoons brown sugar

salt and pepper

BLUEBERRY SALSA

1 cup fresh blueberries,
processed about 5 seconds
in food processor or
coarsely chopped

½ cup finely chopped
fresh pineapple

¼ cup minced red bell pepper

¼ cup minced green bell pepper

¼ cup minced red onion

¼ cup chopped fresh
cilantro leaves

¼ cup chopped fresh mint leaves

1 tablespoon fresh lime juice

2 teaspoons minced, seeded
jalapeño peppers*

¼ teaspoon grated
lime zest (peel)

salt to taste

1. Make salsa first.

2. Prepare barbecue grill or preheat broiler, if needed. Remove as many bones as possible from filets. Heat butter, vermouth, and brown sugar in small saucepan over low heat until butter is melted. Brush both sides of salmon with butter mixture. Season with salt and pepper.

3. To grill: place filets in oiled grilling basket, close. Grill approximately 5-7 minutes per side, turning basket half way through. Baste with butter mixture during cooking. Alternately, broil salmon 3 inches from heat for about 5-6 minutes on each side, or until filets are opaque throughout, basting occasionally with butter mixture. Serve with salsa.

TO MAKE BLUEBERRY SALSA

Combine all salsa ingredients in bowl and season to taste with salt. Allow to stand 1-2 hours at room temperature.

*When mincing jalapeño chili peppers, use disposable or rubber gloves to protect your skin.

Flaming Apples Jubilee with Ice Cream

SERVINGS: 6

Serve in a chafing dish for a spectacular presentation.

vanilla ice cream

4 large cooking apples, peeled, cored, and sliced

1 teaspoon cornstarch

⅓ **cup butter or margarine**

¼ **cup brown sugar**

½ **cup Northwest apple brandy or Calvados; if unavailable, use regular brandy.**

1. Place one or two scoops of ice cream in 6 individual heat-resistant bowls, cover, and place in freezer.

2. Pat apple slices dry and sprinkle with cornstarch. Melt butter in large saucepan or chafing dish. Sauté apples over medium heat until tender, about 15 minutes. Sprinkle brown sugar over apples and continue cooking until sugar is dissolved, stirring frequently. (This part may be done earlier, refrigerated, and reheated.)

3. When ready to serve, take individual ice cream bowls from freezer. (Reheat apple slices if done ahead.) Heat apple brandy in small saucepan until hot, pour over warm apple mixture in chafing dish or saucepan, and ignite. (Long fireplace matches work well.) When flames die down, serve apple mixture over ice cream.

VASHON

Vashon Island, snugly tucked in southern Puget Sound, is filled with quiet scenic beaches, forested hills and glens, and small farms with open fields. In 1792, Captain Vancouver named the island in honor of his friend, Captain James Vashon of the British Navy. Later, the town that grew to meet the needs of the rural islanders also came to be called by the captain's name.

Only a short ferry ride away from Tacoma or Seattle, Vashon is home to some commuters. Many other islanders work in local businesses, such as the making of preserves, ciders, berry products, and processing coffee and tofu.

Vashon Island is famous for its **strawberries**. U-pick farms also feature **raspberries, blackberries,** and a variety of **vegetables.**

Strawberry Brandy Sorbet

SERVINGS. 6

So refreshing and light!

4 cups strawberries

2 tablespoons water

¾ cup granulated sugar

**1½ tablespoons brandy
(fresh lemon or orange juice
may be substituted)**

**fresh strawberries, sliced and
lightly sweetened for garnish**

1. In food processor with steel blade inserted, or blender, puree strawberries. Combine 2 tablespoons puree with 2 tablespoons water and combine with sugar in a small saucepan. Add brandy and cook over low or medium-low heat until sugar is dissolved, stirring frequently. Add rest of fruit puree and stir well. Chill in refrigerator.

2. Place in freezer container and freeze sorbet following manufacturer's directions. To freeze without ice cream maker, pour mixture into 8-inch square pan and place in freezer. Stir every 15 minutes until creamy for about 1½ hours. Cover and freeze. When serving sorbet, it may need to be taken from freezer about 10 minutes before serving. Spoon sliced strawberries around each serving.

TACOMA

A sawmill started in the mid-1800s was the first business of Tacoma, and this industry is still important to the city today. Throughout the years, manufacturing and shipping diversified the city's economy. Now, more than a thousand ships visit busy Commencement Bay each year, carrying goods to and from Pacific Rim countries, South America, and other ports.

Tacomans have built the largest wooden entertainment dome in the world, which draws people from near and far to watch concerts, athletic events, and special shows. The old-time Pantages Theater, a baroque-style beauty, has been restored to serve as a dramatic performing arts center for the city. Nearby Point Defiance Park offers visitors an opportunity to explore the fairy-tale world of "Never, Never Land" and to visit the aquarium and zoo where animals of the Pacific Rim are featured. Tacoma is also home to the Washington State Historical Society museum.

Inland from Tacoma, along the Puyallup River, a number of U-pick farms offer a cornucopia of fresh vegetables including **lettuce, cabbage, cauliflower, broccoli, carrots, beets, corn (Summer Sweet, Kandi, and Golden Jubilee), celery, green beans, zucchini, cucumbers,** and **potatoes.** Freshly picked **raspberries, strawberries, blackberries, and blueberries** tempt buyers who can also find **apples,** mainly **Gravenstein** and **Jonagolds.** Free-range **chickens** are raised nearby. Local farmers bring produce into town to the Farmers' Market, which is held every Thursday on Antique Row, a great place to also find baked goods or an antique copper kettle.

Chris's Broccoli Salad

SERVINGS: 6-8

Toasted pine nuts may be sprinkled on top, in place of, or along with, the bacon.

5 cups coarsely chopped fresh broccoli, both flowers and stalks (the stalks should be peeled before cutting into pieces)

½ cup raisins

¼ cup chopped red onion

2 tablespoons granulated sugar

3 tablespoons white wine vinegar

1 cup mayonnaise, regular or light

8 bacon slices, cooked, crumbled

1. In large salad bowl, combine chopped broccoli, raisins, and onion. In small bowl, combine sugar, vinegar, and mayonnaise. Pour mayonnaise mixture over broccoli, toss to coat. Refrigerate.

2. Before serving, sprinkle with crumbled bacon.

Sautéed Green Beans and Cherry Tomatoes with Basil

SERVINGS: 4

Fresh basil is available almost year round in some markets now, for those times when your garden is not producing this fragrant herb.

1 teaspoon salt

1 pound green beans, cleaned and trimmed

2 tablespoons butter or margarine

1 garlic clove, minced

¼ cup fresh minced basil, divided

16 cherry tomatoes (if very large, cut in half)

freshly ground pepper to taste

1. Fill large saucepan or stock pot with water, adding a teaspoon of salt. Bring to boil, add green beans, and cook for 4-5 minutes or until just tender. Drain and place under cold water (or in bowl with ice water) to stop cooking. Let drain again, then dry with paper towel. (This may be done ahead.)

2. Melt butter in large skillet over low heat and add garlic. Cook until tender stirring frequently, about 2 minutes. Add green beans and 3 tablespoons basil. Cook until beans are heated through. Add cherry tomatoes and cook until tomatoes are heated through, stirring frequently. Grate pepper over. Add salt if needed. Serve with reserved 1 tablespoon basil.

Creamy Sweet Corn Risotto

SERVINGS: 4

Risotto is cooked uncovered, with small amounts of stock added and stirred in until the liquid is absorbed. When finished, the rice should be tender but firm and the dish should have a creamy texture. This risotto will accompany most any meat, poultry, or fish, and I like it as a vegetarian main course.

3 tablespoons olive oil

½ cup chopped onion

¼ cup chopped green pepper

1½ cups Arborio rice*

3¾ cups chicken stock (recipe page 313), or canned broth

½ cup dry white wine or vermouth

½ cup cream, heavy or light (for light cream, see page 322)

1 cup fresh corn kernels (canned may be substituted)

½ teaspoon ground coriander

½ cup freshly grated Parmesan cheese

1 teaspoon salt, or to taste

freshly grated pepper

1. Heat olive oil in large saucepan over medium heat. Add the onion and pepper, and sauté until tender. Add the rice and sauté for 2-3 minutes.

2. In a separate saucepan, heat chicken stock until simmering and keep warm. Meanwhile, add the wine or vermouth to the rice and cook over medium heat, stirring with a wooden spoon until the liquid is absorbed. Continue cooking and stirring constantly, adding ½ cup chicken stock each time and allowing each addition to be absorbed before adding the next. This should take about 20 minutes. Add the cream, corn, and coriander for the last addition. The rice is considered done when it is creamy yet slightly chewy. Stir in cheese. Season with salt and pepper.

*Arborio, an Italian short-grain rice, is available in many supermarkets.

PUYALLUP AND SUMNER

The Native Americans who inhabited this valley were Puyallups, meaning "generous people," and an early settler, Ezra Meeker, chose that friendly word to name this town. Today, these generous people are hosts for one of the ten largest fairs in the United States: each September, more than a million visitors come to the famous Western Washington Fair and "do the Puyallup." Fair goers can ride the roller coaster, see monster pumpkins, pet squeaky-clean hogs, watch top entertainers perform, and generally have a good time.

Nearby Sumner has a rural flavor and is much smaller than Puyallup. Both towns have grand homes dating back to the 1800s. In Puyallup stands the Ezra Meeker mansion, built in 1875, richly decorated with a tile entry, etched glass windows, and original furnishings. In Sumner, the Ryan House, also built in 1875, is now a museum. Many of the fine homes of that era were financed by profitable hop farms. Today, fields of hops have been replaced by daffodils, tulips, Christmas tree farms, and fruits and vegetables.

From April through June, field **rhubarb** is harvested by hand in the Puyallup valley near Mt. Rainier. About 70 percent is frozen, and the rest goes to local markets. The U-pick farms sell **raspberries, blueberries, strawberries, apples, pears,** and **quince.** Yellow Finn **potatoes** and **corn** are available in the fall. Both Puyallup and Sumner have weekly farmers' markets where local produce is available during summer and through early fall.

Rhubarb Strawberry Crisp with Bourbon Sauce

SERVINGS: 8

Rhubarb and strawberries team well together in this crisp, topped with a wonderful bourbon custard sauce. The crisp is also good topped with vanilla ice cream.

¾ **cup brown sugar, firmly packed**

¾ **cup all-purpose flour**

⅓ **cup butter or margarine**

½ **teaspoon cinnamon**

½ **cup rolled oats,
regular or quick cooking**

4 **cups rhubarb, diced
(fresh or frozen)**

2 **cups strawberries, cut in half**

1½ **teaspoons grated
orange zest (peel)**

⅔ - ¾ **cup granulated sugar**

BOURBON SAUCE

½ **cup liquid egg substitutes***

⅓ **cup granulated sugar**

1 **cup heavy or light cream
(for light cream see page 322)**

⅓ **cup milk**

¼ **cup bourbon**

1. To make crisp: preheat oven to 350 degrees. Combine brown sugar, flour, butter, cinnamon, and rolled oats in a small bowl until mixture is crumbly, and set aside. Mix together rhubarb, strawberries, orange zest and sugar in a medium bowl and place in baking dish. Cover with crumb topping.

2. Bake for one hour. Serve slightly warm with Bourbon sauce.

TO MAKE SAUCE

Mix egg substitutes and sugar in top of double boiler, whisking together for 1 minute. Set over bottom with simmering water. Do not let water come to boil. Whisk constantly, over medium-low heat, until slightly thickened, about 5-7 minutes. Add cream and milk gradually. Continue cooking over simmering water, stirring constantly, until mixture coats a spoon. Stir in bourbon. Serve warm. The sauce may be reheated, but do not boil.

*Liquid egg substitutes, pasteurized, are used in this recipe because the sauce is not cooked to a temperature which would prevent salmonella, sometimes present in raw eggs.

Rhubarb Pecan Upside Down Cake

SERVINGS: 6-8

This is one of my favorite "down home" cakes.

**3 tablespoons butter
or margarine, melted**

⅓ cup firmly packed brown sugar

½ cup chopped pecans

**2½ cups rhubarb, sliced
(fresh or frozen)**

1 cup all-purpose flour

1½ teaspoons baking powder

⅛ teaspoon salt

½ cup butter or margarine

1¼ cups granulated sugar

1 egg, beaten

1 cup sour cream, regular or light

1 teaspoon vanilla

**1 teaspoon grated
lemon zest (peel)**

whipped cream for top

1. Preheat oven to 350 degrees. Place melted butter in 8x8-inch square pan. Sprinkle brown sugar evenly over melted butter and press down. Sprinkle pecans over, then sliced rhubarb. Spray sides of pan with vegetable spray or lightly grease. Set aside.

2. Combine flour, baking powder, and salt in a small bowl. In another medium bowl, cream ½ cup butter with sugar until light and fluffy. Add egg, sour cream, vanilla, and lemon zest, and mix together. Fold in dry ingredients to blend.

3. Pour on top of rhubarb mixture and bake 45-50 minutes in oven or until cake tester inserted into center of cake comes out clean. Cool for 10 minutes on rack and invert onto platter. Serve warm with whipped cream. (Cake pieces may be reheated briefly in microwave oven.)

GIG HARBOR

An exploration party, charting the waters of south Puget Sound in 1841, took shelter in a protected harbor during a sudden storm. Those small surveying boats were called gigs, and eventually the quiet bay and town on shore became known as Gig Harbor. The small picturesque village is set amid breathtaking views of the Olympic and Cascade mountain ranges, Mt. Rainier, and a bay filled with brightly colored sailboats.

Salt waters surrounding Gig Harbor Peninsula provide a variety of **clams, mussels,** and **oysters.** The clams commonly found are littlenecks, Manila, butterclams, horse clams, and huge geoducks.

Steamed Clams with Tomatoes and Herbs

SERVINGS: 4

Serve with french bread to dip in the flavorful broth.

3 dozen littleneck or Manila clams

3 tablespoons olive oil

4 cloves garlic, minced

½ cup canned diced tomatoes with puree

½ cup bottled clam juice*

1 bay leaf

1 teaspoon dried oregano

fresh parsley, minced

*Dry white wine may be substituted.

1. Clean and scrub clams well.

2. Heat olive oil in large pan over medium heat. Add garlic and sauté until just tender, do not brown. Add diced tomato with puree, clam juice, bay leaf, and oregano, and bring to boil. Add clams, cover, and cook over medium high heat until clams open, about 5 minutes. Uncover, discard bay leaf, and discard clams that do not open.

3. Place clams in individual serving bowls along with broth and sprinkle with parsley. (If desired, strain broth through 2 thicknesses of cheesecloth before placing in bowls.)

OLYMPIA

Olympia, situated at the foot of Puget Sound, is one of the oldest communities in the Pacific Northwest, serving as the capital since 1853 when Washington Territory separated from Oregon. On a plateau overlooking Capitol Lake is the majestic 287-foot domed capitol building, dominating the skyline. The building is grand and impressive on the outside, and the elegant inside has a Tiffany chandelier hanging from a 101-foot chain in the large marble rotunda. Running the state government keeps people busy in Olympia, as do major industries such as beer brewing, lumbering, and oyster and fish processing.

Famous **Olympic oysters** lie in the shoal bays north and west of town. A large commercial **mushroom farm** is nearby and a U-pick farm offers **sweet corn, pumpkins,** other **vegetables,** and old-fashioned wagon rides. The Farmers' Market in Olympia, begun in 1975 and enlarging in size each year, offers a variety of local products.

PUGET SOUND MYCOLOGICAL SOCIETY

Oyster Stew Enriched with Duxelles

SERVINGS: 5

Duxelles (sautéed, chopped mushrooms) are incorporated into this classic stew for additional flavor, and it needs only a green salad and loaf of warm sourdough bread for accompaniment.

2 cups half-and-half

15 small oysters, cleaned and shucked, with liquid

½ teaspoon salt

white pepper

2-3 dashes Tabasco sauce

3 tablespoons Duxelles (recipe page 312)

1 teaspoon butter or margarine

2 teaspoons sherry (optional)

minced parsley for garnish

1. In top of double boiler over gently boiling water, place all ingredients except sherry and parsley. Cook until oysters float and the half-and-half is hot, from 15-30 minutes, depending on size of oysters. Add sherry.

2. Serve hot and top with a sprinkling of minced parsley.

Appetizer Mushrooms

SERVINGS: 10

These mushrooms can be served as a salad; just place on lettuce leaves with avocado slices.

1 pound fresh mushrooms, cleaned and sliced in half (if large, cut in quarters)

⅓ cup sour cream, regular or light

1 large clove garlic, minced

¼ teaspoon Worcestershire sauce

2 dashes Tabasco sauce

¾ cup mayonnaise, regular or light

2 tablespoons minced parsley, divided

lettuce or kale leaves

1. Place mushrooms in bowl. In separate bowl, combine sour cream, garlic, Worcestershire sauce, Tabasco sauce, mayonnaise, and 1 tablespoon parsley. Pour over mushrooms. Refrigerate 3 hours or longer.

2. Serve in bowl or on lettuce or kale leaves. Sprinkle with reserved 1 tablespoon parsley. Offer cocktail toothpicks.

SUSAN PARISH COLLECTION

CASCADES

Forested hills and valleys, park-like meadows, and secluded lakes burst forth with wild things such as trout, game, mushrooms, and berries. Orchards rim rugged mountains and cattle graze in the highlands.

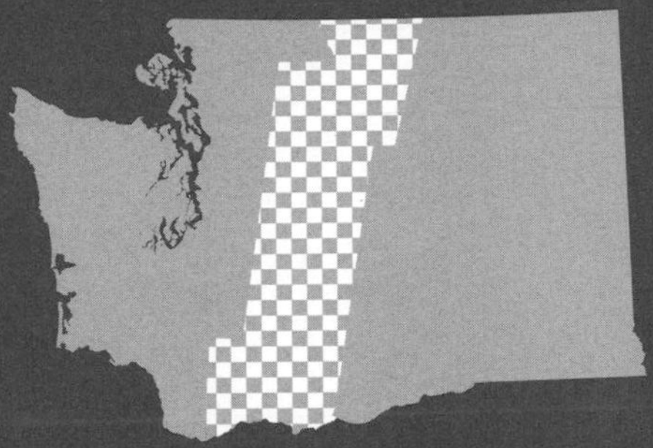

Winthrop

Concrete

Marblemount

Darrington

Skykomish

Leavenworth

Cashmere

Cle Elum

Roslyn

Enumclaw

Packwood

White Salmon

Bingen

WINTHROP

The Old West lives on in Winthrop, where the main street has hitching posts for horses, old-fashioned street lights, covered wooden sidewalks, old-time wooden saloons, shops, and a bakery and general store. Though a fire in 1993 destroyed some shops, most have been rebuilt.

Winthrop is the eastern gateway to the North Cascade Highway and travelers who continue west from here will view one of the most scenic routes in the country. Majestic mountains, deep azure lakes, and wooded settings await those journeying along this breathtaking course.

This is cowboy country; even today cattlemen can be seen driving their herds through the streets—not surprising, for over 30,000 **beef cattle** range in surrounding Okanogan County.

Flank Steak with Blue Cheese, Mushroom, and Sun-dried Tomato Stuffing

SERVINGS: 4

Cut into one-inch slices and serve with Bulgar Risotto and Peas (page 307).

1 (2 or 2½ pound) flank steak

MARINADE

3 tablespoons Dijon or Dijon-style mustard

¼ cup red wine vinegar

2 tablespoons olive oil

1 clove garlic, minced

1 teaspoon freshly ground black pepper

½ teaspoon salt

1½ teaspoons fresh chopped thyme or ½ teaspoon dry thyme

1½ teaspoons fresh chopped rosemary or ½ teaspoon dry rosemary

2 teaspoons brown sugar

STUFFING

1½ tablespoons olive oil

½ cup chopped onion

1 cup chopped mushrooms

1½ cups soft bread crumbs

1 tablespoon minced parsley

½ cup beef stock (recipe page 314) or canned broth

salt and pepper

4 ounces blue cheese, crumbled

8 sun-dried tomatoes, chopped (oil packed and patted dry)

Melted butter or margarine

1. Score steak lightly on both sides by cutting the surface lightly at one-inch intervals in a crisscross pattern. Combine all ingredients of marinade in bowl and stir together. Place steak in non-metallic pan and pour marinade over. Cover and refrigerate at least 2 hours or as long as overnight, turning occasionally.

2. Preheat oven to 350 degrees. Make stuffing by heating olive oil in a medium skillet over medium heat, add onion and mushrooms, and sauté until tender. Take off heat, add bread crumbs, parsley, and beef stock. Salt and pepper to taste.

3. Take steak from refrigerator, discard marinade. Lay flat and spread stuffing mixture over. Crumble blue cheese over, sprinkle with chopped sun-dried tomatoes. Roll lengthwise (like a jelly roll) and tie with cooking string at 2-inch intervals.

4. Brush meat lightly with melted butter or margarine, place in roasting pan or rack, and bake, uncovered, for 65-70 minutes or until meat is cooked as desired. Slice meat and discard string.

Jim's Grilled Spencer Steaks with Béarnaise Sauce

SERVINGS: 6

When the weather is warm and the day calls for outdoor grilling, indulge with these steaks.

6 Spencer steaks

olive oil

salt and pepper

minced garlic for seasoning

BÉARNAISE SAUCE

2 tablespoons white vermouth

1¼ tablespoons tarragon vinegar

1 tablespoon minced fresh tarragon or 1 teaspoon dry tarragon (fresh preferred)

2 teaspoons minced shallots

½ cup butter or margarine

**3 egg yolks or
⅓ cup egg substitutes**

pinch of cayenne

**freshly ground pepper,
a generous amount**

salt to taste

1. Bring steaks to room temperature, trim off excess fat, and brush surfaces lightly with olive oil. Season with salt and pepper and minced garlic. Prepare barbecue grill; rack should be about 3-4 inches from heat. Start charcoals if using charcoal grill. Make Béarnaise Sauce.

2. To make Béarnaise Sauce: combine vermouth, tarragon vinegar, tarragon and shallots in small saucepan and cook over high heat until reduced by about half; set aside. Melt butter in separate small saucepan and set aside. Fill bottom of double boiler with water and bring just to boil, lower heat so water is hot but not boiling. Place eggs (or egg substitutes) in top of double boiler, and place over bottom. Gradually whisk in melted butter and cook, whisking constantly, until mixture lightly thickens. (If using egg yolks, the mixture needs to heat to 160 degrees.) Whisk in reserved vermouth mixture, cayenne, and pepper. Taste and add salt, if needed. Serve immediately (or remove top of double boiler from heat, and partially cover with lid to keep warm). If sauce thickens too much, whisk in droplets of warm water.

3. To grill meat: when charcoals are ashen or gas or electric grill is ready, grill steaks to the way you like them. Suggested cooking time: sear both sides of steak for 1 minute over hot coals, or on high setting for gas or electric grills. Lower heat of grill by raising grid of charcoal grill (or using outside edge of briquettes), or by turning gas or electric grill to medium hot. Continue grilling one side for 5 minutes. Turn and grill other side for about 5 minutes for rare; 7-8 minutes for medium; and 10 minutes for well-done. (Place cooked steaks on a warm serving platter in oven for 5-10 minutes to allow juices to distribute evenly.) Serve with Béarnaise Sauce.

CONCRETE
AND
MARBLEMOUNT

Marblemount and Concrete, located deep in the highlands on the scenic North Cascade Highway, border the Skagit River. Concrete, first named Cement City for the early establishment of a cement plant in town, was later given its existing and equally solid name. Marble in the surrounding mountains inspired the name Marblemount.

Visitors to this area enjoy tours of dams, lakes, and Seattle City Light "company towns." Close by is a 1,500-acre sanctuary for bald eagles, which brings these magnificent birds within viewing distance from the many highway turn-outs.

Wild mushrooms grow in the nearby mountains. Freshwater fishing is popular, as well as hunting for **deer, elk, grouse,** and **wild pigeon.**

Bolete Mushroom Soup

SERVINGS: 4-6

The wild boletus edulis is often dried since dehydration intensifies its earthy fragrance. To the Italians, these are porcini; to the French, they are cèpes; to mushroom lovers everywhere, they are wonderful.

½ **cup cognac, brandy, or water**

3-4 **ounces dried bolete mushrooms (or use dried porcini)**

4 **cups beef stock (recipe page 314) or canned low-sodium beef broth**

1 **tablespoon minced parsley**

½ **cup chopped onion**

2 **tablespoons butter or margarine**

2 **tablespoons all-purpose flour**

freshly ground pepper

1 **cup sour cream, regular or light**

1. Heat cognac, brandy, or water in small saucepan until warm. Add dried mushrooms and soak for 15 minutes. Drain, reserving liquid. Pour liquid through 2 thicknesses of cheesecloth and into a large saucepan. Add stock, parsley, onions, and mushrooms, and bring to gentle boil. Reduce heat and simmer mixture until onions and mushrooms are tender, about 15-20 minutes.

2. Melt butter in separate pan over medium heat, add flour to make roux, stirring and cooking for 1 minute. Stir roux into soup and continue whisking over medium heat until slightly thickened.

3. Season to taste with pepper. (Soup may not need salt, so taste before using.) Stir in sour cream just before serving.

Grouse Breasts with Madeira and Cream

SERVINGS: 4 (OR 2 LARGE SERVINGS)

Grouse are wild woodland birds; if unavailable, use chicken breasts.

4 **grouse breasts, cleaned, boned, skinned, and halved**

salt and pepper

½ **cup heavy (whipping) cream or light cream (see page 322 for light cream)**

¾ **cup Madeira**

¼ **cup finely chopped shallots**

1. Preheat oven to 325 degrees. Place grouse breasts in large casserole that can also be used on top of stove. Season with salt and pepper. Combine cream and Madeira and pour over breasts. Sprinkle with shallots.

2. Cover and bake in oven 40-45 minutes, depending on size of breasts. Take breasts from casserole and keep warm.

3. Place casserole dish on top of stove over high heat, bring sauce to boil and reduce sauce until slightly thickened. Serve sauce with grouse breasts.

DARRINGTON

Darrington, a small community of about 1,000 people, lies in a valley enclosed by the rising, lush Cascade mountains. The forested mountain setting lured loggers from the hills of North Carolina, who brought with them their love of country folk music. A large Bluegrass Festival is staged annually in Darrington, bringing hundreds to hear transplanted Tar Heels play first-rate country bluegrass music.

Darrington is bordered by the Sauk and Stillaguamish rivers, popular for **steelhead** and **trout** fishing. Each season, excellent hunting for **deer, bear,** and **mountain goats** brings sportsmen to the Cascades. **Duck** and **geese** visit the valley on their fall migration, and **grouse** are often found on forest trails. Moist conditions in the heavily wooded area produce an abundance of **wild mushrooms.**

Sautéed Spring Morels

SERVINGS: 4-6

Morel mushrooms emerging from the ground are one of the many delightful signs of spring. Serve these anytime. They are wonderful appetizers.

20-25 morel mushrooms

½ **teaspoon salt**

⅛ **teaspoon ground white pepper**

¾ **cup all-purpose flour**

¼ **teaspoon ground oregano**

¼ **teaspoon garlic powder**

¼ **teaspoon sugar**

½ **cup buttermilk**

2 tablespoons vegetable oil

2 tablespoons butter or margarine

1. To clean morels: brush off dirt or quickly rinse out the pockets (do not soak) and let sit to drain off any moisture before cooking.

2. Combine salt, pepper, flour, oregano, garlic powder, and sugar. Cut dry morels in half, lengthwise. Dip morels in buttermilk and then roll in the flour mixture. Place on paper towels until all morels are coated.

3. Melt oil and butter in one large or two smaller skillets. Sauté mushrooms over medium-high heat until crisp and brown on all sides.

Serve morels for brunch with scrambled eggs, for lunch with a green salad and rolls, or for dinner as an accompaniment to grilled chicken or steaks.

SKYKOMISH

Stevens Pass is a picturesque drive, winding along the Skykomish River and skirting jagged mountain peaks. Along the way are many small towns, including Skykomish, an old logging community near the river. Nearby is Deception Falls, where visitors can see the falls descend the mountainside, and the frothing water rush under the highway bridge. The wary **trout** and **steelhead** in the river are worthy challenges to the many fishers who wade the stream or fish from shore.

Trout with Chive Cream Sauce

SERVINGS: 5

Trout may be fileted after cooking by inserting fish knife at top of backbone and cutting down to tail, then cutting off head and removing backbone from fish. Finally, lift out filets and pour sauce over.

¼ **cup all-purpose flour**

salt and pepper

5 medium-sized trout, cleaned, washed, and fins removed

¼ **cup butter or margarine, melted**

½ **cup heavy (whipping) cream, or light cream (for light cream, see page 322)**

3 tablespoons chives

1. Preheat oven to 450 degrees. Combine flour with about ¼ teaspoon salt and some pepper. Trim, wash, and dry trout, and dust with seasoned flour. Lay on baking dish brushed with melted butter and spoon over more butter to coat fish.

2. Bake in oven for 8-12 minutes, or until opaque throughout, basting once.

3. Meanwhile, boil cream in saucepan over high heat for several minutes to reduce by about ⅓ and thicken slightly. Add chives and salt to taste. When trout are finished cooking, take from oven and serve with sauce.

179

LEAVENWORTH

When loggers left this little lumber town in the 1930s, the community was all but forgotten; that is, until local residents and the University of Washington envisioned and planned a Bavarian village. In 1960, all stores and shops were designed with a country German motif, including roof overhangs, leaded windows, wooden balconies, and carved benches. This Teutonic architecture, combined with a stunning alpine setting in the Cascade mountains, transformed Leavenworth into a slice of old-world Bavaria. Each season features festivities such as the Christmas Lighting, the Autumn Leaf Festival, and Maifest—all of which bring thousands of tourists.

From Leavenworth east to Cashmere large orchards of **apples** and **pears** fill the valley. A few **apricots** and **cherries** are also grown.

Baked Pears in Apple Cider and Cinnamon

SERVINGS: 6

What an easy way to poach pears! Hard pears may be used in this recipe, for after a long, slow cooking time they will become soft and light amber in color. These pears are lovely served in individual glass goblets, surrounded with whipped cream, and topped with toasted almonds.

6 large hard pears, preferably Bosc or Bartletts

3 cups apple cider

2 whole cinnamon sticks

1 teaspoon vanilla

whipped cream for garnish

Toasted slivered almonds for garnish, optional (see page 323 for toasting nuts)

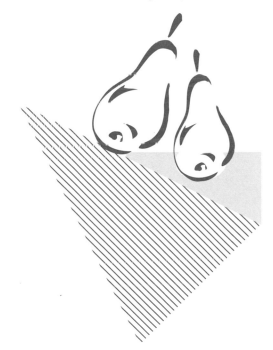

1. Preheat oven to 250 degrees. Peel pears, leaving stems on, and core from the bottom with an apple corer. Place, on sides, in large casserole dish.

2. In a small saucepan, combine cider and cinnamon sticks and bring to boil over medium high heat. Take off heat and add vanilla. Pour mixture over pears, cover casserole, and place in oven for 1½ hours. Turn pears over and return to oven to continue cooking for 1½ hours.

3. When pears are cooked, cool slightly, then place upright in individual serving bowls. (Pears will tend to flatten on one side if not placed upright at this time.) Pour liquid back into saucepan and bring to boil over medium high heat. Lower heat and simmer for about 1 hour or until liquid is reduced to syrupy stage, checking frequently. Pour sauce over pears, cool slightly, and baste each pear occasionally with the syrup.

4. Serve at room temperature or chilled, surrounded with whipped cream piped or spooned around edge, and toasted almonds sprinkled over if desired.

Apricot Bavarian Cream with Apricot Grand Marnier Sauce or Bittersweet Chocolate Sauce

SERVINGS: 8

An impressive and heavenly dessert. Try either the flavorful Apricot Grand Marnier Sauce or the bolder and richer Bittersweet Chocolate Sauce with this Bavarian cream.

½ cup granulated sugar

2 packets unflavored gelatin

1 cup boiling water

1 cup apricot nectar

1 cup heavy (whipping) cream, whipped

1 cup apricot puree*

Additional whipped cream for garnish

Fresh mint leaves for garnish, optional

*Make apricot puree by pureeing drained canned apricot halves in food processor or blender. (A 16-ounce can will usually yield about a cup.) Poached fresh apricots may also be used.

1. In bowl, add sugar and gelatin and mix together. Add boiling water and apricot nectar, mix thoroughly, and refrigerate until partially set, about 60 to 75 minutes.

2. Whip cream and place in refrigerator until ready to use.

3. When gelatin mixture is partly congealed, beat with electric mixer for 2 minutes until mixture is light and fluffy. Whisk in pureed apricots and whipped cream. Pour into a 1½ quart mold, or individual molds, and refrigerate 3 hours or longer. When Bavarian is chilling, make one of the accompanying sauces; recipes follow.

5. To unmold Bavarian, dip mold into hot water in basin or large bowl for 7-10 seconds. Invert serving plate on top of mold and turn over to unmold.

6. Serve with one of the sauces sparingly drizzled over the mold, and pass remaining sauce. Surround mold with whipped cream rosettes and some mint leaves. Or, use individually placed molds, or slices, on pool of sauce with some sauce drizzled over, and garnish with whipped cream and mint leaf.

APRICOT GRAND MARNIER SAUCE

½ cup apricot puree*

⅓ cup Grand Marnier or orange juice

TO MAKE GRAND MARNIER SAUCE

Combine apricot puree and Grand Marnier in bowl.

BITTERSWEET CHOCOLATE SAUCE

¼ cup granulated sugar

½ cup water

3 ounces bittersweet chocolate, broken into small pieces

1 ounce unsweetened chocolate, broken into small pieces

1½ tablespoons butter or margarine

TO MAKE CHOCOLATE SAUCE

1. Place sugar and water in medium saucepan and stir to combine. Bring mixture to simmer over low heat. Cover and simmer 5 minutes. Uncover, remove from heat, and cool to lukewarm.

2. Melt both chocolates with butter in top of double boiler over hot water or in microwave oven on high for about 2 minutes, stirring every 30 seconds.

3. Gradually stir in cooled sugar syrup to chocolate mixture. Keep at room temperature until serving time.

CASHMERE

Strollers take a step back to the turn of the century on Main Street in Cashmere, where residents have chosen an early American Western theme for their community. Old-time buildings and antique street lamps line the street and American flags flutter in the breeze, creating a picture-book scene. At the edge of town stands a Pioneer Village where about twenty authentically restored buildings of the 1800s are assembled, including an 1856 mission cabin and post office built in 1872.

Orchards filled with **apples, pears,** and some **apricots** surround this community. The fruit is shipped all over the world, as well as supplying a local apple juice processing plant and the Aplet and Cotlet candy factory. Nearly 60,000 people visit the factory each year and the confection is sold internationally.

Apple Cream Tart

SERVINGS: 6-8

This apple tart is easy to make, beautiful to look at, and delicious. It was created by Mrs. High, an excellent cook.

CRUST

½ **cup butter or margarine, softened**

⅓ **cup granulated sugar**

¼ **teaspoon vanilla**

1 **cup all-purpose flour**

FILLING

1 **egg**

1 **(8-ounce) package softened cream cheese, regular or light**

½ **cup granulated sugar, divided**

½ **teaspoon vanilla**

3-4 **cups cooking apples, peeled, cored, and sliced about ⅜ inch thick**

½ **teaspoon cinnamon**

⅛ **teaspoon mace or nutmeg**

4-5 **tablespoons apple jelly**

8- **or 9-inch springform pan**

1. Preheat oven to 450 degrees. To make crust: cream softened butter with sugar in a medium bowl. Add vanilla and flour to combine. Press mixture into a springform pan covering bottom and about 1-inch up the sides.

2. To make filling: beat egg and combine well with softened cream cheese, ¼ cup sugar, and vanilla. Pour and spread over unbaked pastry. Arrange sliced apples in concentric circles, slightly overlapping, on filling. Dust with ¼ cup remaining sugar, cinnamon, and mace or nutmeg.

3. Bake 10 minutes at 450 degrees. Reduce heat to 400 degrees and bake for 25 minutes. Remove and cool. Heat apple jelly in small saucepan over low heat to melt. Brush melted jelly on top of apples. Remove sides from pan when thoroughly cooled. Refrigerate.

CLE ELUM
AND
ROSLYN

Roslyn, set back in the mountains off the main highway, has changed little from its early days, when miners dug for coal during the day and frequented the bars at night. The coal mines are closed now, but still open is the Brick Tavern, built in 1898, complete with a bar and an impressive 20-foot spittoon. This town, with its original old buildings, wooden sidewalks, and small wood cabins with high-pitched tin roofs, is a scene that caught the attention of TV producers. Recently, Roslyn was the real setting for the popular television program "Northern Exposure," a series set in the isolated, far-reaching wilderness of Alaska.

Cle Elum, also an early coal-mining town, is located next to a busy interstate highway. The town gradually diversified its economy, increased its population, and kept up with the times. However, it offers a bow to its past each year with its celebration of Pioneer Days, when such festivities as a parade, fireworks, contests, and games are held.

Mushroom hunting, especially for the prized **chanterelles,** is exceptional near here.

PUGET SOUND MYCOLOGICAL SOCIETY

Chanterelles with Marsala and Hazelnuts

SERVINGS: 4

Serve as an accompaniment to meat, in a chafing dish, over toast points, or anytime you are lucky enough to get chanterelles.

1 pound chanterelles

1 tablespoon butter or margarine

½ teaspoon salt

3-4 tablespoons beef stock (recipe page 314) or broth

¼ cup Marsala (dry sherry or additional beef stock may be substituted)

⅓ cup hazelnuts, toasted and coarsely chopped (for toasting hazelnuts, see page 323)

½ cup sour cream, regular or light

pepper, freshly ground

1. Clean chanterelles with a nylon mushroom brush (or toothbrush). To remove small particles of sand or dirt, brush under slowly running faucet water. Do not soak. Slice about ¼-inch thick.

2. On low heat, melt butter in a large heavy skillet. Turn heat to medium high, add sliced mushrooms and sprinkle with salt to draw out moisture. Stir constantly with wooden spoon and cook for 3 minutes. (If chanterelles are moist, dry sauté; refer to page 30).

3. Turn heat to medium low, add stock, and continue cooking 10 minutes or until mushrooms are tender, stirring frequently. Add Marsala and coarsely chopped toasted hazelnuts and cook over low heat for 1 minute. Add sour cream and stir to coat. Season with freshly ground black pepper, and salt if needed, and serve.

ENUMCLAW

Enumclaw, located between the Cascade mountains and plateau farm lands, offers panoramic views of majestic Mt. Rainier. Within a few miles of town are a number of horse farms, as this is one of the largest thoroughbred breeding areas in the country. The fertile plateau lands yield **vegetables** and **berries** and the many **dairy farms** produce a variety of **milk products.** Every July, Enumclaw hosts the King County Fair, with local products, animals, and crafts on display.

Snow-capped Mt. Rainier Pudding

SERVINGS: 6

A cloud of meringue tops this raspberry-filled milk pudding. *

3 cups milk

3 cups fresh white breadcrumbs, crusts removed

1½ tablespoons butter or margarine

¾ cup plus 3 tablespoons granulated sugar, divided

1 tablespoon grated lemon zest (peel)

3 eggs, separated

½ cup raspberry jam

additional sugar for top

Individual puddings can be made in 4-6-inch round soufflé cups, but original baking time needs to be reduced by 10 minutes.

1. Pour milk into a medium saucepan and bring to boil. Remove from heat and stir in bread crumbs, butter, ¾ cup sugar, and lemon zest. Let stand off heat for 20 minutes so breadcrumbs will swell. Preheat oven to 350 degrees.

2. Separate eggs, beat yolks, and add them to the cooled mixture. Set aside the egg whites. Pour pudding into well-buttered 1-quart baking dish. Bake for 30-35 minutes or until set.

3. Meanwhile, melt jam in saucepan over low heat. When pudding is done, remove dish from oven and spread jam carefully over top of pudding. Beat egg whites until stiff, whisk in remaining 3 tablespoons sugar, and spoon meringue over jam, mounding to center. Sprinkle additional sugar over pudding, using about 1½ teaspoons in all.

4. Bake 10 more minutes or until meringue is golden brown. Cool to room temperature before serving.

PACKWOOD

Along the White Pass Highway, motorists and cyclists can view beautiful mountain scenery and rustic small towns. Near the summit is Packwood, the site of a ranger station and supply stores for the many campers, fishers, hikers, and boaters who come to enjoy the Cascade mountains. Nearby Packwood Lake offers an abundant supply of **trout** and other fish. **Wild blackberries** and **mushrooms** grow profusely in the area, and hunters come to track **elk** and **deer** in the Cascades.

Wild Blackberry and Crème de Cassis Ice Cream

SERVINGS: 6

Blackberries and cream are frozen to a smooth dessert in this recipe.

3 cups blackberries (about 1 pound)

¼ cup Crème de Cassis

¾ cup granulated sugar

2 cups heavy (whipping) cream

1. Purée blackberries in food processor or blender. Press and stir berries through strainer into a bowl to remove seeds.

2. Cook puree with the Crème de Cassis in a medium saucepan over low heat for 10 minutes; set aside. Heat sugar with 1 cup of cream in saucepan over medium heat until sugar dissolves, stirring continually. Stir in remaining cream and puree mixture. Chill mixture in refrigerator.

3. Freeze in an ice cream maker according to the manufacturer's directions.

WHITE SALMON
AND BINGEN

White Salmon and Bingen, towns along the Columbia River, have been undergoing work to create a Rhineland atmosphere somewhat similar to that of Leavenworth. A bell tower in White Salmon houses a true glockenspiel, and some buildings reflect a Bavarian influence. Recreationists seek out this area for whitewater rafting, fishing, boating, camping, and prime wind surfing.

The largest **D'Anjou pear** orchard in the world is found nearby as well as orchards of **apples, cherries,** and **peaches. Vineyards** supply the local wineries with premium **grapes,** and **huckleberries** grow on the slopes of Mt. Adams to the north.

SUSAN PARISH COLLECTION

Salad Greens with Pears, Glazed Walnuts, and Blue Cheese

SERVINGS: 6

A variety of greens play host to the well-loved trio of pears, blue cheese, and walnuts. Add some smoked chicken slices to make this an entrée salad.

GLAZED WALNUTS

1 tablespoon butter or margarine

1 tablespoon granulated sugar

¼ teaspoon salt

¼ teaspoon freshly ground pepper

1 teaspoon water

⅔ cup walnuts, halved

DRESSING

1 medium shallot, finely chopped

2 tablespoons rice vinegar (or white wine vinegar)

1 tablespoon Dijon or Dijon-style mustard

3 tablespoons granulated sugar

2 tablespoons walnut oil (or vegetable oil)

½ cup olive oil

⅛ teaspoon salt

freshly ground pepper to taste

SALAD

12 cups assorted torn greens including red leaf lettuce, watercress, arugula, and Bibb lettuce

2 ripe pears, preferably D'Anjou, cored and sliced

¼ cup crumbled blue cheese

1. To make glazed walnuts: combine all ingredients except walnuts in a medium saucepan and cook over medium heat until bubbly. Add walnuts, stir to coat, and cook until sugar begins to caramelize, about 5 minutes. Spread on waxed paper to cool.

2. To make dressing: whisk in bowl or combine in food processor shallot, vinegar, mustard, and sugar. Add oils gradually. Season with salt and pepper.

3. To assemble: combine greens, add sliced pears, and toss with enough dressing to coat. Divide among serving plates or into one large salad bowl. Top with glazed walnuts and blue cheese.

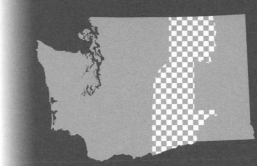

CENTRAL WASHINGTON

Desert lands bloom into fertility with irrigation. Orchards brimming with apples, pears, plums, sweet cherries, nectarines, peaches, and apricots stretch for miles. Fertile fields yield potatoes,

corn,

melons,

berries, beans, vegetables, hops, and grains. Vineyards, laden with

grapes, flourish in the rich soil and ample sun. Farmers raise cattle, sheep, and hogs.

Oroville
Okanogan
Omak
Grand Coulee
Chelan
Ephrata
Wenatchee
Ellensburg
Moses Lake
Othello
Yakima
Wapato
Toppenish
Zillah
Granger
Sunnyside
Grandview
Prosser
Pasco
Richland
Kennewick
Goldendale

OROVILLE

Glimmering gold brought prospectors to the north Okanogan Valley in the early 1880s, and was on the minds of the people who named a small community "Oro," the Spanish word for that precious metal. Later, the townsfolk added "ville" to the name, so it sounded more like a community, not a commodity.

The gold-mining days are over, but artifacts and photographs depicting these early times are found at the Old Depot Museum and Community Hall. Today, Oroville, situated next to serene Lake Osoyoos, has a relaxed atmosphere much different from its busy and boisterous beginnings.

Apple trees burst into bloom in the spring in the more than 10,000 acres of orchards in the surrounding area. **Wheat** fields and **cattle** ranches are scattered throughout Okanogan County.

Beef on Skewers with Peanut Sauce

SERVINGS: 4-6

Inspired by the popular Asian satays, these skewers and sauce may be served as appetizers or as a main dish accompanied by steamed rice and snow peas.

1 cup dry white wine

¼ cup dry sherry

¼ cup soy sauce

1 clove garlic, minced

1 teaspoon freshly
chopped ginger, or
⅓ teaspoon ground ginger

2 pounds beef tenderloin,
sliced in ½-inch strips

bamboo skewers

PEANUT SAUCE

⅔ cup smooth peanut butter

½ cup hot water

¼ cup soy sauce

¼ cup brown sugar

2 teaspoons rice vinegar or
white wine vinegar

½ teaspoon dry hot pepper flakes

2 dashes Tabasco sauce

1. If using bamboo skewers, cover skewers with hot water and soak 1 hour. Combine and stir together in a small bowl the wine, sherry, soy sauce, garlic, and ginger. Thread beef strips on skewer and place in nonmetallic pan and pour marinade over. Cover and marinate for 12 hours or as long as 24 hours in refrigerator.

2. To make Peanut Sauce: blend peanut butter and hot water in a medium bowl until smooth. Add and blend in rest of ingredients.

3. Preheat oven to 400 degrees. Remove meat from marinade, thread 2 strips on each skewer. Bake for 5 minutes, or until done. Skewers may also be grilled, turning once during cooking. Serve with Peanut Sauce.

Festive Apple Walnut Cake with Apple Brandy Glaze

SERVINGS: 10

This cake is rich, moist, full of apples, and nice to serve at holiday time.

4 cups cooking apples, cored, peeled, and chopped

½ cup apple brandy (use northwest apple brandy or Calvados)

2 eggs

1 cup brown sugar, packed

1 cup granulated sugar

1 cup vegetable oil

2¼ cups all-purpose flour

¾ teaspoon salt

2 teaspoons baking soda

2 teaspoons cinnamon

1 teaspoon nutmeg, preferably freshly ground

½ teaspoon cloves

¾ cup raisins

1 teaspoon vanilla

1 cup coarsely chopped walnuts, toasted (see page 323 for toasting nuts)

GLAZE

4 tablespoons butter or margarine

5 tablespoons brown sugar, packed

3 tablespoons heavy or light cream (see page 322 for light cream)

2 tablespoons Northwest apple brandy or Calvados (or apple cider)

1. Preheat oven to 350 degrees. Grease and lightly dust with flour one bundt pan.

2. Place chopped apples in medium bowl and pour apple brandy over; mix and set aside.

3. In a large mixing bowl, beat together eggs, sugars, and oil. In a separate medium bowl, combine flour, salt, soda, and spices together. Stir half of flour mixture into egg mixture and combine well. Combine apples and apple brandy with raisins, along with vanilla and toasted nuts, and mix into batter with spoon. Add final flour mixture and combine well with spoon.

4. Pour batter into prepared bundt pan and bake for 60 to 75 minutes or until cake tester inserted into cake comes out clean.

5. Remove from oven and cool on wire rack for 15 minutes; remove cake from pan.

TO MAKE GLAZE

Melt butter in small saucepan, add brown sugar, cream, and apple brandy, and cook over medium heat until brown sugar is dissolved. Remove from heat and brush glaze over warm cake. Cool.

SUSAN PARISH COLLECTION

OKANOGAN
AND
OMAK

The towns of Omak and Okanogan straddle the Okanogan River high in the plateau lands of north central Washington. This rugged terrain was home for trappers and traders as far back as 1811, when John Astor's Pacific Fur Company built Fort Okanogan. Later in the century, gold fever brought miners to the area. Steamboats chugged the river to the town of Okanogan by 1880, and regular railroad transportation began in 1914. Though settled early, this high country is sparsely populated today. Quiet and serene meadows, secluded lakes, rugged bare mountains, green forests, and peaceful valleys await visitors to the Okanogan highland.

The city limits of the towns of Okanogan and Omak lie only yards from each other, creating one business entity. Okanogan, settled first, is the political center of the county. Omak grew quickly after being chosen as the site for a sawmill in the 1920s and now is the largest town in Okanogan County. Each year, Omak receives attention for its annual stampede and "Suicide Race." This race sends riders on horses down a steep hill at breakneck speeds, across a swift river, and on to the finish line.

Over 39,000 **beef cattle** graze in the county's green fields, and orchards yield **apples, pears, cherries, nectarines, peaches,** and **plums. Garlic** farmers grow superior varieties such as Spanish Roja and Italian Reds. Large herds of **sheep** graze in the Okanogan National Forest and along the foothills of the Cascades.

Grilled Flank Steak with Ginger Marinade

SERVINGS: 3-4

Serve with rice pilaf and Tomato, Cucumber and Gorgonzola Salad (page 204).

3 tablespoons sesame seeds

¼ cup vegetable oil

½ cup soy sauce

1 clove garlic, crushed

½ teaspoon freshly ground pepper

1½ teaspoons grated fresh ginger or ½ teaspoon powdered

¼ cup brown sugar, packed

2 scallions, finely sliced

1 large flank steak, scored*

additional sesame seeds, toasted, optional (see page 323 for toasting nuts)

1. Combine all ingredients, except steak, in a medium bowl or pitcher. Place flank steak in large flat non-metallic baking dish and pour marinade over.

2. Cover and refrigerate 12-24 hours, turning occasionally. Remove steak from marinade. Discard marinade.

3. Grill or broil 5-7 minutes per side. Slice slanted across the grain into about ½-inch strips. Sprinkle with additional toasted sesame seeds if desired.

***TO SCORE FLANK STEAK.**

Cut the surface with diagonal lines about 1 inch apart in one direction, repeat in the other direction, creating a criss-cross pattern. Use a sharp knife which will make it easier to cut just the surface area. This helps prevent the meat from curling when cooked.

Baked Lamb Shanks with Gary's Barbecue Sauce

SERVINGS: 4

These shanks are crispy on the outside and tender on the inside.

4 lamb shanks

salt and pepper

4 cloves of garlic

BARBECUE SAUCE

4 tablespoons brown sugar

2 cloves garlic, minced

½ teaspoon salt

¼ teaspoon freshly
ground pepper

1 teaspoon Dijon or
Dijon-style mustard

¼ teaspoon cayenne pepper

½ cup finely chopped onions

1 cup ketchup

⅓ cup cider vinegar

2 teaspoons Worcestershire sauce

1. Preheat oven to 450 degrees. Place lamb shanks in roasting pan on rack, sprinkle with salt and pepper, and cover each shank with minced garlic, dividing evenly. Bake for 45 minutes, turning once. (To help prevent splattering grease, cover meat loosely with foil and pour off excess fat occasionally.)

2. Make Barbecue Sauce; recipe follows.

3. When shanks have cooked for 45 minutes, remove from oven and reduce oven temperature to 325 degrees. Pour off excess oil and cover shanks with barbecue sauce. Cover pan tightly with foil and bake for 2 hours or until tender.

TO MAKE BARBECUE SAUCE

Combine all ingredients in a medium saucepan over medium high heat. Bring to boil, lower heat, and simmer 15 minutes.

Toasted French Bread with 40 Cloves of Garlic Spread

SERVINGS: 4

Serve as an appetizer or with dinner.

2 cups chicken stock (recipe page 313) or 1 (14½-ounce) can low-sodium chicken broth

40 cloves of garlic, peeled*

2 tablespoons plus 1 teaspoon olive oil

8 slices French bread, toasted

* To peel garlic, place cloves on work surface. Hold a large broad knife blade parallel to board over garlic (sharp edge facing away from you). Strike garlic firmly with flat side of knife blade by whacking knife blade with palm of hand. The outer layer of peel can easily be removed.

1. In heavy, medium saucepan, bring stock to boil over medium heat. Lower heat, add garlic cloves, and simmer, uncovered, until garlic is tender, about 1 hour. Check periodically, adding more stock if necessary.

2. Preheat oven to 200 degrees. Remove garlic from stock and set aside. Reduce stock in pan over medium-high heat to about 1½ tablespoons, if not already reduced to that amount.

3. Place garlic cloves, olive oil, and reduced liquid in food processor and puree. Spread mixture on toasted French bread slices. Place on baking sheet and bake in oven for 20 minutes.

Grilled Nectarines with Honey Wine Glaze

SERVINGS: 4-6

Serve as an accompaniment to grilled chicken or pork, or as a dessert.

1 cup dry white wine (orange juice may be substituted)

2 tablespoons honey

3 large ripe nectarines, halved, pitted, with skins left on

vegetable oil

raspberry puree (see page 89), optional

1 tablespoon granulated sugar, optional

1. In small saucepan, combine wine and honey and bring to boil over medium heat. Reduce to low and simmer mixture about 20-30 minutes, stirring occasionally, until mixture is reduced by two-thirds.

2. Prepare barbecue grill. Rub nectarine halves with vegetable oil. Grill, cut side down, for about 4 minutes or until slightly charred. Brush unpeeled top sides with about half the glaze and grill 30 seconds longer.

3. Remove necatrines from grill, turn nectarines over, and brush on remaining glaze. Cut into thick slices and serve. If using for dessert, drizzle with raspberry puree sweetened with 1 tablespoon sugar.

Nectarine and Almond Tart

SERVINGS: 8

Juicy nectarines are harvested in late summer in Washington; save some for this tart.

PASTRY SHELL

1⅓ **cups all-purpose flour**

¼ **cup granulated sugar**

½ **cup chilled butter,
cut in small pieces
(To chill butter, place in freezer
45 minutes or longer.)**

1 **large egg yolk, beaten**

FILLING

¼ **cup vanilla wafer crumbs**

½ **cup sliced almonds, toasted
(see page 323 for toasting nuts)**

3 **large or about
6 small ripe nectarines,
peeled, pitted, and sliced
(to aid in peeling nectarines,
place in boiling water 15 seconds,
then cool in cold water and
peel off skins.)**

⅓ **cup plus 3 tablespoons
granulated sugar, divided**

1 **cup apricot preserves**

¼ **teaspoon almond extract**

Whipped cream for topping

1. Preheat oven to 300 degrees. Make pastry by combining flour, sugar, and butter pieces in food processor, or place in bowl and combine with pastry blender. Add egg yolk and combine just to stage when dough holds together when pressed. Do not overprocess. Press pastry into 10-inch tart pan with removable bottom and bake for 30 minutes. Cool.

2. For filling: place wafer crumbs over pastry, then toasted almonds. Top with nectarines in concentric pattern with slices close together and sprinkle ⅓ cup sugar on top. Bake for 30 minutes at 300 degrees.

3. Meanwhile strain apricot preserves through sieve and combine with 3 tablespoons sugar in saucepan over medium heat for 2-3 minutes or until sugar is dissolved and syrup is thick enough to coat a spoon with light coating; add almond extract.

4. When tart is baked, cool-to-warm, brush glaze over nectarines, and pour extra glaze over top. Let cool. Chill in refrigerator. Serve with whipped cream, if desired.

GRAND COULEE

The steep-walled chasm in central Washington that was once the bed of the Columbia River chisels its way through miles of rock and soil. Near the head of this coulee stands Grand Coulee Dam, the largest concrete dam in the United States. The dam crosses the Columbia River and creates the greatest single source of water power in the country, providing electricity for hundreds of cities and towns in several states. The associated Columbia Basin Irrigation Project supplies water to irrigate over 500,000 acres. When work on the dam was begun in the 1930s, the surrounding area changed dramatically. Dry desert land became fertile cropland and towns such as Grand Coulee were created overnight. The town continues to serve local farmers and is home to the workers who maintain the dam.

Orchards in the area produce **peaches, apples, pears,** and **cherries. Tomatoes** and other **vegetables** do well in the area's sunny climate. Some farmers also raise **cattle** and grow **wheat.** The Columbia River and adjacent lakes provide such varieties of fish as **rainbow trout, walleye, white sturgeon, yellow perch,** and others which, due to the high level of nutrients in the clean, cold waters, tend to be exceptionally large, trophy specimens.

Tomato, Cucumber, and Gorgonzola Salad

SERVINGS: 4

This salad can be made ahead, covered, and refrigerated, then brought out a half hour before serving. Sprinkle with parsley just before serving.

**2 medium or large tomatoes,
seeded and cut in cubes**

**½ cup finely chopped
green pepper**

½ cup finely chopped red pepper

**½ cup finely chopped onions,
preferably Walla Walla Sweets**

**2 small cucumbers,
cut in small cubes**

¼ cup olive oil

2 tablespoons fresh lemon juice

salt and pepper to taste

**¼ cup crumbled Gorgonzola
cheese (or blue cheese)**

¼ cup minced parsley

1. Combine first five ingredients in serving bowl.

2. Drizzle with olive oil and lemon juice, and season with salt and pepper, and toss together. Sprinkle with cheese and parsley.

Sally's Baked Stuffed Tomatoes

SERVINGS: 6

Serve these savory tomatoes for brunch alongside scrambled eggs; for lunch with a spinach salad, or for dinner as a vegetable side dish.

6 large unpeeled tomatoes

½ cup cooked and crumbled crisp bacon (about 6-8 slices)

¼ cup finely chopped celery

¼ cup finely sliced (or chopped) mushrooms

1 small onion, finely chopped

1 clove garlic, minced

1 cup soft bread crumbs, crusts removed

½ teaspoon salt

½ cup grated cheddar or Parmesan cheese, divided

1 tablespoon butter or margarine

1. Preheat oven to 350 degrees. Cut a slice from the top of each tomato. Scoop out center and place pulp in medium bowl.

2. To pulp, add bacon, celery, mushrooms, onion, garlic, bread crumbs, salt, and ¼ cup grated cheese, and combine. Fill tomatoes with pulp mixture, sprinkle remaining ¼ cup grated cheese on top and dot with butter.

3. Place tomatoes in greased muffin cups or baking dish. Bake, uncovered, 25-30 minutes.

Aunt Emma's Cream Cake

SERVINGS: 6

Aunt Emma created this cake during World War II, when butter was rationed. She continued to make it after the war and served it with fresh peaches and cream.

1 egg

¾ cup (or more) heavy or light cream (for light cream, see page 322)

1 cup granulated sugar

1 cup all-purpose flour

1 teaspoon baking powder

¼ teaspoon salt

½ teaspoon nutmeg

1 teaspoon vanilla

1. Preheat oven to 350 degrees. Place egg in liquid measuring cup and add cream (about ¾ cup) to the one-cup line. Place in medium-sized mixing bowl and stir together.

2. Beat in sugar. Sift together flour, baking powder, salt, and nutmeg, and add to mixture; stir in vanilla. Place in greased 8- or 9-inch round cake pan. Bake 25-30 minutes or until cake tester inserted into cake comes out clean. Set on rack to cool.

Peaches and Cream Trifle

SERVINGS: 8

Fresh peaches, custard, and cream are mingled together in this trifle.

Aunt Emma's Cream Cake
(recipe page 205); or pound cake
(about 11 ounces purchased,
or use recipe page 280)

½ cup sherry

¼ cup granulated sugar

1½ tablespoons cornstarch

4 egg yolks or 6 tablespoons
liquid egg substitutes*

2 cups milk

5 tablespoons Bailey's Irish Cream,
divided

1 teaspoon vanilla

½ cup raspberry jam

4 peaches, peeled, cored,
sliced, and sweetened with
1 tablespoon sugar

1½ cups heavy (whipping) cream

½ teaspoon almond extract

½ cup sliced almonds, toasted
(see page 323 for toasting nuts)

1. Cut cake into 1-inch cubes and place in large glass bowl. Sprinkle sherry over, stir carefully, and set aside.

2. To make custard: whisk together sugar, cornstarch, and eggs or egg substitutes in medium saucepan. Heat over medium heat until warm. Whisk in milk and 4 tablespoons Irish Cream in a thin stream. Cook, whisking constantly, until custard is thickened and lightly coats spoon, about 7-10 minutes. (If using egg yolks, cook custard to 160 degrees.) Remove from heat and stir in vanilla and remaining 1 tablespoon Irish Cream. Set aside to cool.

3. Spoon raspberry jam over cake cubes. Place sliced peaches over jam. Spoon cooled custard over peaches.

4. Whip cream until thick; add almond flavoring. Place whipped cream in pastry bag and pipe over top of cooled custard. (If a pastry bag is unavailable, spoon cream over.) Cover with plastic wrap and refrigerate 4 hours or up to 24 hours. Sprinkle with toasted almonds just before serving.

*Egg substitutes should be used if the mixture is not heated to 160 degrees.

206

CHELAN

The town of Chelan anchors the southern tip of alluring Lake Chelan. Breathtaking mountains surround this a prime resort area, and a leisurely, romantic interlude is possible when cruising up Lake Chelan on an old-fashioned tour boat to Stehekin—a touch of civilization set in the woods—at the head of the lake.

Orchards surround Chelan, and in the springtime the air is filled with the sweet perfume of **apple** blossoms. **Sweet cherries, pears, peaches,** and **apricots** are also grown here.

WASHINGTON STATE HISTORICAL SOCIETY

Spinach Salad with Apples and Ginger Vinaigrette

SERVINGS: 6

Toasted peanuts and raisins top this spinach salad.

VINAIGRETTE

¼ **cup white wine vinegar**

¼ **cup apple jelly**

1 **tablespoon grated fresh ginger, or 1 teaspoon powdered ginger**

½ **teaspoon curry powder**

1 **teaspoon brown sugar**

¾ **cup vegetable oil**

salt and pepper

SALAD

2 **bunches spinach leaves, cleaned and stems removed**

2 **large Red Delicious apples, unpeeled, cored, and sliced**

1 **cup thinly sliced red onion**

½ **cup raisins**

¾ **cup dry roasted peanuts**

TO MAKE VINAIGRETTE

Make vinaigrette by combining vinegar, jelly, ginger, curry powder, and sugar in small bowl or in food processor with steel blade inserted. Slowly add oil in a stream, mixing constantly. Add salt and pepper to taste.

TO MAKE SALAD

Toss spinach leaves, apple slices, and onion slices in bowl with enough dressing to coat. Sprinkle raisins and peanuts on top.

Sweet Cherry and Almond Country Cake

SERVINGS: 6

This country cake, similar to the French clafouti,
is best served warm with whipped cream.

3 cups sweet cherries, pitted

¼ plus ⅓ cup granulated sugar, divided

⅓ cup slivered almonds, toasted (see page 323 for toasting nuts)

½ cup all-purpose flour

⅛ teaspoon salt

3 eggs, whisked together

2 tablespoons butter or margarine, melted

½ cup heavy or light cream or half-and-half (see page 322 for light cream)

½ teaspoon almond flavoring

2 tablespoons confectioners' sugar

Whipped cream for topping

1. Preheat oven to 350 degrees. Place sweet cherries in bottom of buttered 9- or 10-inch round cake pan or shallow fluted baking dish. Sprinkle with ¼ cup sugar and toasted almonds, and set aside.

2. Combine flour, reserved ⅓ cup sugar, and salt in a medium bowl, and stir to combine.

3. In separate medium bowl, combine eggs, butter, cream, and almond flavoring. Add egg-cream mixture to flour mixture, stir until smooth.

4. Pour batter on top of cherries and almonds. Bake 40-45 minutes. Cool slightly. Sieve confectioners' sugar on top. Whip cream, serve with cake.

EPHRATA

Ephrata means "fruit region" and is also an ancient name for Bethlehem. The story goes that in 1892 a Great Northern Railway worker, who had recently been to the Holy Land, so named this community, for it had the only fruit trees in the area. Some orchards remain, but today's farmers have diversified their crops considerably, growing **potatoes, dry beans, wheat, corn, barley, peas, asparagus,** and **carrots.** Orchards still produce **apples, cherries, pears,** and **peaches.** Over 10,000 **hogs** are raised in Grant County, where Ephrata is located. Farming is the important industry here now; but if you want a glimpse of how the early cowboys and railroad workers lived, visit the Grant County Historical Museum in town.

Potato Soufflé

SERVINGS: 6

This is an elegant potato dish to serve with roasts.

¼ **cup butter or margarine**

1 **tablespoon minced shallots**

¼ **cup all-purpose flour**

¾ **teaspoon salt**

⅛ **teaspoon pepper**

⅛ **teaspoon ground nutmeg, preferably freshly ground**

1 **cup sour cream, regular or light**

2 **cups mashed potatoes, warm or room temperature**

4 **eggs, separated**

1 **tablespoon minced chives**

1. Preheat oven to 350 degrees. Melt butter or margarine in medium saucepan over medium heat, add shallots, and sauté until tender, about 2 minutes. Stir in flour, salt, and pepper, and heat for 1 minute, stirring constantly. Take off heat; add nutmeg and sour cream, stirring until thickened. Add mashed potatoes; beat until smooth.

2. Place egg yolks in small bowl and beat well. Add about 6 tablespoons of the potato mixture to yolks, one tablespoon at a time, stirring constantly. Add egg mixture to the remaining potato mixture. Beat egg whites until stiff and fold into potato mixture.

3. Place mixture in buttered 1½-quart dish. Bake for 30-35 minutes. Sprinkle with minced chives and serve. (The soufflé may be made ahead, covered, refrigerated, and brought to room temperature for 30 minutes before final baking.)

White Bean Casserole with Orange and Sage

SERVINGS: 10

The orange and sage add a new taste to an old favorite.

1 pound dried white beans
(navy or Great Northern)

2 bay leaves

1½ teaspoons salt, divided

¼ cup olive or vegetable oil

3 cups chopped onion

3 cloves garlic, minced

¾ cup dark brown sugar, packed

½ cup orange juice
concentrate, undiluted

½ cup ketchup

1 cup reserved bean liquid,
or more

2 tablespoons fresh minced sage,
or ¾ teaspoon dried

⅛ teaspoon freshly
ground pepper

1. Rinse and pick through beans and soak overnight in large bowl with enough water to cover.

2. Rinse the soaked beans under cold water and place in large heavy saucepan along with bay leaves. Cover with water and bring to boil over medium high heat. Reduce heat and simmer beans until tender, about one hour. Drain and reserve liquid.

3. Place beans in large heavy casserole, add 1 teaspoon salt, and set aside. Preheat oven to 300 degrees.

4. In medium saucepan, heat olive oil, add chopped onion and garlic, and sauté over medium-low heat until tender. Add brown sugar and stir in until it has dissolved. Add orange juice concentrate, ketchup, 1 cup reserved bean liquid (reserving remaining liquid), sage, pepper, and reserved ½ teaspoon salt.

5. Combine this mixture with beans in casserole and stir. Cover casserole and place in oven for 3 hours. Stir every ½ hour and check to see if more reserved bean liquid is needed. Remove cover for the last ½ hour.

Medallions of Pork with Apples

SERVINGS: 2 OR 4

This dish takes only minutes to prepare.

4 boneless pork loin chops,
or slices of pork tenderloin
cut ½-inch thick (about 1 pound)

salt and freshly ground pepper

¼ teaspoon ground sage

flour

1 tablespoon vegetable oil

1 tablespoon butter or margarine

1 cup dry vermouth*

1 tablespoon brown sugar

2 cooking apples,
peeled and sliced

*Dry white wine or chicken broth may be substituted for vermouth.

1. Sprinkle pork pieces with salt, pepper, and dry sage, and rub into the meat. Dust both sides with flour. Melt oil and butter in large skillet over medium heat, increase heat to medium high, add pork, and sauté about 4-5 minutes per side, or until done. Place on warm platter and keep warm with foil tent over.

2. To skillet, add vermouth and scrape up any browned bits. Reduce heat to medium, add brown sugar, and cook until sugar dissolves, about 1 minute. Add apples, cover, cook 2 minutes, or until apples are tender. Return pork to pan, lower heat, leave uncovered and simmer 2 minutes. Serve pork with apples and sauce. This serves 4 with one pork chop or slice per person, or 2 with two chops or slices per person.

Filet of Pork with Sweet Cherries and Tarragon

SERVINGS: 4

When I was at the Cordon Bleu cooking school in London, I made a similar recipe. At home, I substituted local products.

pork filets (1½ pounds pork tenderloin cut in ⅜-inch slices)

salt and pepper

1 tablespoon butter

1 tablespoon vegetable oil

2 shallots, minced

1 teaspoon Hungarian paprika

2 teaspoons all-purpose flour

⅓ cup dry white wine

½ cup beef or chicken stock (recipes pages 314 and 313) or broth

1 teaspoon dried tarragon

¼ cup sour cream or Crème Fraîche (recipe, page 312)

1 tablespoon butter

¾ cup sweet cherries, pitted

1. Lightly season pork filets with salt and pepper. Heat butter and oil in large skillet over medium heat and brown meat quickly on both sides. Take out meat and set aside on platter.

2. Add shallots and paprika and cook over medium-low heat for 2-3 minutes. Stir in flour, add wine and stock, and bring to boil. Season with tarragon and salt and pepper.

3. Return browned meat to skillet, cover, and simmer gently for 10-15 minutes or until tender. Remove pork and keep warm on heated platter under foil. Add sour cream or Crème Fraîche to sauce and keep warm; do not boil.

4. In separate small saucepan, melt butter over medium-high heat and sauté cherries in butter until sizzling hot. Top pork filets with sauce and scatter cherries over.

WENATCHEE

Wenatchee hugs the banks of the Columbia River, where apple orchards border both sides of the river a long way up the valley. These orchards yield succulent apples of crimson, green, and gold, giving inspiration for the annual Apple Blossom Festival held each spring.

A small trading post brought white settlers to this area in 1871. These early residents were not the first, however, for in 1987 orchard workers near Wenatchee uncovered Clovis points, a type of spearpoint used about 11,000 years ago by the giant-bison and mammoth hunters who roamed central Washington.

Over one-third of the nation's **apples** are grown in Washington, and Wenatchee boasts that it's the Apple Capital of the World. Many of the apples sold in the United States are from the orchards near Wenatchee. Hardy Red Delicious and Winesap, both great eating apples with long-lasting qualities, are shipped all over the world. Other varieties, better for cooking, include **Golden Delicious, Rome Beauty, Granny Smith,** and **Yellow Pippin. Winter pears, Bartlett pears, sweet cherries,** and **peaches** also grow in the orchards nearby.

High-in-the-Sky Apple Pie

SERVINGS: 8-10

This pie, piled high with apples and baked in a springform pan, is impressive and an apple lover's joy.

CRUST

2 cups all-purpose flour

⅛ teaspoon salt

½ cup vegetable shortening

4 tablespoons butter or margarine, cut into small pieces

4-5 tablespoons ice water

FILLING

8 cups Granny Smith or Gravenstein apples, peeled, cored, and sliced

8 cups Golden Delicious apples, peeled, cored, and sliced

1 tablespoon lemon juice

½ cup brown sugar, packed

1 cup granulated sugar

2 teaspoons cinnamon

½ teaspoon nutmeg, preferably freshly ground

½ teaspoon ground cloves

1 teaspoon vanilla

3 tablespoons all-purpose flour

3 tablespoons cornstarch

¼ cup apple juice

CRUMB TOPPING

1 cup all-purpose flour

½ cup brown sugar, packed

½ cup butter or margarine

vanilla ice cream, optional

1. To make crust: combine flour and salt in bowl, or food processor. With steel blade in food processor, or with pastry blender, cut in shortening and butter until it forms coarse meal. If using food processor, take off cover. Sprinkle in ice water and combine using quick pulses (or combine using forks in bowl) just until it resembles cottage cheese. Press together with hands, form into a disk, and wrap in plastic wrap. Refrigerate while preparing filling and topping.

2. For filling: combine prepared apples with all filling ingredients in a large bowl and set aside. Make crumb topping by combining ingredients with pastry blender or forks in a medium bowl and set aside.

3. Preheat oven to 300 degrees. Roll pie dough out to 15-inch diameter on floured surface and line a 9-inch springform pan with pie dough, overlapping some on sides. Flute edge (see glossary, page 322). Add apple mixture, mounding high in the center. Crumble crumb mixture on top.

4. Bake 2½ hours to 3 hours, until apples are tender. Remove from oven and cool 2 hours. Refrigerate 6 hours or overnight.

5. When serving, remove sides of springform pan. Serve at room temperature, or reheat at 250 degrees, and serve with scoops of vanilla ice cream if desired.

ELLENSBURG

Ellensburg is a relatively quiet town. But the pace picks up on Rodeo Weekend in September when the nation's best cowboys come to town to ride broncos, rope calves, and put on a show that dazzles any rodeo fan. An old-time county fair shares the bill with the rodeo, bringing more festivities and fun to the Labor Day weekend event. When the show-riding cowboys leave, Ellensburg residents and visitors enjoy life in a town that includes many art galleries, antique shops in historic buildings, and the John Clymer Art Museum. Ellensburg's native Clymer was a master artist and a storyteller on canvas. His works range from famous Western art to over 80 Saturday Evening Post cover illustrations. The town also offers repertory drama at the Laughing Horse Theater, a Western Art Show and Auction, a pumpkin festival, and old-time Threshing Bee. Central Washington University, located in town, brings many students during school term. This community's commitment to the arts and its honest Western flavor attracts many visitors.

Some **cattle** and **sheep** graze in fields near Ellensburg and large processing plants for both are located here. **Wheat, corn,** and **potato "chippers"** (potatoes grown for potato chips) are grown in the nearby cropland. Recently, fruit trees have been planted and efforts to raise more cold-resistant **pears** and **apples** have proven successful.

Broiled Ellensburg Lamb Chops with Mint Crust

SERVINGS: 4

Mint, oil, and herbs form a crust that seals in juices in these chops.

¼ cup olive oil

¼ cup finely chopped fresh mint

4 garlic cloves, minced

1 teaspoon salt

1 teaspoon ground cumin

1 teaspoon ground coriander

1 teaspoon cayenne pepper

¾ teaspoon freshly
ground pepper

8 (1-inch thick)
lamb loin chops, trimmed

Fresh mint leaves for garnish

1. Mix all ingredients, except lamb chops and mint leaves for garnish, in small bowl and combine. Spread this mixture on both sides of lamb chops and let stand for 10-15 minutes.

2. Place chops with mixture on broiler pan. Preheat broiler or grill.

3. Broil or grill chops about 4-6 minutes on each side for medium rare. Serve, garnished with fresh mint leaves.

Crunchy-coated Beef Short Ribs

SERVINGS: 4-6

These ribs are tender and crunchy coated. Serve with lightly buttered noodles sprinkled with poppy seeds, and steamed green beans.

6 pounds short ribs,
cracked into serving-sized pieces

1 teaspoon salt

¼ teaspoon freshly
ground pepper

¾ cup Dijon or
Dijon-style mustard

2 cups fresh white bread crumbs

3 tablespoons melted butter
or margarine

1. Preheat oven to 350 degrees. Place short ribs on a rack in roasting pan; season with salt and pepper. Roast in oven until tender, about 2 hours. Cool, transfer to another pan, cover, and refrigerate 4 hours or as long as a day.

2. About 45 minutes before serving, take ribs from refrigerator and trim off fat. Preheat oven to 400 degrees.

3. Spread each rib well with mustard and roll in crumbs. Place coated ribs on a baking or broiler pan and spoon a little melted butter over each piece of coated meat. Bake until golden, about 25-30 minutes.

Beef Wellington with Madeira Sauce

SERVINGS: 8

This is a traditional main course for our Christmas day dinner. Most of the Wellington preparation can be done a day before serving.

4 pounds whole beef tenderloin (Butcher shops usually carry this size, otherwise, do 2 Wellingtons that are 2 pounds each.)

2 tablespoons butter, melted

2 tablespoons brandy

freshly ground pepper

salt

2 sheets frozen puff pastry (1 extra sheet may be used for decoration)

Duxelles (recipe page 312)

1 egg yolk mixed with 2 teaspoons water

1. Preheat oven to 425 degrees. Remove fat and gristle from meat, and tie meat securely with string. Place tenderloin on meat rack in roasting pan. Combine melted butter and brandy and brush over tenderloin. Grind black pepper over meat, pressing in firmly. Sprinkle lightly with salt.

2. Bake 25-50 minutes or until meat is 140 degrees for rare and 160 degrees for medium. Check with meat thermometer periodically. Remove meat from pan and allow to cool on platter. Reserve pan drippings for Madeira sauce. Take off strings from around meat.

3. Bring puff pastry to room temperature. Roll out pastry dough, combining 2 sheets by using water to lightly moisten the dough and help adhere the pieces together. (Dough needs to be rolled large enough to enclose tenderloin.)

4. Spread duxelles over pastry, just enough to cover meat (there will be a border on all sides). Press duxelles firmly into pastry.

5. Place meat, top side down, in center of pastry on duxelles. Wrap pastry around tenderloin, sealing ends and center seam, using water to help seal. Cut off excess pastry. (If using 2 tenderloins, place end to end.)

6. Roll out leftover pastry (and extra sheet of dough, if needed) to decorate Wellington. Some ideas:

a) wrap with ribbon and bow on to
b) place strips crisscrossing over the top
c) create holly and berries with dough and decorate.

Wrap securely with plastic wrap and refrigerate 3 hours or as long as a day.

7. Final baking: unwrap and allow to stand at room temperature for one hour. Preheat oven to 400 degrees. Brush with egg yolk mixture. Bake for 20-30 minutes or until pastry is golden brown. Let stand 10 minutes before carving. Serve with Madeira Sauce, recipe follows.

MADEIRA SAUCE

Pan drippings

butter, as needed

2 cups homemade beef stock (recipe page 314) or canned low-sodium broth

3 tablespoons all-purpose flour

¼ cup Madeira

¼ cup sour cream, regular or light

TO MAKE SAUCE

(This sauce may be made ahead and reheated.)

1. If pan drippings measure less than 2 tablespoons, add enough butter to measure 2 tablespoons. Heat stock (broth) in small saucepan over medium heat until warm.

2. Meanwhile, place pan drippings and butter in separate medium saucepan and heat over medium heat. Add flour to pan drippings, stir together, and cook for 2 minutes. Take pan off heat, add warmed stock (broth) all at once.

3. Return to heat and stir until smooth and thickened. Add Madeira and sour cream. (Sauce will need salt only if the stock is unsalted.)

4. On low heat, cook but do not boil, uncovered, for 10 minutes, stirring frequently. Sauce may be refrigerated, then brought to room temperature and reheated over low heat.

☆

MOSES LAKE

In the 1800s, Neppel was a small town with a few buildings and a post office in the middle of desolate, desert land near a small lake. Things began to change in the 1900s. In 1906 the name was changed when the townfolks decided to name the community after Chief Moses, and Neppel became known as Moses Lake. In the 1940s the surrounding desert blossomed into fertility when water began flowing into the land from Lake Roosevelt, a lake formed by the newly constructed Grand Coulee Dam. People came to farm and the town prospered and grew. In recent years, campers and boaters discovered the area as a great place to fish, camp, hunt, boat, and ride the nearby sand dunes in buggies and four wheelers. Tourists flock to the area in their recreational vehicles. Now Moses Lake is a busy community and claims to be the RV capital of the state.

Potatoes are the predominant crop here. Orchards produce **apples** and **cherries** and fields yield **asparagus, dry beans, onions, peas, potatoes,** and **mint.** Also, **corn** and **wheat** are plentiful. **Sugar beets,** once an important crop in the area, are again being raised by some farmers.

WASHINGTON STATE HISTORICAL SOCIETY

Russet Potato, Zucchini, and Sweet Pepper Ratatouille

SERVINGS: 4

Russet potatoes give this ratatouille (vegetable stew) a deliciously different base, instead of the more commonly used eggplant. Serve as vegetarian main dish or hearty accompaniment to grilled meat or chicken.

4-5 tablespoons olive oil, divided

1½ pounds Russet potatoes, well scrubbed (peeled, if desired), and cut in ¾-inch cubes

salt and pepper

1 large or 2 small zucchini, seeded if large, and cubed

1 medium onion, sliced

1 green pepper, seeded and sliced

1 red pepper, seeded and sliced

2 cloves garlic, finely chopped

4 large tomatoes, peeled, seeded, and chopped

2 tablespoons fresh chopped basil, or 2 teaspoons dry

1½ teaspoons fresh thyme or ½ teaspoon dry

1½ teaspoons fresh oregano or ½ teaspoon dry

¼ cup minced fresh parsley (to sprinkle on top)

2-3 dashes Tabasco sauce

1. Heat 2-3 tablespoons olive oil in large heavy skillet or Dutch oven over medium heat. Add potatoes, season with salt and pepper, and sauté for 25-30 minutes until tender, stirring occasionally. Remove from skillet and transfer to large platter.

2. Heat one more tablespoon olive oil in same skillet, add zucchini, salt and pepper lightly, and sauté over medium heat for about 4 minutes, or until just tender. Place on platter with potatoes.

3. Heat last tablespoon olive oil in skillet, add onion and peppers, and sauté until onions are tender. Add garlic and tomatoes, cook vegetables for 3 minutes, stirring constantly.

4. Add cooked potatoes and zucchini and mix well. Add basil, thyme, oregano, parsley, Tabasco sauce, and combine. Salt and pepper to taste. Cover and simmer over low heat for 30 minutes. Serve with minced parsley on top.

Syl's Potato Latkes with Rosemary and Spicy Applesauce

SERVINGS: 6

Latkes (pancakes) are a special tradition and treat when celebrating Hanukkah.

4 pounds Russet potatoes, well scrubbed, trimmed, but unpeeled (dry with paper towel)

2 medium onions,* finely chopped

4 eggs, beaten

⅔ cup Matzo meal (or flour)

1 teaspoon dry rosemary, rubbed between hands

2 teaspoons salt

freshly grated pepper

oil for frying, preferably peanut oil

spicy applesauce, recipe follows

sour cream, regular or light

Do not chop onions in food processor.

1. Make applesauce earlier and refrigerate.

2. Grate potatoes on coarse grater or shred in food processor. Drain potatoes, if necessary. Place in large bowl and add eggs, chopped onion, Matzo meal, rosemary, salt, and pepper, mixing well.

3. In large heavy skillet (or two) place oil about ¼- to ½-inch deep and heat until very hot but not smoking. Drop about ¼ cup potato mixture into hot oil. Do not flatten. Fry about 3-4 minutes on each side, or until golden brown and crisp. Drain on paper towels, patting both sides, and serve immediately, or keep warm on rack in pan in a 200 degree oven for up to 25 minutes. Serve with spicy applesauce and sour cream.

SPICY APPLESAUCE

1½ cups apple cider or juice

10 Golden Delicious apples, peeled, cored, and cut in chunks

10 Granny Smith or Gravenstein apples, peeled, cored, and cut in chunks

½ cup brown sugar, packed

½ teaspoon ground cloves

½ teaspoon ground nutmeg, preferably freshly ground

2 teaspoons cinnamon

TO MAKE APPLESAUCE

1. In large saucepan, place apple cider and apple chunks. Bring to boil over medium heat, turn down heat, and simmer over medium low heat, partially covered, for 45 minutes or until apples are tender, stirring frequently.

2. Add brown sugar and spices and continue cooking and stirring to desired consistency. (About 5-8 minutes for chunky applesauce.) Serve at room temperature, or chilled.

WASHINGTON STATE HISTORICAL SOCIETY

Potato and Corn Chowder

SERVINGS: 4

Two vegetables combine to make this a flavorful and nourishing chowder.

2 medium Russet potatoes, peeled and diced

1 medium onion, thinly sliced and separated into rings

½ cup chopped celery

1 cup chicken stock (recipe page 313) or canned broth

1½ cups corn kernels, fresh uncooked or cooked, or canned

½ teaspoon granulated sugar

1½ cups milk

¼ teaspoon dried marjoram

salt and pepper

4 slices bacon, cooked and crumbled, optional

l. Combine potatoes with onion, celery, and chicken broth in large saucepan. Bring to boil over medium high heat, turn heat to low, and cook about 20 minutes or until vegetables are soft.

2. Stir in corn, sugar, milk, marjoram, and salt and pepper to taste. Heat through. (If fresh corn is used, heat for 5 minutes or until corn is tender.) Serve with crumbled bacon on top.

OTHELLO

An early resident, inspired by the works of William Shakespeare, named this small community after one of the playwright's famous plays. Located in the heart of the Columbia Basin, the area was sparsely populated until irrigation brought water to the barren fields and farmers came to till the soil. The town grew, offering goods and services to farmers and visitors. Today, Othello is a convenient place for fishermen to buy goods before heading off to the Potholes area, where a large reservoir and many lakes hold **walleye, rainbow trout, large mouth bass, perch,** and **crappie.** Bird hunters come in the fall to hunt **pheasant** in the dry fields and **ducks** near ponds and canals. Local farmers grow Russet **potatoes, corn,** other **vegetables** and **apples.**

Freshwater Perch with Orange Parsley Sauce
SERVINGS: 4

These ingredients can be taken along camping if you plan to cook the perch over a campfire. Good with sole also.

freshwater perch filets, enough for 4 people (about 2 pounds)

salt and freshly ground pepper

flour

1 tablespoon vegetable oil

1 tablespoon butter or margarine

juice of 3 medium or 2 large oranges

1 tablespoon grated orange zest (peel)

pinch ground allspice

1 clove garlic, minced

1 tablespoon minced parsley

1. Sprinkle fish filets with salt and pepper and dust with flour. Heat oil and butter in large skillet until hot, over medium high heat. Add filets and cook about 2-3 minutes on each side, or until fish is opaque throughout. Remove to warm platter and cover loosely with foil.

2. To skillet add orange juice, orange zest, allspice, and garlic, and cook over high heat for about 1-2 minutes, stirring constantly with wooden spoon, until juice is reduced to a light syrup. Stir in parsley and spoon sauce over filets.

Pheasants with Apples, Cream, and Apple Brandy

SERVINGS: 4

Many lovers of good food favor the pheasant over all other game birds.

2 pheasants, cut in pieces
(as you would a small chicken)

about ½ cup flour,
seasoned with ½ teaspoon salt
and ⅛ teaspoon pepper

2 tablespoons butter or margarine

1 tablespoon vegetable oil

1 cup heavy or light cream
(for light cream, see page 322)

1 cup cooking apples,
peeled, cored, and diced

½ cup apple brandy
(Northwest apple brandy
or Calvados) or apple juice

1. Preheat oven to 325 degrees. Roll pheasant pieces in seasoned flour (or shake in plastic bag) to coat. Melt butter and oil over medium heat in large skillet. Add pheasant pieces and cook until pieces are browned on all sides. Remove pheasant pieces and place in baking pan or large casserole dish.

2. Remove fat from skillet. To skillet add cream, chopped apples, and apple brandy, stir, heat to simmer, and pour over pheasant. Bake, covered, for 1 hour and fifteen minutes or until pheasant is tender. Remove pheasant to warm platter and cover with loosely vented foil. Heat sauce in small saucepan, over medium high heat, stirring frequently until sauce has reduced and is slightly thickened. Serve over pheasant pieces.

Duck Breasts in Orange Ginger Sauce

SERVINGS: 3 (WITH 2 BREASTS EACH), 6 (WITH 1 BREAST EACH)

A rich full-flavored orange sauce tops these duck breasts.

**6 duck breasts,
cleaned and skinned
(from 3 ducks)**

**¼ cup flour,
seasoned with ½ teaspoon salt
and ⅛ teaspoon pepper**

2 tablespoons soy sauce

1 tablespoon granulated sugar

2-3 teaspoons ground ginger

¼ teaspoon dry mustard

½ teaspoon cinnamon

¼ teaspoon salt

⅛ teaspoon pepper

**⅔ cup undiluted frozen
orange juice concentrate
(brought to room temperature)**

2 tablespoons butter or margarine

1. Preheat oven to 350 degrees. Roll breasts in seasoned flour (or shake in plastic bag) to coat; set aside.

2. In a small bowl, mix the soy sauce, sugar, ginger, mustard, cinnamon, salt, pepper, and orange juice concentrate.

3. Heat butter in large stove-top and oven-proof casserole dish. Sauté duck breasts 5 minutes on each side or until browned. (Breasts may also be sautéed in skillet, then placed in baking dish.) Stir the orange juice mixture and pour over duck breasts.

4. Place casserole pan in oven and bake, uncovered, for 30 minutes, or until breasts are done. Serve duck breasts coated with sauce.

YAKIMA

Native Americans lived in the fertile green valley east of the Cascade mountains for many years before pioneers came to till the soil. The valley's good hunting, fishing, and rich soil served the Indians well. Local Indians called themselves "Yakimas," a name later given the valley, a river, and the city that grew to meet the needs of the valley people.

Confusion still exists over the Native American meaning of the word "Yakima." Some scholarly etymologists say the name means "big belly, beginning of life, bountiful," while an equally scholarly group believes the name means "runaway," referring to the rushing waters of the Yakima River. Whichever, the Yakima River's runaway waters bring moisture to the valley to produce bountiful crops.

The city of Yakima's population was about 3,000 in 1884 when the Northern Pacific railroad decided to extend services to the area. Some of the townspeople refused to meet certain of the company's demands, so the Northern Pacific routed the tracks four miles north of the community, and named the new location "North Yakima." The railroad company offered to move any building to the new community, thus some 50-60 buildings were moved north. The courthouse, banks, saloons, stores, and some houses were moved on rollers, and as the wheels rolled on, so did business. A hotel was on the road for a month pulled by a mule team. Business continued in the dining room and guests slept in the hotel's rooms. Eventually, North Yakima became simply Yakima, and the original site is now called Union Gap.

Yakima Valley's rich volcanic soil, abundant sunshine, and more than adequate water supply produce a prolific supply of quality agricultural products. **Apples, apricots, cherries, grapes, peaches, pears, plums, cantaloupes, and nectarines** are the main fruits cultivated by Yakima farmers. Many of the more than six billion apples harvested each year in Washington state come from this valley.

"Yakimas" or "Yaks," words known world-wide in the brewery business, identify the famous **hops** that originate here. Seventy-five percent of the nation's hops are grown in the Yakima Valley. Though only about ¼ pound of hops is used to brew a 31-gallon barrel of beer, the importance of the flavor it brings to any ale is without challenge. The two main **mint** growing areas in the United States are the Yakima Valley and the Columbia River Basin, both in Washington state. The peppermint and spearmint crops are shipped internationally. Yakima Valley, along with the Columbia River Basin and the Walla Walla area, grow most of Washington state's **asparagus** crop. Approximately 32,000 acres in the state are devoted to this noble vegetable, comprising 30 percent of the nation's supply. Increasingly, this lush valley is becoming well-known for its wines, producing both quality red and white wines. **Vineyards** are multiplying throughout the valley and the wine world is taking notice. **Beef cattle** range in the nearby hills, and **dairy cattle** graze in pastures, adding yet another dimension to the area's prodigious array of agricultural products.

WASHINGTON STATE HISTORICAL SOCIETY

Cream of Asparagus Soup with Coriander

SERVINGS: 6

If you have used the tips of asparagus for some other purpose, this is a good way to use the rest of the stalk. This soup is terrific served either hot or chilled.

3 tablespoons butter or margarine

2 cups chopped onion

4 cups chicken stock
(recipe page 313) or broth

1¼ pounds fresh asparagus,
cut in ¼-inch pieces

1 tablespoon minced parsley

¾ teaspoon ground coriander

¼ cup heavy cream,
light cream, or half-and-half
(for light cream see page 322)

½ teaspoon salt, or to taste

⅛ teaspoon white pepper

chopped chives for garnish

1. Melt butter in large stockpot and add chopped onion. Cook over medium heat until soft, about 7-10 minutes. Add chicken stock and bring to boil. Drop asparagus pieces into boiling stock. Reduce heat to medium low and boil gently until asparagus is very soft, about 30 minutes.

2. Cool for 10 minutes; puree mixture in food processor or blender. (This may be done in batches.)

3. Return soup to pan and add parsley and coriander. Simmer for 10 minutes over medium low heat. Stir in cream and add salt and pepper. Serve warm or refrigerate and serve chilled. Garnish with chopped chives.

Ginger Chicken Wings with Fresh Plum Sauce

SERVINGS: 4-6; PLUM SAUCE YIELDS ABOUT 1 CUP

This plum sauce is also good served with roast pork, grilled poultry, or game.

12 chicken wings

½ cup soy sauce

⅓ cup fresh plum sauce
(recipe follows)

3 scallions finely sliced

1½ teaspoons grated fresh ginger
or ½ teaspoon ground ginger

1 tablespoon rice vinegar

1 tablespoon brown sugar

1. Cut chicken wings apart at joints, discarding tips.

2. Combine remaining ingredients in large shallow glass dish and marinate chicken pieces in mixture for a day or overnight, refrigerated.

3. Preheat oven to 400 degrees. Discard marinade. Place chicken pieces in a single layer on oiled foil in very shallow pan. Bake for 15 minutes. Turn and bake until tender, about 10 minutes longer. Serve with fresh plum sauce.

FRESH PLUM SAUCE

2 cups Italian plums,
pitted and coarsely chopped

2 teaspoons butter or margarine

2 tablespoons finely
chopped onion

2 tablespoons orange juice

½ cup granulated sugar

½ teaspoon dry mustard

⅛ teaspoon salt

⅛ teaspoon freshly
ground pepper

1½ tablespoons freshly
grated ginger, or
1¼ teaspoons ground ginger

2 tablespoons white wine vinegar

TO MAKE PLUM SAUCE

1. Process plums in food processor until finely chopped, but do not puree.

2. Melt butter in medium saucepan, add chopped onion, and sauté until soft, over medium-low heat. Add finely chopped plums and orange juice. Bring to boil, lower heat, and simmer 10 minutes, stirring frequently. Add sugar, mustard, salt, pepper, and ginger, and simmer 10 more minutes. Stir in vinegar and simmer 5 minutes.

3. Remove from heat. Serve warm or at room temperature.

Sesame Beef and Asparagus Stir-fry

SERVINGS: 4

In spring, when fresh asparagus is in season, I try to come up with all sorts of ways of using it. Since asparagus should be cooked briefly, it is an excellent choice for a quick stir-fry.

**1 pound beef
(sirloin or flank steak)
cut across the grain into
thin strips**

4 tablespoons sesame seeds

1 pound asparagus

2 scallions, thinly sliced

**1 yellow or red pepper,
thinly sliced**

4 tablespoons soy sauce

**1 cup beef stock
(recipe page 314)
or canned beef broth**

**2 tablespoons
minced fresh ginger, or
½ tablespoon ground ginger**

2 cloves garlic, minced

2 teaspoons cornstarch

½ teaspoon dry red pepper flakes

**4 tablespoons vegetable oil,
divided**

steamed white rice

1. Place beef strips in bowl, sprinkle with sesame seeds, toss to coat.

2. Cut or break off tough ends of asparagus; reserve for soup or discard. Slice prepared stalks diagonally into ½-inch pieces. Combine asparagus pieces with scallions and pepper strips in bowl and set aside.

3. Combine rest of ingredients, except vegetable oil and rice, in separate small bowl. Stir until cornstarch dissolves.

4. Heat 2 tablespoons oil in wok or heavy skillet over high heat. Add beef and brown all sides for about 3 minutes. Remove to plate. Add remaining 2 tablespoons oil, add asparagus, scallions, and pepper strips, and stir-fry one minute. Cover and cook until just tender, about one more minute. Return meat to pan. Stir liquid mixture again, add to pan, cooking and stirring until thickened. Serve with steamed white rice.

Spicy Baked Apple Sundaes with Cinnamon Sour Cream Ice Cream

SERVINGS: 4

If the ingredients are ready, this dessert is fun to make after dinner with friends. Some can make the ice cream, while others prepare the baked apples.

2 large cooking apples, preferably Rome Beauties, peeled, cored, and cut in half crosswise

3 tablespoons confectioners' sugar

3 tablespoons brown sugar

¾ teaspoon cinnamon

½ teaspoon nutmeg, preferably freshly ground

3 tablespoons chopped walnuts

1 tablespoon butter or margarine

Cinnamon sour cream ice cream, recipe follows

1. Place apple halves cut-side-up in microwave-safe dish. Combine sugars, cinnamon, nutmeg, nuts, and sprinkle mixture over apples. Dot the surface with butter and cover dish with plastic wrap. (May be refrigerated at this point.)

2. Make cinnamon sour cream ice cream.

3. When ready to cook apples, keep the plastic wrap on and microwave the apple halves for 6 minutes on high, or until apples are tender, rotating halfway through cooking.

4. Serve apple halves in glass goblets or individual serving dishes, topped with sauce from apples, and cinnamon sour cream ice cream.

CINNAMON SOUR CREAM ICE CREAM

1 cup light sour cream, well chilled

1 cup heavy (whipping) cream, well chilled

¼ cup brown sugar, packed

1 teaspoon ground cinnamon

TO MAKE ICE CREAM

1. Combine chilled creams with brown sugar and cinnamon in medium bowl and stir together.

2. Place in chilled ice cream maker and freeze according to manufacturer's directions. This ice cream is especially good served slightly soft. If the ice cream is frozen solid, bring out of freezer about 15-20 minutes before serving.

Poached Pears with Raspberry and Crème de Cassis Glaze

SERVINGS: 6

Rosy red-glazed pears served in a pool of Crème de Cassis syrup,
with Crème Fraîche spiraling around, make this a spectacular dessert.

2 cups dry white wine

1 cup water

1 cup granulated sugar

**1 cup raspberries
(fresh, or frozen and thawed)**

½ cup Crème de Cassis

**6 ripe but still firm pears
peeled, cored from the bottom,
leaving stems on
(Bosc or Bartlett preferred)**

**Crème Fraîche, about ¾ to 1 cup,
commercial or homemade,
recipe on page 312**

1. To poach pears: combine wine, water, and sugar in 3-quart saucepan and bring to boil over medium heat. Reduce heat and simmer until sugar is dissolved. Add raspberries and poach for 2 minutes. Strain syrup through a sieve into bowl. Place drained raspberries in food processor and puree. Strain puree through nylon sieve into separate bowl by stirring and pushing through nylon sieve to remove seeds from puree. Set puree aside.

2. Return syrup to saucepan, adding Crème de Cassis, and bring to simmer. Place pears in pan and poach 40-45 minutes, or until tender. (Pears may be poached on their sides, rotating with 2 pastry brushes occasionally, with care not to bruise fruit.)

3. When cooked, remove pears with slotted spoon and place upright on plate. Take out ½ cup of syrup and add to raspberry puree to make it a coating consistency. Spoon puree over upright pears, coating each, and set aside. Pears may by refrigerated, covered loosely.

4. Increase heat to medium high under pan with rest of syrup and cook 30-45 minutes to reduce syrup to about 1½ cups. (Check every 5 minutes; heat may need to be reduced.) When syrup has reduced, it may be kept at room temperature for a few hours or refrigerated overnight.

5. To assemble: pour a layer of syrup onto 6 dessert plates. Fill plastic squeeze bottle (one with a small tip opening to make a thin line) with Crème Fraîche. Practice making a line on a small plate with Creme Fraîche by squeezing bottle. The Crème Fraîche may need to be thinned a bit with milk. Beginning at the center of sauce on plate, pipe a spiral of Crème Fraîche over sauce, working toward the edge of sauce. After the spirals have been formed, drag the back of a thin knife from the center of plate to the edge at about 1-inch intervals all around the plate.

6. Place poached pear in center of sauce on dessert plates and drizzle some Crème Fraîche over pears, sparingly, to show the contrast between the rosy pears and white Crème Fraîche.

Garden Fresh Mint Cream

SERVINGS: 6

A smooth, creamy, and refreshing mint dessert.

¾ cup granulated sugar

1 cup water, divided

1 cup lightly packed fresh mint leaves, stems removed

1 packet unflavored gelatin

1 cup sour cream, regular or light

1 cup heavy or light cream (for light cream see page 322)

¼ cup Crème de Menthe

fresh mint leaves for garnish

1. In medium saucepan combine sugar and ¾ cup water; cook over medium high heat stirring frequently until mixture boils. Add mint leaves and cook 10 minutes longer reducing heat to medium low, stirring occasionally. Remove from heat and strain mixture into a medium bowl, pressing down on mint leaves; set aside. (Discard mint leaves.)

2. In small saucepan, sprinkle gelatin over ¼ cup remaining cold water; let stand 1 minute. Place over low heat and stir until gelatin is completely dissolved. Stir gelatin into syrup mixture. Add sour cream, cream, and Crème de Menthe, and combine well.

3. Pour into individual glass serving goblets and refrigerate at least 2 hours. Garnish with fresh mint leaves.

LOWER YAKIMA VALLEY
WAPATO, TOPPENISH, ZILLAH, GRANGER, SUNNYSIDE, AND GRANDVIEW

As the Yakima River flows south, the dry hills spread further apart, widening the verdant valley. Several small communities serve the valley farmers. First is Wapato, a town named for potatoes by the Chinook Indians because the area originally was devoted to growing these tubers. Now, the fertile fields and orchards bear a wide variety of vegetables and fruits, and Wapato calls itself the "Salad Bowl of the Valley."

Continuing south through the valley, another stop is Zillah, where a self guided "Fruit-Loop" tour is offered to visitors. The tour winds through vineyards, farms, wineries, orchards, and concludes atop a hill for a sweeping view of the entire valley.

In Toppenish, Western-style buildings and spectacular historic outdoor murals set the scene for this Western town. Well-known artists came in 1989 to paint scenes of the Old West on the sides of many of the older buildings. The project was wildly successful, and now Mural Days has become an annual event where thousands watch artists transform bare walls into Western art.

In Granger, another small community in the valley, folks celebrate a Cherry Festival each May with three days of fun and entertainment paying tribute to the area's sweet, juicy cherries.

Residents of Sunnyside, located in the heartland of the Lower Yakima Valley, enjoy over 300 days of sunshine a year, with mild winters and dry summers. They celebrate this warm climate annually with "Sunshine Days," a three-day event with a street fair, parade, and fun in the sun.

Grandview, so named for its grand view of Mt. Adams and Mt. Rainier, lies in the southern stretch of the bounteous valley. This community has the distinction of being 185 miles from Seattle, Portland, and Spokane. The oldest wine-making facility in the Northwest, the Chateau Ste. Michelle Winery, is located here. The local grape harvest is celebrated each year with a festive Grape Stomp sponsored by the Grandview Chamber of Commerce. This is when enthusiastic team members stomp barefooted into wooden barrels in a fervent effort to turn pounds of grapes into juice.

Yakima County boasts more fruit trees than any other county in the United States. The lower valley produces **apples, pears, cherries, plums, peaches, apricots,** and **nectarines** in abundance. **Mint** is grown and facilities for supplying peppermint and spearmint worldwide are located near Toppenish. Rows of **hop** vines on trellises dot the landscape. **Vineyards** produce grapes for more than twenty wineries located throughout the valley. Fields of **asparagus, corn, potatoes,** and some **wheat** are found here. Truck farmers raise a variety of vegetables including **peppers, green beans, beets, broccoli, cabbage, corn, cucumbers, eggplant, garlic, okra, squash, tomatoes,** and **zucchini. Watermelons, cantaloupes,** and other **melons** do well in this warm climate. The Granger Berry Patch offers over 15 varieties of **berries** as well as red and black **currants.** Over 1,300 pounds of Gouda and other **cheeses** are produced daily at the Yakima Valley Cheese Company in Sunnyside.

SUSAN PARISH COLLECTION

Apple Coconut Muffins with Cinnamon Sugar Topping

YIELD: 9 MUFFINS

These are my favorite breakfast muffins.

½ cup butter or margarine, at room temperature

½ cup granulated sugar

1 egg

½ cup milk

1½ cups all-purpose flour

1½ teaspoons baking powder

½ teaspoon salt

¼ teaspoon nutmeg, preferably freshly ground

1 cup cooking apples, peeled and finely chopped

½ cup flaked coconut

2 tablespoons granulated sugar mixed with ¼ teaspoon cinnamon for tops

1. Preheat oven to 350 degrees. In mixing bowl cream butter and sugar until light and fluffy. In separate small bowl whisk together the egg and milk. Combine flour, baking powder, salt, and nutmeg in another bowl or on waxed paper.

2. Add egg-milk mixture alternately with the flour mixture to the butter and sugar. Blend until just combined. Stir in apples and coconut.

3. Spray muffin tins with vegetable spray or grease and flour. Fill cups ¾ full and sprinkle tops with sugar-cinnamon mixture. Bake for 25-30 minutes. Place on wire rack to cool for 10 minutes. Remove muffins from tins.

Asparagus with Sauce Vidil

SERVINGS: 4-6

Janie Lanier, a friend and French teacher, brought this recipe back from France after one of her extended visits. The sauce has become known as Sauce Vidil because Janie got the recipe from her good friend, Dr. Vidil. The original recipe calls for a raw egg, but for safety reasons (to prevent the possibility of salmonella) the yolk and white have been cooked briefly in the microwave in this adapted version. Dr. Vidil and Janie serve this with asparagus, but it's so good you may want to try it with artichokes or chilled tomatoes. For an appetizer, dip chilled asparagus spears into sauce. As a vegetable dish, arrange chilled or hot asparagus on serving dish and top with sauce.

1 pound asparagus

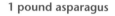

TO COOK ASPARAGUS

Take each spear and gently bend; it will snap about where the tenderness begins. Reserve stem ends for soup or other purposes and cook tender spears; or cut off ends (about ½-inch) and peel asparagus to tender flesh area.

Fill a large bowl with ice water and set aside. Add water to large skillet to a depth of about 1-inch and bring to a gentle boil. Add asparagus in single layer and cook, uncovered, until just tender, about 3-6 minutes. Take from heat. Immediately immerse spears in cold water if serving chilled. Drain and wipe dry.

This Sauce Vidil recipe is for those who crave a good classic, yet safe, homemade mayonnaise sauce. Though this recipe is rather long, it is easy. The directions include placing egg yolks and egg whites in and out of the microwave oven several times.

SAUCE VIDIL

1 egg, separated

1 tablespoon and
1½ teaspoons water, divided

2 tablespoons Dijon mustard

½ teaspoon salt

⅛ teaspoon pepper

½ cup (scant) sunflower oil

1 tablespoon (3 teaspoons)
white wine vinegar, divided

TO MAKE SAUCE

1. Combine egg yolk and 1 tablespoon water in small microwave-safe bowl and whisk well. Cover bowl with small plate and microwave on high for 10 seconds. Take out and whisk. Continue to cook, covered, for 5 seconds and take out and whisk. Cover and return again to microwave for 5 more seconds and take out and whisk. Cover, and let sit 10 minutes. Remove cover and whisk egg yolk again; add mustard and seasonings to yolk and whisk to incorporate.

2. Place this mixture in food processor bowl with steel blade inserted. Add the oil slowly with motor running to form a mayonnaise. Stir in 1½ teaspoons vinegar.

3. In small microwave-safe bowl, whisk together egg white and reserved 1½ teaspoons water and vinegar. Cover the bowl with a small plate and microwave on high for 10 seconds. Uncover and whisk well. Cover and microwave on high for 5 seconds. Whisk again and allow to cool. Before incorporating into sauce, whisk again to soft peak stage. Fold into sauce, leaving any liquid residue in bowl and discard. Serve at room temperature with asparagus.

Pasta with Roasted Peppers, Tomatoes, and Garlic Croutons

SERVINGS: 4

Garlic croutons add a marvelous crunch to this pasta dish.

1 green pepper, medium sized

1 red pepper, medium sized

4 tomatoes

4 cloves garlic, minced, divided

1 tablespoon butter or margarine

5 tablespoons olive oil, divided

2½ cups cubed
Italian or French bread,
(cut in ½-inch cubes)

salt

1 pound linguine

3 tablespoons chopped fresh basil

pepper, freshly ground

¼ cup or more freshly grated
Parmesan cheese

1. To roast peppers: remove stem and cut peppers in half; remove seeds and ribs and press down to flatten. Place skin-side-up on oiled, heavy baking sheet and place about 3-4 inches under broiler. Broil until skins become blackened and blistered, watching carefully. Place in paper bag to cool. When cooled, peel and cut in strips and set aside.

2. Prepare tomatoes by placing in pot of boiling water for 10 seconds. Remove from boiling water and place in cold water in bowl and cool. Peel, and seed by cutting crosswise and squeezing or scooping out seeds. Chop coarsely.

3. Combine chopped tomatoes, pepper strips, and 2 cloves of minced garlic in a medium bowl and set aside.

4. To make croutons: preheat oven to 400 degrees. Heat butter and 2 tablespoons olive oil in large saucepan over medium-low heat until butter is melted. Add reserved 2 cloves of minced garlic and cook until garlic is just tender, about 2 minutes. Take off heat, add bread cubes and mix together until cubes are coated. Place on baking sheet and bake for 10 minutes or until golden brown. Remove from oven and cool.

5. Bring 4 quarts of water to boil, add salt and linguine and cook, stirring occasionally until just tender. (Check manufacturer's directions; cooking time will vary depending on whether the pasta is fresh or dried.)

6. Drain pasta, place in bowl. Add tomato mixture, 3 tablespoons remaining olive oil, basil, salt and pepper to taste, and freshly ground Parmesan cheese. Top with croutons.

Yakima Valley Gouda Beer Bread

YIELD: 1 MEDIUM LOAF

This crusty bread is made in minutes; the self-rising flour is essential. The Yakima Valley produces both the Gouda cheese and the famous hops that flavor the beer used in this recipe.

3 cups self-rising flour

3 tablespoons granulated sugar

1 (12-ounce) can of beer, room temperature

1 cup grated Yakima Valley Gouda cheese, divided*

*Other grated hard cheese may be substituted.

1. Preheat oven to 350 degrees. Grease and flour a 9x5-inch bread pan. Combine flour, sugar, and beer in bowl and place ½ of dough in prepared bread pan. Sprinkle with ¾ cup grated cheese. Add remaining dough and top with remaining ¼ cup grated cheese.

2. Bake one hour. Remove from oven and cool on rack.

Minted Cantaloupe Soup

SERVINGS: 6

This chilled soup is refreshing on a warm summer day. Serve for lunch before a hearty green salad and rolls, or start off a brunch with this fruit soup.

2 medium-sized ripe cantaloupe, peeled, seeded, and coarsely chopped

2 tablespoons chopped fresh mint leaves

2 tablespoons granulated sugar

4 tablespoons sour cream, regular or light

½ cup orange juice

Mint leaves for garnish

1. In food processor with steel blade inserted, or in blender, puree cantaloupe with mint and sugar until sugar is dissolved. Transfer to a medium non-metallic bowl and whisk in sour cream and orange juice.

2. Place bowl in refrigerator, covered, and chill at least 4 hours.

3. Stir again before serving and ladle soup into chilled bowls, or sieve into tall glasses, and garnish with a sprig of mint.

Spicy Grilled Chicken Breasts with Fresh Peach Salsa

SERVINGS: 4

A spicy fruit salsa tops these well-seasoned chicken breasts.

SALSA

1 cup peeled and chopped peaches

¼ cup chopped onion, preferably Walla Walla sweets

½ cup chopped, seeded, and peeled cucumber

2 teaspoons lime juice

2 tablespoons chopped fresh cilantro

⅛ teaspoon salt

1 tablespoon granulated sugar

CHICKEN

4 large chicken breast halves, boned and skinned

1 tablespoon olive oil

1 teaspoon cayenne pepper

1 teaspoon finely chopped cilantro

1 teaspoon minced parsley

1 teaspoon ground cumin

¼ teaspoon salt

1. Combine all ingredients for salsa and let stand at room temperature, up to 1 hour.

2. Pat chicken breasts dry. Combine olive oil, pepper, cilantro, parsley, cumin, and salt in bowl. Brush mixture on chicken breasts and set aside.

3. Prepare barbecue or stove-top grill and cook breasts 10-15 minutes or until done, turning once. Serve with peach salsa.

Bing Cherry and Chocolate Ganache Tarts

YIELD: 18-20 MINIATURE TARTS

These miniature "finger food" tarts are great to serve at buffet dinners.
When cherries are out of season, use strawberries.

PASTRY

½ cup butter, softened

3 ounces regular or light cream cheese, room temperature

1 cup all-purpose flour

GANACHE*

8 ounces semisweet or bittersweet chocolate, finely chopped (chocolate chips may be substituted)

⅔ cup heavy or light cream (for light cream, see page 322)

2 tablespoons Crème de Cassis, optional

10 Bing cherries, pitted and halved (or halved strawberries)

Tart shell pans with 1¾-inch tart cups

*Leftover ganache may be used as a fudge frosting or heated in a double boiler over a pan of simmering water and served as a topping for ice cream.

1. Preheat oven to 350 degrees. In a medium mixing bowl, cream butter and cream cheese until light; add flour and mix until well blended. Form into a ball and place on sheet of waxed paper. Take small balls of dough and press into 18 or 20 ungreased miniature tart shells. Bake shells for 25-30 minutes or until tarts are golden brown. Remove from oven and cool pan on rack for 10 minutes. Remove tart shell cups from pans.

2. To make ganache: place chocolate pieces in heat-proof bowl and set aside. Bring cream to boil in saucepan over medium heat, whisking frequently. When at boil, pour cream over chocolate pieces in bowl and whisk until chocolate is completely melted. (Or combine chocolate pieces with cream in microwave-safe bowl, and microwave on medium for 2 minutes or just until chocolate turns shiny but not melted. Remove from oven and stir until melted.) Whisk in Crème de Cassis and cool to room temperature.

3. Place a bit of chocolate ganache in tart and top with cherry half, cut-side down. Surround cherry half (or strawberry) with more chocolate ganache.

Tarts are best served the day they are assembled; however, they may be made a day earlier and the filling placed in the tarts early in the day.

245

PROSSER

A stately old courthouse takes up an entire city block in the quiet, rural community of Prosser. This historic building commands respect and makes it clear Prosser is the seat of Benton County. The area grew in the 1940s, when the Roza Project brought irrigation to the dry fields, and a variety of new crops were introduced such as **hops, cherries, currants, apples, potatoes, asparagus,** and **mint.** A local company dries cherries and distributes them nationally. **Grapes,** an increasingly important crop, supply premium wineries nearby. Local wines and gourmet foods are offered at the Prosser Wine and Food Fair, held every August.

Red Currant Jelly

YIELDS ABOUT 4 CUPS

Use this currant jelly on muffins, fresh-from-the-oven bread, or as a glaze on a fruit tart.

2 quarts fresh red currants

½ cup water

3 cups granulated sugar, approximately

candy thermometer

4-5 (1-cup) sterilized jelly glasses, with 2-piece lids

1. Remove leaves from currants, but do not stem. Wash and drain. Mash with potato masher; add water. Put in a medium saucepan and cook 10-15 minutes or until currants are quite soft, stirring frequently.

2. Strain through jelly bag or cheese cloth, pressing with spoon to extract all juices. For every cup of juice, use ¾ cup of sugar and heat currant juice-sugar mixture over medium-high heat, in large pot, stirring constantly until sugar dissolves. Without stirring, cook to 220 degrees on candy thermometer. Pour into hot, dry, and sterilized jelly jars with 2-piece lids and process for 5 minutes in water bath canner. (Refer to page 324 for water bath procedure.)

Romaine Salad with Toasted Almonds and Dried Cherry Vinaigrette

SERVINGS: 6

Hearty romaine lettuce leaves are perfect for this dried cherry vinaigrette. Marinate the dried cherries in the raspberry vinegar before making the vinaigrette, and top the salad with fresh cherries when they are in season.

VINAIGRETTE

½ **cup dried cherries**

½ **cup raspberry vinegar**

½ **cup orange juice, more if needed**

1 **tablespoon Dijon or Dijon-style mustard**

⅓ **cup olive oil**

⅓ **cup vegetable oil**

salt and pepper to taste

SALAD

1 **large or 2 medium-sized romaine lettuce heads, cleaned, dried, and torn into bite-sized pieces, or tender leaves of 2 heads separated**

⅓ **cup sliced almonds, toasted (see page 323 for toasting nuts)**

18 **fresh pitted sweet cherries, when in season**

1. To make vinaigrette: place cherries and raspberry vinegar in a small bowl and let stand 8 or more hours. Transfer both cherries and vinegar to food processor with steel blade inserted, add orange juice and mustard, and combine until mixture is almost smooth.

2. Add oils in small, steady stream with machine running. (If too thick, add more orange juice.) Add salt and pepper to taste.

3. Toss prepared romaine lettuce with vinaigrette and sprinkle toasted almonds and fresh cherries on top. Or, small romaine leaves may by placed on individual serving plates with the dressing drizzled down the middle and almonds and cherries sprinkled over.

247

Auntie Gertrude's Chilled Bing Cherry and Sherry Mold

SERVINGS: 8

Jellied molds are rarely served these days, but this one is so cool and refreshing that it is in a class by itself. Gertrude Bendix, my great aunt, loved to cook and if she were alive today would be using such things as arugula and radicchio. However, this recipe is from the 1950s, reflecting a time when desserts and salads were often molded. (The amount of sherry is correct.)

1 (17-ounce) can Bing or Dark Sweet cherries, pitted

water

3 envelopes unflavored gelatin

2 cups orange juice, divided

¾ cup granulated sugar

1½ cups dry sherry wine

2 tablespoons lemon juice

1. Drain juice from cherries; add water to make 2 cups. Reserve cherries. Dissolve gelatin in ½ cup orange juice.

2. Bring cherry juice and sugar to boil in saucepan over medium heat, stirring frequently until sugar is dissolved. Add gelatin-orange juice mixture and stir to combine. Let cool for 5 minutes. Add remaining 1½ cups orange juice, sherry, and lemon juice, and stir well.

3. Pour mixture into a 1½ quart mold and add cherries. Chill until set, about 4 hours or longer. Place chilled mold in bowl of hot water for about 5-10 seconds, place serving plate on top of mold, and invert on plate.

Muscat Blanc Sorbet

SERVINGS: 8

A sweet wine incorporated into a cool citrus sorbet makes this a perfect light summer dessert.

2 cups water

1 cup granulated sugar

juice of 2 lemons

juice of 2 oranges

2 cups Muscat Blanc

whipped cream, slightly sweetened, for top

1. Simmer water and sugar in saucepan over medium heat for 5 minutes or longer, until sugar is dissolved.

2. Add other ingredients, except whipped cream topping, and chill. Freeze in ice cream freezer according to manufacturer's directions. This will freeze to a granita (slushy) stage.

3. Serve this refreshing sorbet in glass goblets with a dollop of whipped cream on top.

TRI-CITIES
PASCO, RICHLAND, AND KENNEWICK

The Columbia, Snake, and Yakima rivers join forces in south-central Washington, driving waters to the Pacific Ocean. In the same area, three cities—Pasco, Richland, and Kennewick—also join forces and combine into a large community known as the Tri-Cities.

Pasco is the oldest of the three. It began in the 1800s when the building of a railroad on the desert land brought workers to settle here. Local historians claim that one of the railroad surveyors, suffering from the intense heat, named the town after Cerro de Pasco, a town high in the Peruvian mountains where the cool breezes blow. Undoubtedly, he longed for the chilly climate to accompany the name. The cool winds stayed in Peru, but the name "Pasco" lingered here.

Richland grew from a small farming village of about 300 people to a town of over 11,000 during World War II when workers were needed to supply the nearby Hanford Atomic Plant. Today, the Hanford site continues to play a major role in Richland's economy.

Kennewick, the largest of the Tri-Cities, is port to the many pleasure boats that moor on the banks of the Columbia. This river and others nearby provide an aquatic playground for those seeking fun in a warm and sunny climate.

Over two dozen wineries are located within a 50-mile radius of the Tri-Cities, giving credence to the area's boast of being the "Heart of the Washington Wine Country." Rich volcanic soil, long summer days, and plentiful irrigation produce an outstanding **grape** crop for the making of wines. Other crops grown here include **carrots, potatoes, dry beans, sweet corn, asparagus, cherries,** and **apples.**

Vegetable Bisque

SERVINGS: 4

Potatoes and carrots from the Columbia River Valley give this soup a rich flavor.

1 tablespoon vegetable or olive oil

1 medium onion, diced

1 clove garlic, minced

¼ cup chopped red pepper

1 rib celery, diced

½ cup finely chopped cauliflower

2 carrots, diced

2 cups peeled and diced potatoes

4 cups chicken stock
(recipe page 313) or
vegetable stock (recipe page 315),
or canned broth

¼ teaspoon cayenne pepper

¼ teaspoon freshly ground
pepper

½ teaspoon salt

pinch ground nutmeg,
preferably freshly ground

½ cup smooth peanut butter

minced parsley for garnish

1. Heat oil in large saucepan. Add onion, garlic, and red pepper, and sauté over medium heat until tender. Add celery, cauliflower, carrots, potatoes, and stock. Bring to boil, reduce heat, cover pan, and simmer about 15 minutes or until vegetables are tender.

2. Add cayenne, black pepper, salt, nutmeg, and peanut butter, and stir together. Place mixture in food processor (or blender) and puree. Serve, or return to pan and keep warm, over low heat, until serving time. Sprinkle with minced parsley.

Garbanzo Bean, Celery, and Red and Green Pepper Salad

SERVINGS: 6

This salad has a remarkably fresh taste. It may be made ahead a few hours, then topped with onion rings and parsley and served.

2⅔ cups cooked or canned garbanzo beans, drained

1 cup thinly sliced celery

¼ cup chopped red pepper

½ cup chopped green pepper

freshly ground pepper

salt, optional

½ cup mayonnaise, regular or light

1 tablespoon prepared horseradish

lettuce leaves

6 thinly sliced onion rings, preferably Walla Walla Sweets

minced parsley for garnish

1. Combine garbanzo beans, celery, and chopped peppers in medium bowl. Season with pepper and salt, if needed. (If canned beans are used, no salt may be necessary.)

2. Combine mayonnaise with horseradish and stir into bean mixture. Arrange salad on lettuce leaves and top with onion rings and minced parsley.

Roasted Asparagus and Red Pepper Noodle Salad

SERVINGS: 4-6

Roast the asparagus and red pepper strips in the oven before adding to the noodles.

2 tablespoons rice vinegar or white wine vinegar

1½ tablespoons brown sugar

2 tablespoons sesame oil, divided (if unavailable, use vegetable oil)

¾ teaspoon freshly grated ginger or ¼ teaspoon ground

1 clove garlic, minced

2-4 teaspoons hot chili garlic sauce,* depending on hotness desired

1 pound asparagus, tough ends broken off

1 red pepper, seeded and cut in 1-inch strips

1 tablespoon olive oil

salt

12 ounces linguine, Chinese noodles, or spaghetti

4 scallions thinly sliced

*Hot chili garlic sauce is found in some supermarkets. If unavailable, use 3–4 dashes of Tabasco sauce.

1. To make dressing: combine vinegar, brown sugar, 1 tablespoon sesame oil, ginger, garlic, and hot chili garlic sauce in food processor with steel blade inserted, or blender, and combine.

2. Cut prepared asparagus into 1-inch pieces. Preheat oven to 500 degrees. Combine asparagus and red pepper strips in large bowl and toss with olive oil. Transfer and spread asparagus and red pepper pieces onto baking sheet and sprinkle with salt. Cook for 7 minutes or until asparagus is tender. (Very thin spears will take less time.) Return to bowl.

3. Cook pasta in large pot of boiling salted water, according to directions on the package. Drain and rinse under cold water; drain again. Place in bowl with vegetables, add remaining 1 tablespoon sesame oil, and combine.

4. Add scallions, reserving some to sprinkle on top. Stir dressing again before adding to pasta. Let salad stand a few minutes to absorb dressing; toss again. Sprinkle with reserved scallions. This dish may be served warm, room temperature, or cold.

Plum and Port Crumble

SERVINGS: 6

If you have plums on hand, this dessert can be made in minutes.

3 pounds plums,
washed, pitted, and quartered

¼ cup brown sugar, packed

¼ cup Port
(orange juice may be substituted)

1 cup all-purpose flour

1 cup granulated sugar

½ teaspoon salt

½ teaspoon cinnamon

1 egg, beaten

½ cup butter or margarine,
melted

heavy (whipping) cream,
whipped, or as is, to pour on top

1. Preheat oven to 375 degrees. Combine prepared plums with brown sugar and Port and spoon into a quart-and-a-half baking dish.

2. Stir together the flour, granulated sugar, salt, and cinnamon in mixing bowl; add beaten egg and toss until crumbly. Sprinkle over plums. Drizzle with melted butter and place in oven to cook for 45 minutes. Serve slightly warm with cream.

Classy Carrot Cake with Dried Cherries and Walnut Cream Filling

SERVINGS: 16

An old favorite with some new changes.

WALNUT CREAM FILLING

¾ **cup brown sugar, packed**

¾ **cup granulated sugar**

¼ **cup all-purpose flour**

½ **teaspoon salt**

2 **cups heavy or light cream (for light cream, see page 322)**

¼ **cup butter or margarine**

1¼ **cups chopped walnuts, toasted (see page 323 for toasting nuts)**

2 **teaspoons vanilla**

1. To make filling: in heavy large saucepan, mix together sugars, flour, and salt. Gradually stir in cream over low heat; add butter. Continue cooking over low heat, stirring frequently until butter is melted. Simmer for about 20 minutes or until mixture is slightly thickened, stirring frequently.

2. Take off heat and cool. Stir in toasted walnuts and vanilla. Place in refrigerator to thicken and chill for 3 hours or as long as overnight. Bring to room temperature and if too thick add drops of cream or milk.

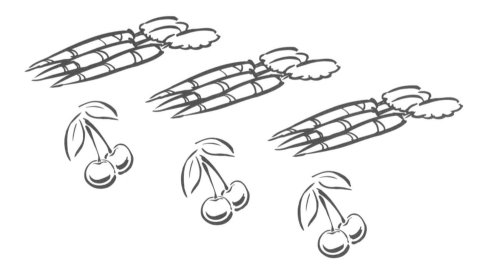

CAKE

2½ cups all-purpose flour

2 teaspoons baking powder

1 teaspoon baking soda

½ teaspoon nutmeg,
preferably freshly ground

1 teaspoon ground cinnamon

¾ teaspoon salt

4 eggs

1½ cups granulated sugar

1 cup brown sugar, packed

1½ cups vegetable oil

2 tablespoons lemon juice

2 tablespoons orange juice

1 tablespoon grated
lemon zest (peel)

2 tablespoons grated
orange zest (peel)

1½ cups cooked, pureed carrots

1 cup shredded coconut, optional

1 cup dried cherries

3. To make cake: preheat oven to 350 degrees. Sift together flour, baking powder, soda, nutmeg, cinnamon, and salt in a medium bowl and set aside. In large mixing bowl, beat eggs. With mixer, gradually beat in sugars on high speed until mixture is thickened and lighter in color, about 2-3 minutes. At low speed, or with a rubber spatula, gradually stir in oil, lemon and orange juices, and grated zests. Add and blend in flour mixture, pureed carrots, coconut, and cherries. Divide among 3 greased, floured, 9-inch round layer pans. Bake 25 minutes or until cake tester comes out clean after being inserted in cake. Cool in pan 10 minutes on wire rack. Turn out on racks to cool. Make Cream Cheese Glaze; recipe follows.

4. To assemble: place one cake layer on serving platter and top with half of Walnut Cream Filling; repeat with second layer. Place third layer on top and pour and spread glaze on top. Surround the edge of cake with chopped walnuts. Cover with plastic wrap and refrigerate until serving time.

CREAM CHEESE GLAZE

1 (8-ounce) package
cream cheese, regular or light

1 tablespoon lemon juice

1½ cups confectioners' sugar

½ cup finely chopped walnuts
for garnish

TO MAKE GLAZE

In a medium mixing bowl, combine cream cheese, lemon juice, and confectioners' sugar. Beat mixture until smooth.

Pinot Noir and Pear Sorbet

SERVINGS: 6

A lovely dessert; best served the day it is frozen. The pears may be poached and pureed the day before.

2½ pounds ripe pears,
such as Bosc or Bartletts

1 bottle (750 ml) Pinot Noir

¾ cup granulated sugar

2 cinnamon sticks

3 tablespoons lemon juice

raspberries for garnish

1. Peel, core, and slice pears; set aside. Place wine, sugar, and cinnamon sticks in a large saucepan. Bring just to a boil over medium heat, lower heat, and simmer until sugar is dissolved. Place sliced pears in syrup and simmer until pears are very tender, about 30-45 minutes. Allow to cool completely. Remove cinnamon sticks.

2. Puree mixture in food processor or blender until smooth. Add lemon juice and refrigerate until well chilled, about 5 hours.

3. Freeze in chilled ice cream machine according to manufacturer's directions. Serve in goblets with fresh (or frozen and thawed) raspberries on top.

SUSAN PARISH COLLECTION

GOLDENDALE

Situated on a high grassy plateau north of the Columbia River is the small town of Goldendale. Here, stargazers can get a spectacular celestial view through the nation's largest public telescope at the Goldendale Observatory.

Traveling east, visitors discover a startling scene. High on a bluff sits a lonely but magnificent Flemish castle, overlooking all the countryside and the Columbia River. In 1914, wealthy Sam Hill built this elegant manor and named it Maryhill, after his daughter. He also purchased 7,000 acres of surrounding land, envisioning the establishment of a Quaker agricultural community. The venture proved unsuccessful, and eventually Maryhill was turned into a museum and the land rented to local farmers. Today, the museum is filled with Rodin sculptures, paintings by Manet and Cezanne, rare Native American art objects, and other treasures. Sam Hill's dream to attract Quakers failed, but more than 80,000 people from all over the world come each year to enjoy an impressive art collection in a magnificent mansion.

Farmers grow **wheat, barley,** and **oats** as field crops; orchards produce **pears, apples, cherries, apricots,** and **peaches.** Ranchers raise **cattle, sheep,** and **hogs.** Some **vineyards** are here, and the area is popular for **huckleberries** found on the southern slopes of Mt. Adams.

Blintzes with Huckleberry Sauce

SERVINGS: 4

If huckleberries are unavailable, use blueberries in the sauce.

FILLING

1 pound low or
non-fat cottage cheese

1 egg, beaten

⅛ teaspoon cinnamon

¼ cup granulated sugar

¼ teaspoon salt

HUCKLEBERRY SAUCE*

2 cups huckleberries

½ cup water, plus 1 tablespoon, divided

½ cup plus 2 tablespoons granulated sugar

½ teaspoon cinnamon

2 tablespoons lemon juice

1 teaspoon cornstarch

Sauce may be made ahead.

BATTER FOR BLINTZES

1 cup all-purpose flour

¼ teaspoon salt

3 eggs

⅓ cup water

3 tablespoons melted butter or margarine

crepe pan

oil for pan

1. Combine filling ingredients in food processor or blender until almost smooth. Refrigerate until needed. (May be made a day earlier and refrigerated.)

2. To make sauce: In a medium saucepan, combine huckleberries, ½ cup water, sugar, and cinnamon. Simmer over medium heat until sugar is dissolved. Stir in lemon juice. Blend cornstarch and 1 tablespoon water together and add to mixture. Heat to boiling over medium high heat, stirring constantly. Boil for 2 minutes. Remove from heat. Serve warm or at room temperature.

3. To make blintz batter: combine flour and salt in food processor with steel blade inserted and process briefly. In pitcher or bowl, combine eggs, water, and melted butter together. With motor running in food processor, add liquids and process until smooth. Keep at room temperature until ready to cook.

4. To cook and assemble: heat a 6- or 7-inch non-stick crepe pan over high heat. Brush lightly with oil. Pour in small amount of batter and tilt pan to coat bottom. Reduce heat to medium high and cook blintz until it begins to pull away from the sides of pan, about 45 seconds. Loosen sides of blintz with spatula and turn it out onto paper towel or clean towel, cooked-side-up. (Do not turn over and cook other side as you would for crepes.) Repeat with remaining batter, brushing pan occasionally with oil. Place blintzes, cooked-side-up, on work surface. Put 1 heaping tablespoon filling in center of blintz and cover by folding over 2 opposite sides. Then fold in the two side ends by about ¾-inch; this will resemble an envelope. (At this point, the blintzes may be refrigerated overnight.) For final cooking: in large nonstick skillet, add oil to depth of ⅛-inch and heat over medium high heat. Fry on both sides until brown and crisp. Remove and place on paper towel. Serve with sauce.

Red Grape and Chicken Salad with Apple Chutney Dressing

SERVINGS: 4-6

The chutney, curry, and ginger make this chicken salad special.

1 cup mayonnaise, regular or light

½ cup apple chutney
(may use Easy Apple Raisin
Chutney, page 106)

1 teaspoon curry powder

1 tablespoon grated fresh ginger
or 1 teaspoon powdered ginger

1 teaspoon lemon juice

4 cups white chicken, cooked
and cut in bite-sized pieces

1 cup seedless red grapes

½ cup sliced celery

½ cup slivered almonds, toasted
(for toasting nuts, see page 323)

1. Combine mayonnaise, chutney, curry, ginger, and lemon juice in large bowl. Add chicken, grapes, and celery, and refrigerate up to 3 hours.

2. Serve on individual plates or in serving bowl. When serving, top with toasted slivered almonds.

Roast Leg of Lamb with Merlot Mint Sauces

SERVINGS: 8

Serve lamb with one or both sauces.

1 leg of lamb,
(about 6 pounds) bone-in

2 cloves garlic, peeled
and cut in thin slices

salt

freshly ground pepper

½ teaspoon dry rosemary
(rub between palms of hands
to crumble)

1 tablespoon soy sauce

⅓ cup Dijon or
Dijon-style mustard

3 tablespoons vegetable oil

1. Preheat oven to 350 degrees. Wipe lamb dry and remove excess fat. Pierce meat about ½-inch deep with small sharp knife and push a slice of garlic into cut until it is embedded. Continue to pierce and insert garlic slices over surface of lamb at about 2-inch intervals. Season with salt and pepper. Place on rack in roasting pan.

2. Mix rosemary, soy sauce, and mustard in a small bowl; beat in oil by droplets to make a thick sauce. (This may be done in a food processor.) Coat lamb with mixture.

3. Place in oven and roast about 2 hours or until internal temperature reads 140 (rare) to 150 (medium).

MERLOT MINT SAUCE 1

½ cup mint jelly

2 tablespoons Merlot wine

1 teaspoon rice vinegar
or white wine vinegar

1 tablespoon minced fresh mint

TO MAKE MINT SAUCE 1

Whisk together jelly, wine, and vinegar in small bowl. After whisking, small pearls of mint jelly may remain. Add fresh mint. Serve with lamb.

MERLOT MINT SAUCE 2

½ cup water

2 tablespoons
confectioners' sugar

⅓ cup minced mint leaves

¼ cup Merlot wine

1 tablespoon balsamic vinegar

TO MAKE MINT SAUCE 2

Heat water in small saucepan over medium heat until warm; add sugar and stir until dissolved. Remove from heat; cool. Add rest of ingredients. Serve with lamb.

Oatmeal Coffee Cake with Streusel Topping

SERVINGS: 12

Try oatmeal for breakfast in this moist coffee cake.

1 cup rolled oats, quick-cooking

1½ cups boiling water

½ cup butter or margarine

¾ cup brown sugar, packed

¾ cup granulated sugar

2 eggs

1 teaspoon vanilla

1½ cups all-purpose flour

1 teaspoon cinnamon

1 teaspoon baking soda

¼ teaspoon nutmeg,
preferably freshly ground

1 teaspoon salt

STREUSEL TOPPING

½ cup chopped pecans

2 teaspoons cinnamon

½ cup brown sugar, packed

¼ cup all-purpose flour

¼ cup rolled oats,
regular or quick-cooking

3 tablespoons butter,
room temperature

1. Preheat oven to 350 degrees. Combine rolled oats and boiling water in a small bowl and let stand 15 minutes.

2. Cream butter in a large mixing bowl, add sugars, and beat until light; add eggs and vanilla and combine. Combine flour, cinnamon, soda, nutmeg, and salt, and stir into batter. Fold in oatmeal mixture.

3. Pour batter into a greased and floured 9x13 pan. Combine all streusel ingredients in bowl and mix together with pastry blender or forks. Sprinkle over top of cake. Bake 30-35 minutes or until cake tester inserted into middle of cake comes out clean. Cool slightly and serve warm.

INLAND EMPIRE

*Rolling hills of rich
wheatland reach as far
as the eye can see. Lentils,
dry peas, and barley vie for
acreage. Wild game find
refuge in the rugged
mountains to the north
and south.*

Colville

Newport

Davenport

Spokane

Cheney

Ritzville

Colfax

Pullman

Clarkston

Pomeroy

Dayton

Walla Walla

COLVILLE

Forested mountains surround Colville in northeast Washington. Small farms with large barns grace the mountain scenery to the south, in the Colville Valley. Here, cattle and sheep graze in pastures creating a tranquil pastoral scene. Hay is grown in some fields, but high-tech agriculture is not visible in the valley.

The largest population of **whitetail deer** in the state live in the surrounding mountains. **Trout** thrive in local streams, helped along by the nearby fish hatchery.

SUSAN PARISH COLLECTION

264

Venison with Juniper Berry Sauce

SERVINGS: 6

The juniper berry has a slightly pungent flavor, complementing game animals such as venison.

2 cups dry red wine

4 tablespoons
vegetable oil, divided

1 medium onion, sliced

1 bay leaf

1 tablespoon juniper berries

1 teaspoon allspice

3-4 pounds venison roast,
neck or rump

½ cup chopped carrots

½ cup chopped celery

½ cup chopped onion

2 tablespoons butter or margarine
at room temperature

2 tablespoons all-purpose flour

Juice of one orange

zest (peel) of one orange,
shredded in strips

1 tablespoon currant jelly

salt and pepper, to taste

1. Combine red wine, 2 tablespoons oil, sliced onion, bay leaf, juniper berries, and allspice in medium saucepan and bring to boil. Remove from heat and let cool.

2. Place roast in non-metallic dish and pour marinade over. Cover and refrigerate for 2-3 days. Turn twice daily.

3. Preheat oven to 350 degrees. Take roast from marinade and pat dry. Heat remaining 2 tablespoons oil in large skillet and brown meat on all sides over medium high heat. Place chopped carrots, celery, and onion in large casserole with lid. Place roast on top of vegetables and pour marinade over; cover.

4. Cook 3 hours or until tender, basting occasionally. Remove from oven, take meat from casserole pan, and keep warm on warmed platter. Cover with foil.

5. Strain marinade. Put strained liquid in saucepan and boil for 5 minutes over medium heat. Mix together room-temperature butter with flour and add to hot liquid in saucepan. Simmer until thickened, stirring constantly. Add orange juice, zest, jelly, and combine. Add salt and pepper to taste. Slice roast and serve with sauce.

Look for juniper berries in specialty food shops and large grocery stores in the spice department.

NEWPORT

Newport, next to the Idaho border in northeast Washington, became an important port in the late 1800s and early 1900s. Steamers traveling up the Columbia and Pend Orielle rivers anchored at the landing dock built in 1890. Now, pleasure boats use the dock, and highways and railroads serve as links to the outside.

This rugged northeast corner of Washington is home to **moose, deer, elk, caribou, grizzly bears,** and **bighorn sheep.** A **buffalo** herd, one of the few in the entire country, roams in the nearby Kalispel Indian Reservation. Lakes and rivers hold **perch, bass, whitefish, crappie,** and **trout.** Many **geese, ducks, pheasants,** and **partridges** inhabit the area. Local farmers raise some **beef** cattle in the meadow areas.

Hungarian Partridge with Cream and Currant Sauce

SERVINGS: 4

This sauce may also be used with Cornish Game hens.

4 partridges, cleaned and prepared

2 tablespoons butter or margarine, room temperature

salt and pepper

2 cups heavy or light cream (for light cream, see page 322)

2 tablespoons currant jelly

4 tablespoons cooked ham, diced

1. Preheat oven to 350 degrees. Rub partridges with butter or margarine and season with salt and pepper. Place in roasting pan and roast in oven 40-50 minutes or until done (180 degrees at inner thigh). Remove from oven, place birds on warmed platter, and keep warm under foil.

2. Add cream to pan juices, place pan over burner, and cook until liquid in reduced by one-third and slightly thickened. Add currant jelly and ham and stir until jelly is melted. Serve partridges with sauce.

Roast Goose with Savory Apple Stuffing and Cumberland Sauce

SERVINGS: 4

The Cumberland Sauce is also good with roast pork or ham.

1 adult wild goose (3-5 pounds)

juice of one medium lemon

salt and pepper

2 tablespoons butter or margarine

½ cup chopped celery

½ cup chopped onion

1 cup soft bread crumbs

4 tart apples,
peeled, cored, and chopped

¼ cup raisins

½ teaspoon salt

freshly ground pepper

¼ teaspoon ground sage

¼ teaspoon dried rosemary

¼ cup apple juice

vegetable oil or margarine

1. Preheat oven to 325 degrees. Rub inside and outside of goose with lemon juice and sprinkle with salt and pepper.

2. Melt butter or margarine in small saucepan and sauté celery and onion over medium heat until tender. Combine in large bowl with rest of ingredients, except vegetable oil, to make stuffing. Spoon stuffing lightly into goose cavity. Close opening and truss with skewers and string. (Extra stuffing can be baked separately, covered, for the last 45 minutes.)

3. Place goose, breast up, on rack in roasting pan and brush bird liberally with vegetable oil. Place in oven and baste occasionally. Cook for approximately 1½ hours, or until done. (Temperature registers 175-180 degrees in breast.) Serve with Cumberland Sauce.

CUMBERLAND SAUCE

zest (peel) and juice
of one orange

1 cup port

1 tablespoon lemon juice

½ cup currant jelly

¾ teaspoon freshly grated ginger
or ¼ teaspoon ground ginger

1 teaspoon cornstarch

1 teaspoon water

TO MAKE SAUCE

1. Cut the zest off the orange and chop zest finely. Juice the orange and set aside.

2. Cook zest with port in small saucepan over medium-high heat until the liquid is reduced by one-third. Reduce heat, add orange juice, lemon juice, currant jelly, and ginger, and stir.

3. Dissolve cornstarch in water in small bowl and add to sauce. Cook over medium-high heat, stirring constantly, until slightly thickened. Remove from heat and serve warm.

DAVENPORT

The farming community of Davenport dates to the 1800s when the site was known as Cottonwood Creek. Early settlers came to farm; today, the Lincoln County Museum in the town exhibits old-time farm machinery, including a wooden pull-combine and a stationary threshing machine.

Most of the 800,000 fertile acres around Davenport produce **wheat** and **barley** and some **corn.** A number of **cattle** ranches are located in the surrounding scablands.

WASHINGTON STATE HISTORICAL SOCIETY

Barley, Lentil, and Sun-dried Tomato Soup

SERVINGS: 10-12

This hearty soup combines the wonderful flavor and texture of barley and lentils.
It freezes well, so you may wish to make the entire recipe. Serve with
whole grain rolls and a simple green salad for a complete meal.

2 tablespoons vegetable oil

½ cup chopped red pepper

½ cup chopped onion

1 cup chopped celery

¼ cup chopped carrots

1 clove garlic, minced

¼ teaspoon salt, and freshly ground pepper to taste

5 (14½-ounce) cans chicken broth or 8½ cups homemade chicken stock (recipe page 313)

1 (28-ounce) can crushed tomatoes, with juice

1 cup pearled barley or whole grain barley (for whole grain barley, see page 324)

1 cup dry lentils, rinsed and drained

1 cup tomato juice

2 cups water

2 teaspoons dried basil

1 teaspoon dried oregano

1 bay leaf

½ teaspoon dried thyme

8 oil-packed sun-dried tomatoes, drained and chopped

1. In large kettle or stock pot, add oil and over medium heat sauté red pepper, onion, celery, carrots, and garlic until tender.

2. Add salt and pepper and cook for 1 minute longer. Add remaining ingredients and bring to boil. Reduce heat and simmer, covered, for 1½ hours. (If using whole grain barley, cook for 2 hours or until barley is tender.) Check and stir occasionally. May be thinned with broth or water. Ladle into soup bowls.

Marinated Beef, Bulgar, and Snow Pea Salad

SERVINGS: 4

If snow peas are unavailable, use cooked green beans.

DRESSING

1 clove garlic, minced

6 tablespoons olive
or vegetable oil

3 tablespoons red wine vinegar

1½ teaspoons Dijon
or Dijon-style mustard

1½ teaspoons granulated sugar

salt

pepper

2 tablespoons capers, optional

SALAD

3 cups cooked beef,
cut in bite-sized strips

2 cups cooked bulgar, cooled

1 cup cooked white
or brown rice, cooled

⅓ pound snow peas

1 large tomato, seeded and diced

⅓ cup sliced celery

½ teaspoon salt, or to taste

freshly ground pepper

¼ cup minced fresh parsley

⅓ cup crumbled blue cheese

1. Make dressing by whisking together garlic, olive oil, vinegar, mustard, and sugar in small bowl, or by combining in food processor with steel blade inserted. Stir in salt, pepper, and capers. Set aside.

2. To make salad: combine beef, bulgar, and rice in large bowl and mix in all but 2 tablespoons of dressing. Refrigerate mixture, covered, for 2 hours or longer.

3. In large saucepan or stockpot bring about a quart of water to boil. Add the snow peas and cook (blanch) for 5 seconds. Remove and place under cold tap water, pat dry, and remove strings. Set aside to cool.

4. At serving time, add snow peas to salad, along with all other ingredients. Add reserved 2 tablespoons dressing and combine.

☆ SPOKANE

Spokane, the hub of the Inland Empire, is located in an area covering rich agricultural, lumbering, and mining land. It is the largest city between Seattle and Minneapolis and between Calgary, Canada, and Salt Lake City. The Native American word, Spokane, means "Children of the Sun," a fitting name for a place where people see the sun year round. Situated far east of the Cascade Range, Spokane is shielded from the damp, coastal weather. Dry, desert-type air covers the area in summer, while winter airs are cold and clear. Winter precipitation falls mainly as snow.

Nicknamed "The Lilac City," Spokane each year sponsors a spectacular Lilac Festival with a colorful parade and a multitude of other events. During the lilac festivities, nearly 60,000 runners come to Spokane to race in the Bloomsday Run.

Many parks beautify Spokane, including Riverfront Park which was developed out of old railroad yards for the world's fair, Expo '74.

Wheat, barley, dry peas, and **lentils** grow in the large fields surrounding Spokane. The Greenbluff area, north of the city, is famous for its **apples, sweet cherries, pie cherries, peaches, pears,** and many **berries.** Those who seek out **gooseberries** can find some at one of the many local truck farms. Local vintners make wines from **grapes** grown by the "Children of the Sun."

Spicy Bulgar Wheat and Vegetable Chili

SERVINGS: 6-8

This vegetarian chili is hearty enough for all appetites.
Serve with corn muffins and Joanie's Cherry Pie.

2 (1-pound) cans tomatoes

4 tablespoons olive oil

1½ cups finely chopped onion

4 cloves garlic, peeled and minced

1 cup finely chopped carrots

¾ cup finely chopped green peppers

1 cup finely chopped mushrooms

2 (15-ounce) cans,
plus 1 (8-ounce) can
undrained kidney beans

½ teaspoon dry red pepper flakes

1-2 tablespoons chili powder,
depending on desired hotness

1 tablespoon ground cumin

½ teaspoon Tabasco sauce

¼ cup chopped parsley

1 tablespoon
Worcestershire sauce

1 cup bulgar wheat

⅓ cup red wine

2 tablespoons fresh lemon juice

½ teaspoon salt, or to taste

freshly ground pepper

grated cheddar cheese (optional)

sour cream,
regular or light (optional)

1. Strain liquid from canned tomatoes and reserve. Dice tomatoes.

2. Heat oil in large skillet over medium heat, add onions and garlic, and cook until tender.

3. Add diced tomatoes, reserved juice, and all other ingredients except grated cheese and sour cream. Bring mixture to boil, reduce heat, and simmer for 20 minutes uncovered. If too thick, add more tomato juice. Serve in bowls and top with grated cheese and/or sour cream, if desired.

Curried Lentils with Apples

SERVINGS: 4

Serve as an adjunct to roast lamb or as a vegetarian main dish along with rice and fresh fruit on a skewer. Washington state is well known for producing many apples but not so well known for producing lentils. Eastern Washington and northern Idaho produce over 90 percent of the country's lentils.

1 cup dry lentils,
rinsed and drained

1 bay leaf

3 cups chicken stock
(recipe page 313) or broth

3 tablespoons vegetable oil

1½ cups chopped onion

1 cup cooking apple,
peeled and chopped

½ cup chopped celery

2 cloves garlic, minced

1 tomato, peeled and chopped

1½ teaspoons curry powder

1 teaspoon coriander

½ teaspoon cinnamon

½ teaspoon ginger

¼ -½ teaspoon salt,
according to taste

coconut for garnish, optional

1. Combine lentils, bay leaf, and stock in large saucepan, and bring to boil over medium heat. Reduce heat and simmer, covered, until lentils are tender, about 30 minutes. Remove from heat and set aside; do not drain. Preheat oven to 350 degrees.

2. Meanwhile, in medium skillet heat oil over medium heat. Add onion, apple, celery, and garlic, and sauté until vegetables are tender.

3. Combine undrained lentils and cooked vegetables in medium baking dish and add tomato, curry, coriander, cinnamon, ginger, and salt. Place, uncovered, in oven and cook 1 hour. Remove bay leaf. Serve with coconut sprinkled in a row, down the center, if desired.

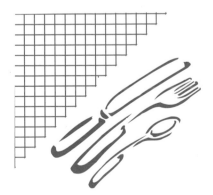

Gooseberry Tart

SERVINGS: 6

This simple tart is a perfect way to savor the unique flavor of gooseberries.

Pastry for one-crust pie, recipe page 310

4 cups gooseberries, washed and ends removed (both stems and blossom nubs cut off)

1¼ cups granulated sugar

¾ cup heavy (whipping) cream, divided

1 egg yolk

1. Preheat oven to 350 degrees. Line 9-inch tart pan with rolled-out pastry dough. Fill with gooseberries, sprinkle sugar on top, and bake for 20 minutes.

2. Combine ¼ cup of cream with egg yolk and pour over tart. Continue to bake for 20-25 minutes.

3. Whip reserved whipped cream and serve with warm or room-temperature tart.

Joanie's Cherry Pie

SERVINGS: 6

Joanie Staiger's pie crusts are always flaky. Her secret is to "never touch the dough with your hands." Use fresh-picked tart (sour) pie cherries for this treat.

FILLING

4-5 cups pitted fresh (sour) pie cherries

1⅓ cups granulated sugar

3 tablespoons tapioca

¼ teaspoon almond extract

4 drops red food coloring

1 tablespoon butter

CRUST

2 cups all-purpose flour

¼ teaspoon salt

1 cup Crisco

⅛ -¼ cup cold water

1. To make filling: combine filling ingredients, except butter, in bowl and mix together. Let stand 15 minutes to thicken before placing in pie shell.

2. To make crust: preheat oven to 400 degrees. Put flour and salt in bowl and cut in shortening (Crisco) with knives until mixture looks like corn meal. With fork, stir in just enough cold water to bind. *Never touch dough with hands.*

3. Take out ½ dough, using waxed paper to cover hand. Roll dough out between 2 pieces of waxed paper into an 11-inch circle. (Take top sheet of waxed paper off gently and then replace. This is done so paper will not adhere.) Turn dough and pieces of waxed paper over, and remove top sheet and discard. Turn over and carefully place dough over 9-inch pie plate and press down to fit. Lift off remaining sheet of waxed paper.

4. Add filling and dot with butter. Roll out remaining dough in the same manner, between two sheets of waxed paper. Place over filling and lift off remaining sheet of waxed paper. Trim and flute edges to seal. Fork decoratively to make air vents in crust. Place a 2-3 inch strip of foil over crust edge and bake 30 minutes on a pie sheet. (For pie sheet used in this recipe, refer to the glossary, page 323. If pie sheet is unavailable, place cookie sheet or drip catcher on the rack underneath the rack that the pie is on.) Remove foil and bake 20-25 minutes longer.

CHENEY

Education and agriculture share the spotlight in the rural community of Cheney. Eastern Washington University plays a prominent role in shaping the character of the town. However, rural roots run deep as witnessed by the grain elevators and Centennial flour mill that dominate the skyline. Centennial Mills processes millions of bushels of the area's **wheat** into flour. While wheat serves as the centerpiece of this farming region, farmers also grow **peas, oats,** and **barley,** and raise **beef** and **dairy cattle.**

Excellent fishing in "the fifty lakes within fifty miles" of Cheney brings **trout** to the lines of many fishermen.

The Turnbull National Wildlife Refuge lies just six miles south of town. This 17,000-acre secluded sanctuary offers migratory birds and other wildlife a protected haven, and gives visitors a place to observe nature in a pristine setting.

Bulgar Wheat Pilaf with Mushrooms

SERVINGS: 4

This versatile pilaf accompanies poultry, meat, or game.

4 tablespoons butter or margarine

½ cup scallions, chopped, including green tops

1 clove garlic, minced

½ cup chopped celery

¾ cup sliced mushrooms

1 cup bulgar wheat

2 cups chicken or beef stock (recipes pages 313, 314) or broth

⅛ teaspoon freshly ground pepper

½ teaspoon salt

¼ teaspoon dry basil

1 tablespoon parsley, minced

1. Melt butter or margarine in a medium saucepan over medium heat, add scallions, garlic, celery, and mushrooms, and sauté until tender. Add bulgar and stir until the wheat becomes coated with butter.

2. Add stock or broth, pepper, salt, and basil. Bring the mixture to a boil. Stir briefly with a fork, cover the saucepan, and reduce heat. Simmer about 20 minutes or until liquid is absorbed. Fluff and add parsley. Serve, or keep warm with lid ajar for up to 30 to 45 minutes off burner.

Trout with Toasted Hazelnuts

SERVINGS: 4

Hazelnuts add crunch to this pan-fried trout.

½ cup milk

½-¾ cup Japanese panko crumbs*

4 trout, cleaned, gutted, and fins removed (approximately 12 inches long or 8-10 ounces each)

½ teaspoon salt

freshly ground pepper

5 tablespoons butter or margarine, divided

2 tablespoons oil

3 tablespoons chopped hazelnuts

2 tablespoons lemon juice

1 tablespoon minced parsley

1. Place milk and panko crumbs in separate shallow pans. Dip trout in milk, then dredge in panko crumbs. Season with salt and pepper and lay on large tray to rest a few minutes.

2. Heat 2 tablespoons butter and oil in large frying pan over medium heat. Add fish and cook about 4-5 minutes on each side. Do not crowd when cooking. (Check in cavity of fish to see if it is cooked and opaque throughout.)

3. Remove fish from pan and place on warmed serving platter. Loosely cover with foil. Wipe oil-butter mixture out of pan and add remaining 3 tablespoons of butter. Add hazelnuts and sauté for 2-3 minutes. Add lemon juice, heat through, and pour over fish. Sprinkle with parsley and serve.

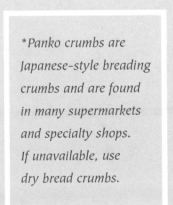

Panko crumbs are Japanese-style breading crumbs and are found in many supermarkets and specialty shops. If unavailable, use dry bread crumbs.

RITZVILLE

☆

Stories still linger that the famous Ritz cracker, first introduced in 1934, was named after Ritzville; however, no evidence is available to support these tales. Probably the only connection that links the two is that eastern Washington's white wheat is a primary source for making crackers.

The Washington Association of Wheat Growers' headquarters is located here for good reason, as miles of **wheat** fields surround Ritzville. Local farmers keep busy harvesting wheat and other products including **barley, dry beans, onions,** and **potatoes.** Nearby in the more arid regions are large **cattle** ranches.

COURTESY GARY HOUSER

Old-fashioned Pot Roast with Onions and Mushrooms

SERVINGS: 6

A robust and flavorful sauce accompanies this pot roast.

1¾ teaspoons salt, divided

2 large cloves of garlic, minced

3 or 3½ pound chuck roast or bottom round

freshly ground pepper

2½ tablespoons vegetable oil

1 celery rib, diced

1 carrot, diced

1½ cups dry red wine

1⅔ cups beef stock (recipe page 314 or 1 (14½-ounce) can beef broth

1 (14½-ounce) can ready-cut tomatoes, undrained

½ teaspoon dry thyme

½ teaspoon dry oregano

1 large bay leaf

½ teaspoon dry tarragon

½ pound sliced mushrooms

1 medium onion, peeled and sliced

6 carrots, peeled and cut in chunks, or 12 small carrots, left whole

3 large potatoes, peeled and quartered

½ cup water

5 tablespoons all-purpose flour

¼ cup minced fresh parsley

1. Place ¾ teaspoon salt on a cutting board and place minced garlic over the salt. With a paring knife, scrape back and forth over the salt and garlic to mash together, forming a paste.

2. With sharp knife, cut several small incisions in meat and fill with garlic mixture. Grate pepper over. Heat oil in Dutch oven or large heavy pot and brown meat slowly on all sides over medium heat. Add diced celery and carrots and sauté for about 1 minute.

3. Pour in the wine and add stock, tomatoes, thyme, oregano, bay leaf, tarragon, and pepper to taste. Bring mixture to boil, then reduce heat to low and simmer. Cover and continue simmering for three hours.

4. Add mushroom and onion slices and continue simmering, covered, for 1 hour or until meat is fork tender. About ½ hour before serving, steam carrots and potatoes in separate steamer basket in large saucepan until tender. Salt and pepper to taste.

5. When meat is cooked, remove to heated platter and top with vented foil to keep warm. Discard bay leaf from liquid. Combine flour and water in medium bowl and whisk together until blended. Slowly add 1 cup warm liquid from Dutch oven to flour mixture in bowl, whisking constantly until well blended. Add mixture to liquid in Dutch oven; bring to boil over medium heat, stirring constantly. Reduce heat and stir until slightly thickened. Add reserved 1 teaspoon salt and more freshly ground pepper.

6. Surround meat on platter with carrots and potatoes. Pour some sauce over pot roast and vegetables. Pass the rest of sauce in sauceboat. Sprinkle minced parsley over meat and vegetables.

Ritz Torte

SERVINGS: 6

The famous Ritz Cracker is basis for this torte.

3 egg whites

1 cup granulated sugar

1 teaspoon baking powder

½ teaspoon vanilla

¾ cup chopped pecans

1 cup Ritz Cracker crumbs

TOPPING

1 cup heavy (whipping) cream

1 tablespoon confectioners' sugar

1 teaspoon almond flavoring

1 cup coarsely chopped strawberries, well drained

whole strawberries for garnish

1. Preheat oven to 350 degrees. Beat egg whites until stiff. Add sugar, baking powder, vanilla, and mix in well. Fold in nuts and cracker crumbs. Mix all carefully and pour into well greased 9-inch springform pan.

2. Bake 30 minutes. Remove from oven and cool.

3. Before serving, whip cream, whisk in confectioners' sugar and almond flavoring. Fold in chopped and well-drained strawberries.

4. With knife, go around inside of pan to loosen torte. Remove sides of pan, top with cream mixture, and garnish with whole strawberries. Cut in wedges.

Pound Cake

SERVINGS: 8-10

This is a dense, yet light pound cake. Most of the wheat in eastern Washington is a soft white variety, which is used in making cake flour, an important ingredient in this cake.

1 cup butter or margarine, room temperature (butter preferred)

2 cups granulated sugar

5 eggs

2¼ cups cake flour (sifted or stirred before measuring)

¼ teaspoon salt

1 teaspoon almond extract

¼ teaspoon ground nutmeg, preferably freshly ground

1. Preheat oven to 325 degrees. Grease and lightly flour a 9-inch loaf pan or bundt pan.

2. Cream butter in a large bowl until light; gradually add sugar, beating until light and fluffy. Add 4 eggs, one at a time, beating well after each addition. Stir in flour, salt, almond extract, and nutmeg. Blend in remaining egg and pour mixture into prepared pan.

3. Bake until cake tester inserted in cake comes out clean. For 9 x 5 loaf pan, bake 1 hour and 20-30 minutes; for bundt pan, check after 1 hour and 5 minutes. Cool cake in pan on rack for 10 minutes. Turn out on rack to cool.

COLFAX

The North and South Fork of the Palouse River meet in a serene valley surrounded by hills of fertile land and basalt cliffs, providing a perfect setting for a town. The community was first called Belleville by James A. Perkins in 1870. It is said he named it in honor of his sweetheart, but when the bachelor's affections changed he thought it wise to also change the town's name. So Perkins and other early residents renamed it Colfax, in honor of Schuyler Colfax, vice president under Ulysses S. Grant. The house Perkins built in 1884 has been restored and is open to the public during the summer months, maintained by the Whitman County Historical Society.

In the fields surrounding Colfax **wheat** crops yield as high as 100 bushels an acre, and **barley** is close behind with 80 bushels per acre. This is done without the help of irrigation. **Hogs** and **cattle** are raised by some farmers in Whitman County. Independent **sheep** farmers tend their flocks throughout all of Washington state, with the largest farms found on the eastern side, some in the scablands west of Colfax.

COURTESY ROBERT HOUSER LARSON

Bulgar Wheat Pilaf with Red Peppers and Sour Cream

SERVINGS: 4

This is a colorful and flavorful pilaf to accompany meat, poultry, or fish.

2 tablespoons butter or margarine

1 tablespoon vegetable oil

½ red pepper, cut in strips

¾ cup chopped onion

½ cup shredded carrots

½ cup chopped celery

1 clove garlic, minced

2½ cups chicken stock (recipe page 313) or canned broth

1 cup bulgar

¾ teaspoon salt

freshly ground pepper, to taste

1 tablespoon dried dill

¼ teaspoon dried thyme

¼ cup sour cream, regular or light

1. Melt butter with oil in large saucepan over medium heat. Add red pepper strips, onions, carrots, celery, and garlic, and cook 5 minutes. Cover, reduce heat to low, and cook 10 minutes longer.

2. Add stock and bring to boil over medium high heat. Stir in bulgar and reduce heat to low. Cover and simmer until bulgar is tender, about 20-25 minutes.

3. Take off heat and let pan stand, covered, for 10 minutes. Season with salt, pepper, dill, and thyme, stirring in with fork. Add sour cream and stir in before serving.

Barley, Rice, and Smoked Turkey Salad

SERVINGS: 6

If smoked turkey is unavailable, use regular cooked turkey in this flavorful salad.

2 tablespoons olive oil

¼ cup orange juice

1 tablespoon grated
orange zest (peel)

1 clove garlic, minced

1 teaspoon ground cinnamon

¾ teaspoon ground cumin

dash Tabasco sauce

½ pound smoked turkey, cubed

¾ cup thinly sliced celery

½ cup thinly sliced scallions

½ cup raisins, or dried currants

1 cup cooked pearled or
whole grain barley
(for whole grain barley,
see page 324)

1 cup cooked white rice

½ teaspoon salt, or to taste

freshly ground black pepper,
to taste

¼ cup pine nuts, toasted
(optional)
(for toasting nuts, see page 323)

1. Combine first 7 ingredients in a large serving bowl and whisk together. Add rest of ingredients and toss to combine.

2. Refrigerate, covered, until serving time. (May be refrigerated up to 24 hours.)

County Fair Barbecued Pork Sandwiches
SERVINGS: 8

Lemonade and barbecued pork or beef sandwiches satisfy hungry appetites at many Washington county fairs, such as the Palouse Empire Fair held each year in Colfax. In this recipe, the pork is simmered in a broth for hours before adding to a spicy barbecue sauce. The barbecue sauce works nicely with other meats also.

4 pounds pork shoulder or butt pork roast

2 cloves garlic, minced

freshly ground black pepper

salt

1 cup chicken stock (recipe page 313) or canned broth

1 bay leaf

8 Kaiser rolls

SAUCE

2 (8-ounce) cans tomato sauce

2 cups tomato ketchup

2 tablespoons liquid smoke (natural hickory seasoning)

1 cup white wine vinegar

1 cup brown sugar, packed

¾ teaspoon Tabasco sauce

2 teaspoons Worcestershire sauce

⅓ cup chopped onion

1 tablespoon Dijon or Dijon-style mustard

2 cloves garlic, minced

1. Trim fat from pork roast. Rub pork with minced garlic, grate black pepper over, and sprinkle lightly with salt. Place in large heavy stockpot; add chicken broth and bay leaf. Bring broth to boil over medium heat. Reduce heat to low, lower temperature of mixture to simmer, cover, and simmer for 3 hours. Check occasionally to see that broth is just simmering. Turn meat about every ½ hour.

2. Make barbecue sauce as meat simmers: combine all sauce ingredients in large saucepan, bring to boil over medium high heat, turn heat to low, and simmer for 30 minutes.

3. When pork has cooked for 3 hours, take meat out and place on cutting board. Pour broth in bowl and refrigerate. Tear or slice pork into pieces and return to stock pot along with barbecue sauce. Leave uncovered and simmer over low heat for 1 hour. Take broth from refrigerator, skim fat from top, remove bay leaf, and add amount desired to barbecue sauce and pork. Continue simmering, uncovered, for 2 more hours, adding more broth if needed. Warm Kaiser rolls and serve barbecued pork between buns. Offer napkins and forks.

Grilled Butterflied Leg of Lamb

SERVINGS: 6-8

Grill or broil this flavorful leg of lamb.

1 leg of lamb, butterflied (boned and cut in butterfly shape). Ask butcher to butterfly lamb.

MARINADE

½ **cup olive or vegetable oil**

½ **cup red wine vinegar**

3 cloves garlic, minced

2 teaspoons Dijon or Dijon-style mustard

1½ teaspoons fresh chopped thyme or ½ teaspoon dry thyme

1½ teaspoons fresh chopped rosemary or ½ teaspoon dry rosemary

½ **teaspoon dry oregano**

1 tablespoon soy sauce

1 tablespoon dry sherry

1 teaspoon salt

½ **teaspoon freshly ground pepper**

1. Trim excess fat from lamb and place in a non-metallic pan. Combine marinade ingredients and cover meat with marinade, cover pan, and refrigerate for 6 hours or as long as 24 hours. Turn meat occasionally.

2. Remove meat from refrigerator and from marinade.

TO PREPARE BARBECUE OR BROILER GRILL

◆ *For open grill:*
When grill is hot, grill meat 4 inches from heat, for 10 minutes. Turn, baste with marinade, and grill for 10 more minutes on other side. Raise grill slightly to about 5 inches from heat and continue basting and cooking until done to liking, about 15-20 minutes more on each side.

◆ *For covered barbecue:*
Cook lamb 50 minutes, basting and turning after the first 30 minutes.

◆ *Broiling:*
Lamb may also be broiled 4 inches from heat on both sides until browned, then roasted in an oven turned to 425 degrees for 20-30 more minutes or until done.

Discard unused marinade.

PULLMAN

Bolin Farr came to the Washington Territory in 1876 searching for the perfect place to settle. One night, stopping to camp in fields of grass where three creeks joined, he knew he had found his destination. Seeing not only beauty but also farming opportunity in these grassy meadows, Farr settled by the creeks and started a small community originally called Three Forks. Later the name was changed to Pullman in honor of George Pullman, the Chicago industrialist who invented the railroad sleeping car.

Today, this site is both a farming community and the home of a state university. In 1892, a small land-grant college opened its doors, the forerunner of today's Washington State University. Now more than 17,000 students attend WSU for a liberal arts education, as well as specializing in programs such as hotel and restaurant management, agriculture, engineering, communications, and veterinary medicine. The large campus, set on a hill overlooking the three forks, dominates the scene of this picturesque rural town, deep in Palouse territory.

The Indians first inhabiting the region took their name from their major village, on the Snake River. "Palus" described a rock formation near the village site, and, after white settlement, "Palouse" became the place name of a town, a region, a river, and an Indian people.

Whitman County surrounding Pullman produces more **wheat** per acre than any dryland farming area in the United States. An acre of this rich soil yields as much as 100 bushels each harvest. Ninety percent of the **lentils** and **dry peas** in the entire country are grown here and in neighboring Idaho. Crops of **barley, oats,** and **rapeseed** are also harvested in the scenic rolling hills. **Beef cattle** and **hogs** are raised by local farmers. Ferdinand's, the dairy operated by the WSU creamery, specializes in ice cream and a variety of cheeses. Foremost among them is **Cougar Gold**, a white cheddar, named after WSU's mascot and the inventor of the cheese, Dr. Golding.

Wheat Berry and Vegetable Salad

SERVINGS: 6

Wheat berries are whole kernels with a terrific nut-like flavor and are found in many grocery stores and specialty shops, as well as fields throughout the Palouse.

1 cup uncooked wheat berries

5 cups water

SALAD

2 cups cooked wheat berries

½ red pepper, chopped

½ green pepper, chopped

1 cup thinly sliced celery

3 scallions, sliced

1 cup frozen peas, slightly thawed

1 cup coarsely chopped dry-roasted cashews

salt and pepper to taste

DRESSING

1 tablespoon Dijon or Dijon-style mustard

¼ cup white wine vinegar

1 teaspoon granulated sugar

½ teaspoon salt

⅛ teaspoon freshly grated pepper

3 sprigs parsley (no stems)

¼ cup olive oil

¼ cup vegetable oil

1. To cook wheat berries, combine wheat berries and water in 3-quart saucepan. Bring to full boil over medium heat. Cover and boil for 2 minutes. Remove from heat and let stand 1 hour covered. Bring to boil again over medium heat, lower heat, and simmer until berries are tender, about 20-30 minutes. Drain and rinse. Any leftover berries may be frozen and used later.

2. Combine all salad ingredients, except salt and pepper, in a serving bowl.

3. To make dressing, place mustard, vinegar, sugar, salt, pepper, and parsley in bowl of food processor, insert steel blade, and combine. (Or combine in bowl with whisk, mincing the parsley before adding.) Slowly add oils.

4. Coat salad with dressing, add salt and pepper to taste. Serve, or refrigerate and bring to room temperature 30 minutes before serving.

Cougar Gold, Apple, and Onion Soup

SERVINGS: 4-6

This soup is lighter and more delicate than most cheese soups.
The apples add a slight sweetness.

**5 cups chicken stock
(recipe page 313) or
canned broth**

1 cup peeled and chopped potato

**2 cooking apples,
peeled, cored, and chopped**

½ cup chopped onion

¼ cup chopped carrot

¼ cup chopped celery

⅛ teaspoon ground thyme

2 tablespoons cornstarch

2 tablespoons cold water

**4 cups grated Cougar Gold
Cheese (or other cheddar)**

**¼ cup heavy or light cream
(for light cream, see page 322)**

**⅛ teaspoon nutmeg,
preferably freshly ground**

⅛ teaspoon white pepper

¼ cup dry white wine (optional)

thin apple slices for garnish

1. Combine chicken stock or broth, potato, apples, onion, carrot, celery, and thyme in a medium stock pot. Bring just to boil, reduce heat, and simmer 45 minutes or until vegetables are tender. Puree mixture in food processor. (May need to be done in batches.)

2. Return soup to stock pot. Mix cornstarch with cold water, stir into soup, and cook over medium heat until slightly thickened, stirring constantly. Add cheese and cook, stirring until cheese is melted. Add cream, nutmeg, white pepper, and simmer 5 minutes to incorporate flavors. Taste for salt and add, if necessary.

3. Stir in wine just before serving. Top each serving with 3 unpeeled slices of apple.

Marinated Lentil Salad with Mint

SERVINGS: 6

This salad is an excellent accompaniment to lamb kabobs. It can be made early in the morning, left to marinate in the refrigerator, and brought out about 30 minutes before dinner.

**1 cup dry lentils,
rinsed and drained**

1½ teaspoons salt, divided

1 bay leaf

**4 tablespoons vegetable oil,
divided**

½ cup chopped onion

1 cup cooked rice

**½ cup green pepper,
finely chopped**

½ cup scallions, sliced

**1 large tomato,
peeled, seeded, and diced**

¼ cup chopped fresh mint

freshly ground pepper to taste

1 tablespoon granulated sugar

⅛ teaspoon cumin

½ teaspoon coriander

3 tablespoons lime juice

lime wedges

1. Place lentils in large saucepan with 2 cups water, ½ teaspoon salt, and bay leaf. Heat to boiling, reduce heat, cover, and simmer 25-30 minutes or until just tender. Drain, if necessary.

2. Heat 2 tablespoons oil in saucepan over medium heat and sauté onion until tender. Take off heat and combine lentils, rice, and onion in bowl. Add remaining 2 tablespoons oil and 1 teaspoon reserved salt, and all other ingredients except lime wedges, to lentil mixture.

3. Refrigerate at least 2 hours to blend flavors. Serve with fresh lime wedges to squeeze over salad.

Palouse Split Pea Soup

SERVINGS: 8-10

Make enough of this hearty soup to reheat the next day.
Serve with Yakima Valley Gouda Beer Bread (page 243).

2 tablespoons vegetable oil

½ cup onion, chopped

½ cup baked ham, chopped

1 pound dry split peas*
(rinsed and drained)

a ham hock (optional)

5 cups water

6 cups chicken stock
(recipe page 313) or broth

1 cup chopped celery

1 cup peeled and chopped carrots

1 medium potato,
peeled and diced

1 bay leaf

1 tablespoon granulated sugar

1 tablespoon lemon juice

2 tablespoons parsley, minced

⅛ teaspoon nutmeg,
preferably freshly ground

⅛ teaspoon marjoram

1 teaspoon salt, or to taste
(amount of salt depends on the
salt content in chicken stock)

freshly ground pepper, to taste

dry sherry, to taste (optional)

1. Place oil in large stock pot over medium heat. Sauté onion in oil until tender, and add chopped ham, peas, optional ham hock, water, broth, celery, carrots, potato, bay leaf, sugar, and lemon juice. Bring to boil, reduce heat, and simmer, partially covered, for 2 hours over low heat. Remove bay leaf.

2. Place solids in food processor, with steel blade inserted, and puree; or press through coarse sieve to get puree. Combine puree with remaining liquid in stock pot and mix together.

3. Add parsley, nutmeg, marjoram, and season with salt and freshly ground pepper to taste. Serve in soup bowls. Add about ½ teaspoon sherry to each bowl, if desired.

*One pound of dry peas equals
2 cups, plus 2 tablespoons.

Roast Pork Tenderloins with Apricot Orange Glaze

SERVINGS: 4

A glistening apricot glaze lightly covers this tenderloin roast, with the remaining glaze used to sauce the pork at serving time.

1 tablespoon butter or margarine

1 teaspoon dried thyme

1 teaspoon dried rosemary

2½ pounds pork tenderloin, trimmed of excess fat

salt and freshly ground pepper

1 cup dry white wine

1 cup apricot spread or jam

6 tablespoons orange juice

3 tablespoons brandy
(or more orange juice)

1. Preheat oven to 350 degrees. Melt butter in small saucepan over low heat; add thyme. Rub rosemary between palms of hand to crush and add to melted butter.

2. Place pork in shallow roasting pan, sprinkle with salt and pepper, and brush herb-butter mixture on top. Pour in wine and roast in oven for 1 hour, basting occasionally.

3. Meanwhile, combine apricot spread, orange juice, and brandy in small saucepan over low heat and heat until warm. Pour ⅓ cup of apricot mixture over pork after meat has cooked for 1 hour. Remove the remaining apricot mixture from heat and set aside. Continue roasting meat for about 15 minutes or until meat thermometer registers 155-160 degrees.

4. When meat is ready to serve, reheat reserved apricot mixture and serve with pork.

CLARKSTON

Captains William Clark and Meriwether Lewis traveled down the Snake River through this area in 1805; later, residents honored the two explorers by naming towns after them. On the Washington side of the Snake is Clarkston, and on the Idaho side is Lewiston. These cities are located where the Snake and Clearwater rivers join and head for the Columbia. Today, Clarkston is the most inland seaport in Washington state.

South of these communities, the Snake River winds through Hell's Canyon, the deepest gorge in the United States. For forty miles the canyon is over 5,000 feet deep and at one point, Dry Diggins, the depth reaches 7,900 feet. Hikers climb up the sides of the canyon for breathtaking views. Whitewater rafting and jet boating are popular on the river, as are fishing for **steelhead, sturgeon, bass,** and **trout.** Orchards near Clarkston produce **cherries, apricots, apples,** and **peaches.**

WASHINGTON STATE HISTORICAL SOCIETY

Sweet Cherry and White Chocolate Cream Cake

SERVINGS: 8

Use fresh, sweet cherries in this dessert.

1½ cups sweet cherries

1½ cups heavy (whipping) cream

12 ounces white chocolate,*
melted and cooled to lukewarm

Pound Cake, recipe page 280,
or purchased pound cake
(about 14 ounces)

extra cherries for garnish, about 5

*Semi-sweet dark chocolate may be used in place of white chocolate.

1. Pit and cut cherries in half, except those for garnish.

2. Whip cream in medium bowl, make a small well in the cream and gradually whisk chocolate into the cream.

3. Using a long serrated knife, cut the cake into 3 layers horizontally.

4. Into 1 cup of whipped cream mixture, add 1½ cups cherries. Spread ½ of this mixture on bottom layer of cake. Repeat, ending with un-iced cake layer on top. Frost top and sides of cake with remaining whipped cream. Refrigerate until serving time.

5. For garnish, pit whole cherries, with stems intact. This can be done by cutting a slit in bottom of cherry and gently pressing out pit. (Very ripe cherries are easier to pit this way.) Place decoratively on top.

Smoked Steelhead Dip

MAKES APPROXIMATELY ⅔ CUPS

Smoked salmon may be substituted for the steelhead.

4 ounces smoked steelhead,
flaked

⅓ cup heavy or light cream
(for light cream, see page 322)

½ teaspoon capers

freshly ground black pepper

Place all ingredients in food processor or blender and combine until smooth. Grind pepper over dip and serve with crackers.

HOUSER MILL IN POMEROY, COURTESY GARY HOUSER

POMEROY

In a valley rimmed with hills, carpeted in wild grass or fields of grain, lies the farming community of Pomeroy. Its business center is small, and is dwarfed by the grain elevators jutting to the sky, filled with wheat and barley from the surrounding fields. Growing wheat and milling flour have a long history here. Three miles east of town is located the old Houser Flour Mill, begun in 1878, now deserted but listed on the National Register of Historic Places.

Recently Pomeroy residents got together and planted trees, shrubs, and flowers where unsightly old train tracks lay unused. Now a brilliant profusion of lilacs, petunias, geraniums, marigolds, and other plantings extend from one end of town to the other in the middle of Railroad Street, one block from Main Street.

Local farmers plant and harvest **wheat** and **barley**. **Wild mushrooms** grow in the nearby Blue Mountains; the most prized and popular are morels. Good hunting for **upland birds** in the wheat fields, and for **deer** and **elk** in the Blue Mountains south of Pomeroy, bring hunters to the area in the fall.

Houser Mills Graham Bread

YIELD: 2 LOAVES

This bread is delicious toasted, with butter and honey. John Houser, my great-grandfather, milled graham flour and steadfastly refused to make white flour, insisting the nutrients were lost in the process. In making graham flour, the bran outer layer is left coarse and the inner part of the kernel is ground fine. It has a nutty flavor and can be used interchangeably with regular whole wheat flour. Most supermarkets carry it. Following is an adaptation of my great-grandmother Houser's old family recipe.

2¼ cups very warm water

2 packages active dry yeast

⅓ cup honey

2 teaspoons salt

⅓ cup butter or margarine, at room temperature

about 7 cups graham flour

1. Combine water, yeast, and honey in large bowl and let stand 2 minutes. Add salt and butter and blend or whisk together.

2. Add 2 cups of graham flour; beat with wooden spoon until smooth. Stir in enough of the remaining flour to make a soft dough. (Dough should be the consistency of biscuit dough.)

3. Turn dough out onto lightly floured surface and knead 5 minutes until smooth and elastic. (To knead, fold dough toward you, using fingers of both hands, then push ball of dough away from you using the heel of your hands. Turn dough one quarter way around on board and repeat steps.)

4. Place in oiled bowl and turn to oil all sides of dough. Cover with waxed paper and a tea towel. Set in warm place until double in bulk, about one hour.

5. Punch down with fist in center of dough and pull sides into center. Turn dough out on lightly floured board and rest for 3 minutes.

6. Divide dough in half and shape into loaves. Place in 2 well-oiled 9x5-inch pans. Cover and let rise in warm place until almost double in bulk, about 30 minutes.

7. Place in unheated oven and turn on oven to 400 degrees. Bake 35-40 minutes, or until done. Cool loaves on wire rack.

Barley Pilaf with Morel Mushrooms

SERVINGS: 6

Other dried mushrooms may be used in place of the morels.

2½ tablespoons butter
or margarine

1 cup pearled barley
or whole grain barley
(for whole grain barley,
see page 324)

½ cup chopped onion

1 clove garlic

3 cups chicken stock or beef stock
(recipes pages 314 and 315), or
canned broth

⅓ cup dried morels*
(other dried mushrooms may
be used)

½ cup minced parsley

1. Preheat oven to 350 degrees. Melt butter in large stove-top casserole dish.

2. Sauté barley, onion, and garlic in butter or margarine over medium heat, until barley is lightly browned, about 7-10 minutes, stirring constantly with wooden spoon. Add stock and dried mushrooms, and bring to boil.

3. Cover and bake for one hour (for whole grain barley, cook 1 hour and 45 minutes). Add minced parsley, stir, and serve.

(If stove-top casserole is unavailable, sauté barley, onion, and garlic in skillet, add stock, and bring to boil. Then transfer to casserole dish, cover, and bake as directed.)

*TO DRY MORELS

String mushrooms like beads on a thread, using a needle with a button at the bottom of the thread. Hang in a warm dry place until dried. Or use a dehydrator. Before placing in a sealed bottle, let mushrooms dry for a few days in a paper bag hung in a warm place. This allows all moisture to escape.

Marie's Beef, Vegetable, and Barley Soup

SERVINGS: 8

A hearty and flavorful soup.

1½-2 pounds beef soup bones (shank, short ribs, chuck bones)

6 cup water, divided

1 cup shredded cabbage

1 cup sliced carrots

1 cup diced celery

1½ cups chopped onion

2 cans (14½-ounce) ready-cut tomatoes with juice

½ cup pearl barley or whole grain barley (for whole grain barley, see page 324)

¼ teaspoon dry thyme

1½ teaspoons chopped fresh basil or ½ teaspoon dry basil

1 bay leaf

3 tablespoons chopped fresh parsley or 1 tablespoon dry parsley

1 clove garlic, minced

1 teaspoon dry green pepper flakes

3 cans (14½-ounce) beef broth

freshly ground pepper

3-4 beef bouillon cubes for salt and flavoring

1. Place meat bones in large stock pot. Add 4 cups water. Bring to boil over medium high heat, reduce heat and simmer, covered, for 1½ to 2 hours or until meat is tender. Skim fat from top. (At this point, the meat and liquid may be refrigerated and the congealed fat more easily removed.)

2. Take bones from liquid, remove meat, and return meat pieces to broth in stock pot. Discard bones. Add the rest of ingredients, including 2 cups reserved water, and mix well. Bring to boil over medium heat, reduce heat, cover, and simmer at least one hour. (If whole grain barley is used, simmer one hour longer, or until barley is tender.) Add more water if needed.

DAYTON

Stagecoaches stopped at the station of Dayton as far back as the mid-1880s. Settlers came early, and today over eighty local houses are included in the National Register of Historic Places. Dayton's two-story wooden depot, the oldest in the state, is surrounded by a tree-shaded brick courtyard. No longer in use as a railroad station, it now houses a museum. Across the street from the depot stands the oldest courthouse still in use for county government in Washington. Both buildings have been well-preserved and handsomely refurbished.

Wheat and **barley** are the big crops here and **asparagus** is grown nearby and processed in the local cannery. A few **sheep** farms are in the area.

SUSAN PARISH COLLECTION

Asparagus Napoleons with Orange Hollandaise Sauce

SERVINGS: 6

Cindy Breilh adapted some recipes and came up with this impressive dish.
At the SAUTÉ (Seattle Area Ultimate Tasting Experience) CLUB, she served this as a first course.

½ **pound frozen
puff pastry, thawed**

**1 large egg yolk beaten with
2 teaspoons water**

**1½ pounds asparagus,
trimmed and peeled**

1. To make Napoleons: preheat oven to 400 degrees. Roll out pastry ⅛-inch thick on lightly floured surface. Cut out six 5-inch by 2-inch rectangles, and transfer them to dampened baking sheet. Brush the tops of the rectangles with some of the egg-water wash. Do not let egg wash drip down the sides. Score napoleons in crosshatch pattern with the back of a paring knife and brush again with egg wash.

2. Bake in upper third of oven for 12 to 15 minutes, or until golden. Transfer cooked pastry rectangles to rack, and cool. Halve the rectangle horizontally with knife and carefully pull out any uncooked dough. (These may be made a day in advance and kept in airtight container at room temperature, then reheated.)

3. Make Orange Hollandaise Sauce (see recipes on following page.

4. To cook asparagus: in large skillet, add water to depth of about 1 inch and bring to gentle boil. Add asparagus and cook until stalks are just tender, about 3-6 minutes. Drain well.

5. To assemble: place bottom layer of Napoleons on individual serving plates. Divide asparagus spears evenly for servings and top with Orange Hollandaise Sauce. Place top of Napoleons over sauce.

ORANGE HOLLANDAISE SAUCE

1 cup orange juice

½ cup (1 stick) unsalted butter

3 egg yolks*

pinch of cayenne pepper

salt and freshly ground white pepper, to taste

*Hollandaise Sauce can be made with egg substitutes, which are pasteurized, and do not need to reach the 160 degrees necessary in cooking with raw eggs, which may contain salmonella. Egg substitutes are also low in cholesterol.

TO MAKE HOLLANDAISE SAUCE (WITH FRESH EGGS)

1. Pour orange juice in a small heavy-bottomed saucepan and place over medium heat. Reduce juice to 2 tablespoons. Set aside.

2. Melt butter in another small saucepan and set aside to cool to room temperature. Add water to bottom of double boiler and bring to a simmer. Mix egg yolks and reduced orange juice in the top of the double boiler and place the top pan over bottom of double boiler. Whisk mixture until smooth. Gradually whisk in the butter in a slow, steady stream. Insert candy thermometer and continue cooking and whisking until mixture has reached 160 degrees and is thickened. Add seasonings. Take off heat and cover to keep warm until serving.

TO MAKE HOLLANDAISE SAUCE WITH EGG SUBSTITUTES

1. Put ½ cup egg substitutes, reduced 2 tablespoons orange juice, and cayenne pepper in food processor or blender. Blend.

2. Heat ⅓ cup margarine to boiling, but not browned, either in saucepan on stove or in a glass measuring cup in microwave. Turn on food processor or blender and pour boiling margarine slowly through lid opening, blending until slightly thickened. Place in saucepan and cook over low heat, whisking constantly, to thicken more if desired. Add salt and pepper.

Bulgar Wheat Salad with Dates and Pecans

SERVINGS: 4

Dates, orange juice, and cinnamon add a spicy sweetness to this salad.

2 cups water

½ teaspoon salt

1 cup bulgar

⅓ cup chopped scallions

½ cup thinly sliced celery

½ cup chopped dates

½ cup coarsely chopped pecans, toasted

3 tablespoons orange juice

1 tablespoon lemon juice

1 teaspoon grated orange zest (peel)

½ teaspoon cinnamon

3 tablespoons olive oil

1. Bring two cups of water to boil in large saucepan; add salt and bulgar. Boil 5-10 minutes or until bulgar is just tender. Drain the bulgar in a sieve and let cool.

2. Place in a serving bowl, fluff bulgar with fork, and add scallions, celery, dates, pecans. Pour orange and lemon juice over the mixture, add grated orange zest and cinnamon. Drizzle with olive oil and toss well. Taste for seasoning and add more salt if needed. Serve at room temperature.

Curried Lamb Chops

SERVINGS: 2

The following recipe is from Bruce and Heather Hebert, owners and chefs of the Patit Creek Restaurant in Dayton. Their restaurant has received many plaudits and awards and this recipe is a winner! Sheep farms are found throughout the state; several are in southeast Washington.

1 teaspoon olive oil

4-6 loin lamb chops

salt and pepper

½ teaspoon minced garlic

2 tablespoons brandy

½ cup dry red wine

1 cup beef stock
(recipe page 314)

1 teaspoon curry powder

½ teaspoon dried mint or
2 teaspoons fresh chopped mint

2 tablespoons butter

extra fresh chopped mint
to sprinkle on top, if desired

1. Heat the olive oil in a large frying pan. Add lamb chops and sauté over medium heat until done (about 5 minutes per side for medium). Remove chops from pan, salt and pepper, and keep warm on heated platter. Cover loosely with foil.

2. Remove most of the oil from the pan and add garlic. Sauté garlic for a minute over medium heat and add brandy and red wine. Bring to a boil over high heat and add beef stock, curry powder, and mint. Boil until thick and syrupy.

3. Remove pan from heat and whisk in butter. Serve sauce with the lamb chops. Sprinkle with minced fresh mint, if desired.

WALLA WALLA

The entertainer Al Jolson once called Walla Walla "the town they liked so much they named it twice." It is a friendly community, but the truth is that numerous streams nearby inspired early Native Americans to name the area Walla Walla, meaning "many waters." White settlers came early; seven miles west of the present-day town of Walla Walla is the site of a mission founded in 1836 by Marcus and Narcissa Whitman. Eleven years later, Cayuse Indians killed the Whitmans and twelve others. Many Native American children lay dying of measles, a disease brought in by new missionary settlers, and the Cayuse believed the missionaries were poisoning their sons and daughters. Later, this mission site became an important station on the Oregon Trail. Nearby Fort Walla Walla, built in 1858, is now a museum that includes a reconstructed pioneer village. These early beginnings are the basis for Walla Walla's title of "The Cradle of Northwest History."

Wheat, green peas, and barley are the main crops covering many of the rolling hills surrounding Walla Walla. Famous Walla Walla Sweet onions are cultivated here. Other local crops are asparagus, shallots, other vegetables, and some berries.

A Note about Walla Walla Sweets: the valley soil conditions near Walla Walla give onions a mild and succulent flavor. Since the late 1920s, farmers experimented and interpollinated onions searching for an ideal variety. The most prized were the Sweet Spanish onions which later became known simply as, "Walla Walla Sweets." To be labeled a genuine Walla Walla Sweet, an onion must be grown within a specific geographic boundary encompassing only Walla Walla County and a part of adjoining Umatilla County in northeastern Oregon.

Walla Walla Sweet Onion Salad with Tomatoes and Basil

SERVINGS: 4-6

Walla Walla Sweets are so mild that they are best uncooked, as in this simple salad.

3 large ripe tomatoes

1 large Walla Walla Sweet onion

2 tablespoons red wine vinegar

5 tablespoons olive oil

½ teaspoon salt

freshly ground pepper

¼ cup crumbled feta cheese (or blue cheese)

¼ cup shredded fresh basil

1. Peel tomatoes if desired by immersing in boiling water for 7 seconds, then cooling under cold tap water, then peeling off skins.

2. Cut tomatoes across into ¼-inch slices. Arrange slices, overlapping slightly, on a platter.

3. Peel onion and cut into ⅛-inch slices, separate into rings, and arrange over the tomatoes.

4. Combine vinegar, oil, and salt in bottle with lid, and shake. Drizzle over tomatoes and onion rings. Grind black pepper over salad, and sprinkle top with cheese and shredded basil.

Debra's Tossed Salad with Walla Walla Sweets

SERVINGS: 4-6

There is a Greek influence to this salad with the feta cheese and the Calamata olives.

2 medium-sized heads of romaine lettuce leaves, cleaned and dry, torn into small pieces

2 small tomatoes, quartered and sliced (peel, if desired)

1 cucumber, peeled, halved, and sliced

1 green pepper, sliced in ½-inch pieces

½ Walla Walla Sweet onion, sliced

3 ounces feta cheese, crumbled (leave 1 ounce for top)

⅓ cup pitted Calamata olives

½ cup olive oil

¼ cup red wine vinegar

1 garlic, minced

salt and pepper to taste

1. Place lettuce, tomatoes, cucumber, green pepper, onion slices, 2 ounces feta cheese, and Calamata olives in large salad bowl and toss.

2. Combine olive oil, vinegar, and garlic in small bowl; pour on salad to coat leaves. Season with salt and pepper. Sprinkle reserved 1 ounce of feta cheese on top.

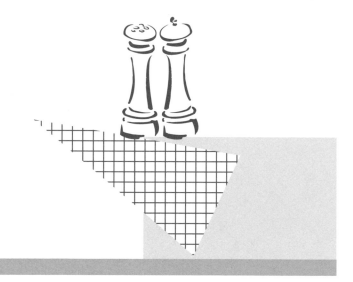

Walla Walla Sweet Onion Confit

SERVINGS: 4

Use large, mature Walla Walla Sweets for this. Serve with grilled steak, chicken, or lamb.

2 large Walla Walla Sweet onions, peeled and sliced

1 cup chicken stock (recipe page 313) or broth

2 tablespoons butter or margarine

salt

Freshly ground black pepper

1 tablespoon whole grain mustard

1. Place sliced onions, stock, butter, salt, and pepper in 2-quart saucepan. Bring to boil over medium heat, stirring to break up onion "rings." Turn heat to low or medium-low and simmer, covered, for 15 minutes, stirring twice. Onions should be soft, but not mushy.

2. Uncover, add mustard, and continue cooking until liquid is almost absorbed, about 5-10 minutes.

Bulgar Wheat Risotto with Peas and Parmesan Cheese

SERVINGS: 4

Use bulgar instead of the traditional Italian arborio rice for this risotto.
Chopped ham or chicken may be added to this just before serving to make it a main dish.

2 tablespoons butter, divided

2 tablespoons olive oil

1 cup chopped onion

1 cup bulgar wheat

2-2½ cups chicken stock
(page 313) or canned broth

½ cup white wine or vermouth

½ cup freshly grated
Parmesan cheese

½ cup freshly cooked peas,
or frozen and thawed

freshly ground pepper

additional grated
Parmesan cheese

1. Heat 1 tablespoon butter and olive oil in heated 3-quart sauté pan or skillet. Add onions and sauté until tender over medium heat; do not brown. Add bulgar and stir until all kernels are coated with oil.

2. In small separate pan, heat chicken stock to simmering.

3. Cook bulgar over medium heat and add wine or vermouth. Stir with wooden spoon until liquid is absorbed. Continue cooking and stirring, adding ⅓ cup chicken stock each time and allowing each addition to be absorbed before adding next.

4. Cook until bulgar is just tender. Stir in 1 tablespoon reserved butter, cheese, and peas. Sprinkle with pepper and additional cheese.

BASIC RECIPES

LOW-FAT
SUGGESTIONS

GLOSSARY

SELECTED
BIBLIOGRAPHY

BASIC RECIPES

Pie Crust

Before making pie crust place butter and shortening in freezer for at least a half hour and up to a day. Place ice in glass with water to chill just before making.

1-CRUST PIE SHELL

1¼ cups all-purpose flour

¼ teaspoon salt

¼ cup frozen or well chilled shortening, cut in ½-inch chunks

¼ cup frozen or well chilled butter, cut in ½-inch chunks

3 tablespoons ice water

WITH FOOD PROCESSOR

Place flour and salt in bowl with metal blade inserted. Distribute shortening and butter over flour. Begin motor and cut in shortening and butter until particles look with small peas. Remove lid and sprinkle measured ice water over mixture. Add lid, and using pulsing action, pulse mixture just to a point that it looks like cottage cheese, do not allow mixture to form into a ball. Turn mixture onto a piece of plastic wrap and pull up corners of wrap to form dough into a ball. Flatten to form disk and refrigerate for an hour.

WITH A PASTRY BLENDER

Place flour and salt into a bowl, distribute butter and shortening over, and combine to form meal. Add water to combine and turn onto a piece of plastic wrap and proceed as above.

Remove dough from refrigerator, lightly flour dough and put on lightly floured board or between two pieces of lightly floured waxed paper. Roll out dough to ⅛-inch thickness. Fold in half and place in pie pan. Unfold dough and crimp or flute edges.

FOR BAKED PIE CRUST

Preheat oven to 425 degrees. Using a table fork, prick bottom and sides of pastry thoroughly and bake in oven 12-15 minutes or until lightly browned.

OR: Line dough with foil and fill with rice or beans. Bake in oven for 8 minutes, remove beans or rice and lining. Prick bottom of dough with fork and bake 10 minutes longer or until lightly browned.

2-CRUST PIE SHELL

2½ **cups all-purpose flour**

½ **teaspoon salt**

½ **cup frozen or well chilled shortening, cut in ½-inch chunks**

½ **cup frozen or well chilled butter, cut in ½-inch chunks**

6 **tablespoons ice water**

FOR 2 CRUST PIE

Line pie pan with pastry, trim overhanging edge of pastry to ½-inch from rim of pan. Place in filling. Roll out second disk of dough, fold in half and cut slits for steam to escape, and place on top of filling. Unfold, trim edge ½-inch from rim of pan. Form stand-up rim on edge of pan to seat and flute. (To prevent excessive browning, cover edge with strip of foil and remove last 15 minutes of baking.

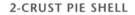

Duxelles

Use to flavor sauces, soups and meats.

1 pound fresh mushrooms

4 tablespoon, butter or margarine

¼ cup finely chopped shallots
(or onion)

½ cup dry sherry

2 tablespoons minced parsley

½ teaspoon salt

freshly ground pepper

⅛ teaspoon ground nutmeg

Finely chop mushrooms in food processor or by hand. Melt butter in large skillet, add chopped mushrooms, shallots, sherry and parsley. Cook over medium heat until liquid is absorbed. Season with salt and pepper. Add nutmeg. Cool.

Créme Fraîche

2 cups heavy cream

2 tablespoons buttermilk

Pour cream into a glass container and whisk in buttermilk. Cover with plastic wrap and leave at room temperature until thickened. (The time will vary depending on the temperature of the room; this can take 7 hours or as long as a day.) When thickened, place in refrigerator and use within a week.

Stocks

Make a batch of any of the following stocks and freeze what is not initially used in ice cube trays. The frozen cubes can be then stored in containers to use in recipes calling for stock.

Chicken Stock

3 quarts water

3 pounds chicken wings
(or 3-4 pound chicken,
cut in quarters)

1 large carrot,
cleaned and cut in large pieces

3 ribs celery with leaves,
cut in about 3-inch lengths

1 large onion, cleaned,
but left unpeeled, and quartered

1 sprig parsley

1 bay leaf

3 peppercorns

1 whole clove

¼ teaspoon dried thyme

salt (or chicken bouillon cubes*)
to taste

In large stockpot, place all ingredients, except salt. Bring to boil, skim off foam from surface, reduce heat and simmer, partially covered, for 3-4 hours. Remove chicken from pot and reserve for other use. Discard large vegetable pieces and strain stock through sieve into bowl, add salt (or bouillon cubes) to taste. (If you are planning to reduce stock more, salt slightly, or salt at time of reduction.) Let cool in refrigerator, uncovered, in shallow container(s). When cold, cover. Refrigerate stock or freeze for later use.

*Chicken bouillon cubes are mainly salt and may be used as the salt in the recipe.

Beef Stock

5 pounds beef bones

2 large onions, cleaned and left unpeeled, quartered

3 tablespoons vegetable oil

water

1 leek, well cleaned and cut in 1-inch pieces

3 large carrots, cut in large pieces

3 cloves garlic, unpeeled and sliced in half

3 ribs celery, cut in about 3-inch lengths

2 whole cloves

2 bay leaves

½ teaspoon dried thyme

6 peppercorns

a sprig of parsley

3 quarts water

salt to taste

1. Preheat oven to 450 degrees. Combine bones and onion quarters in large roasting pan and pour oil over. Place in oven and roast, stirring occasionally, until bones are brown, about 45 minutes.

2. Place bones and onions in stockpot. Pour off fat from roasting pan and pour about 1 cup of the water into roasting pan and bring to boil over medium heat. Scrape pan with wooden spoon to loosen browned bits in pan. Pour this mixture into stock pot with bones. Add all other ingredients, except salt. Heat over medium heat to boiling. Skim off any foam. Reduce heat and simmer, partially covered, for about 6 hours.

3. Remove from heat, and strain stock through sieve into metal bowl or heat resistant container. Salt to taste. (If you are planning to reduce stock more, lightly salt or salt at time of reduction.) Cool quickly in cold water bath (place bowl in large container or basin full of cold water.) Refrigerate until cold. Remove fat from surface. Refrigerate, covered, or freeze for later use.

Vegetable Stock

**1 medium cleaned
but unpeeled onion, quartered**

**2 stalks of celery,
cut in 1-inch pieces**

**2 carrots, cleaned but unpeeled
carrots, cut in 1-inch pieces**

1 parsnip, cut in 1-inch pieces

**2 medium sized red potatoes
with skins, cut in quarters**

4 springs parsley

3 whole cloves

1 bay leaf

**1½ teaspoon chopped fresh
thyme or ½ teaspoon dry thyme**

½ teaspoon salt, or to taste

6 black peppercorns

dash cayenne

water to cover, about 8 cups

l. Place all ingredients in large, heavy stockpot. Bring to boil, reduce heat and simmer, partially covering the pan, for 1½ hours.

2. Strain broth through sieve into heat resistant bowl, pressing the vegetables to extract liquid. Place bowl in cold water bath (put bowl in cold water in basin or large container.) Refrigcrate until cold, then cover and continue refrigerating up to 5 day. (Freeze for later use.)

LOW-FAT SUGGESTIONS

*For those who wish to lower the fat content in their cooking,
the following substitutions or tips should be helpful.*

HEAVY (WHIPPING) CREAM

In recipes where the cream is to be reduced to make a sauce, the following substitutions may be used: evaporated skim milk, light cream, or half-and half. Evaporated skim milk will reduce and thicken; however, the taste of the dish will be altered. Light cream is sold in some places in the United States, and is basically equal parts heavy cream and half-and-half. It reduces well, has a bit lighter taste than heavy cream, but still contains a butterfat content too high for some diets. Half-and half does not reduce as well as light cream but has less butterfat.

Evaporated skim milk may be used as a whipped topping by chilling the milk in a bowl, along with the mixers, in freezer for 20 minutes or until crystals start to form around the edge of the bowl. Whip milk, sweeten to taste, and generously flavor with vanilla or other extract. This topping has a different taste than regular whipped cream.

CREAM CHEESE

Use low-fat (Neufchatel) or non-fat cream cheese.

SOUR CREAM

Use light or non-fat sour cream, or make non-fat yogurt cheese. To make yogurt cheese, place 2 cups plain non-fat yogurt in basket style paper coffee filter (or double thickness cheesecloth) in a strainer. Place strainer over bowl, cover, and refrigerate 12 hours or longer. Drain liquid from bowl and use the thickened yogurt. This makes about ¾ to 1 cup of yogurt cheese. (I find the yogurt cheese has a "chalky" taste and is best combined with other flavorings.)

MILK Use non-fat, 1 percent, or non-fat buttermilk.

MAYONNAISE Use light mayonnaise, or try non-fat sour cream or yogurt. A non-fat mayonnaise is available and can be enhanced by a squeeze of lemon and a few drops of olive oil. (Otherwise, I think it tastes awful.)

EGGS In many cases, two egg whites or ¼ cup commercial egg substitutes may be used for a whole egg.

WHITE (BÉCHAMEL) SAUCE One cup of white sauce usually has 2 tablespoons of butter or margarine. The following recipe has no fat and may be substituted for 1 cup white sauce:

1 cup non-fat milk
1 tablespoon flour
1 tablespoon cornstarch
salt, pepper, or other seasonings to taste

Blend milk with flour and cornstarch in food processor or blender until smooth. Heat heavy saucepan over medium heat, watching carefully, until the bottom is warm to the touch. Add milk mixture to the pan all at once and whisk constantly until thickened. Season as needed.

PAN SAUTÉING Heat a good quality non-stick pan over medium heat, watching carefully, until the bottom of the pan is warm to the touch. Add about ½ the oil called for in the recipe, add the food to be sautéed, and continue cooking, stirring food. Or "water" sauté by using a liquid such as a broth or wine, and cook food. Vegetables such as celery, carrots, and onions should be chopped finely to cook quickly and evenly.

BAKED GOODS CALLING FOR BUTTER, MARGARINE, OR OIL Replace oil with applesauce or part applesauce and oil. The texture and taste will be altered.

CHOCOLATE Since cocoa powder does not contain cocoa butter, it is fat free. Combining and heating cocoa powder, sugar, and non-fat milk will form a paste (or sauce) which may be substituted in some recipes. Different proportions may be used, the following is approximate: Combine ¼ cup unsweetened cocoa and ⅓ cup sugar in saucepan, gradually whisk in milk, and cook over medium or low heat until sugar dissolves, stirring constantly.

POULTRY AND MEAT For poultry, remove excess fat before cooking and remove skin before eating or cooking. For meat, remove as much fat as possible before cooking. Skim fat from pan juices before deglazing or thickening.

SALAD DRESSING

Many low- or non-fat salad dressings are on the market. Two recipes for homemade dressings follow:

LOW-FAT YOGURT CUCUMBER DRESSING

1 clove garlic

½ teaspoon salt

1 teaspoon Dijon or Dijon style mustard

1 tablespoon white wine vinegar

1 tablespoon vegetable or olive oil (optional)

1 cup non-fat plain yogurt

2 tablespoons grated cucumber, seeds removed

1 teaspoon minced parsley

1 teaspoon chopped fresh dill or ⅓ teaspoon dry dill

Freshly ground black pepper

pinch of sugar (optional)

1. Slice garlic in two and place on cutting board. With paring knife, press salt into garlic, mashing together to make paste. Place in bowl and mix with mustard and vinegar. Whisk in oil and yogurt. Stir in rest of ingredients.

2. Refrigerate until ready to use.

NON-FAT HONEY MUSTARD DRESSING

⅔ cup water

1 teaspoon cornstarch

2 teaspoons Dijon or Dijon-style mustard

1 tablespoon honey

3 tablespoons rice vinegar or white wine vinegar

salt and freshly ground pepper to taste

1. In small saucepan, whisk together water and cornstarch. Place pan over medium high heat and bring to full boil. Boil one minute, whisking constantly. The heat may need to be lowered so the mixture will not boil over.

2. Take off heat and whisk in remaining ingredients until well blended. Chill in refrigerator for 2 hours or longer.

GLOSSARY

SELECTED COOKING PROCEDURES, TOOLS, AND FOOD PRODUCTS

Baste: To moisten foods as they cook.

Blanch: To plunge food (usually vegetables or fruit) into boiling water for a brief period. The food is then refreshed under cold water.

Boil: The cooking liquid bubbles rapidly.

Bulgar: Wheat that is steamed and dried before being crushed into various grinds.

Butter: Butter burns at a low temperature, so when sautéing with butter, it helps to add another oil such as vegetable or olive oil to help prevent burning. Also, butter may be clarified to prevent burning.

    To clarify: Melt butter over low heat. Let it settle, remove the foamy fat. Pour clear liquid, which is the clarified butter, in container; discard solids that remain at the bottom of the pan. The clarified butter will tolerate the high temperature needed to sauté.

Butterflied: Split and spread apart, often done to whole fish or leg of lamb.

Canadian theory for cooking fish: The recommended time for cooking fish is 10 minutes per inch of thickness. Author's note: an additional 2 minutes may be needed to cook fish to "opaque throughout" stage. If fish is baked at medium temperature (350 degrees), it may need a few more minutes of cooking time. Fish should not be cooked until it flakes, as it will be too dry. Cook only until it is opaque throughout.

Capers:	The flower buds of a hyssop shrub, usually pickled. The small flavorful buds are unique in flavor and it is difficult to suggest a substitute.
Chèvre cheese:	Cheeses usually made with all goat's milk; however, some are mixed with cow's milk. Some excellent goat cheeses are made in Washington and many are available at large supermarkets. Cream cheese may be substituted for soft goat cheese. Any white cheese may be substituted for a hard goat cheese.
Confectioners' sugar:	Powdered sugar. This sugar is made by grinding white sugar. Most powdered sugars have some cornstarch added.
Cracked wheat:	Coarsely ground wheat berries. It cannot be used in place of the more processed bulgar.
Crimp:	When working with pie dough, crimp edge of pie crust by pinching dough together decoratively with fingers.
Cube:	To cube food, cut into cube-shaped pieces from ¼- to 1-inch in size.
Dash:	A small quantity, less than ⅛ teaspoon. Two quick shakes yield a dash, often used when measuring Tabasco sauce.
Deglaze:	To add liquid such as broth or wine to a pan in which a food such as meat, fish, or chicken has been cooked and stir and scrape the browned bits from the bottom of the pan into the liquid.
Degrease:	To remove fat from the surface of a liquid.
Dice:	Cut food in cube size pieces about ¼ inch, or smaller, in size.
Emulsified:	Thickened; as when adding oil to a salad dressing. To turn an oil into an emulsion (a mixture of liquids that do not dissolve in each other).
Feta cheese:	Sheep's milk cheese, which usually comes in firm chunks that are soft enough to crumble. Blue cheese may be substituted.

Flute:	To make a decorative pattern on something such as the edge of a pie shell. Fluting a pie shell is usually done by crimping the pastry between the thumb and the index finger to make a scalloped pattern.
Framboise:	A liqueur made from raspberries.
Hazelnuts, toasting:	See Toasting.
Heavy cream:	Whipping cream used for whipping and in sauces.
Julienne:	To cut food, usually vegetables, into thin match-stick strips.
Light creams:	Old in some places in the United States. Light cream is essentially a combination of equal parts heavy cream and half-and-half. Light cream reduces well for sauces, but does not whip.
Margarine:	Margarine may be used for sautéing by itself or in combination with an oil, such as vegetable or olive oil, or butter. Light margarin that contains less than 60 percent oil should not be used for baking as it will affect the texture and quality of the product.
Mascarpone:	A rich, smooth, and creamy cheese. If unavailable, use cream cheese.
Mustard:	The recipes in this book request using a Dijon or Dijon-style mustard. Dijon is a city in France noted for making fine mustards. A true Dijon mustard is a creamy, spicy product and not always available. A good quality cream mustard or coarse grain mustard may be used in the recipes in this book, unless specifically stated.
Mince:	Cut food into very fine pieces, ⅛ inch or smaller in size.
Nap:	To cover with a sauce that is thick enough to coat or adhere to food.
Pearled barley:	Barley that has been milled, removing outer layers until it resembles small pearls.

Pie sheet:	The pie sheet suggested in some recipes in this book is circular with a rimmed hole in the center. The pie tin is elevated by this rim and the hole allows air to circulate under the pie tin. Therefore, the tin should be placed directly on the pie sheet. This pie sheet is different from a "drip" pan. It is available in some cooking or gourmet shops.
Pine nuts:	The small edible seeds of the stonepine. Toasted walnut pieces or sunflower seeds may be substituted.
Roux:	A cooked mixture of flour and butter or some other fat used to thicken a sauce.
Sauté:	To fry foods quickly in a small amount of fat.
Scallions:	Green onions. These onions do not form a large bulb.
Score:	To cut shallow grooves or slits into the surface of meat to prevent it from curling as it cooks.
Shallots:	A small vegetable related to the onion. The flavor is more subtle than that of an onion and less harsh than that of garlic. Mild onions are most often substituted.
Simmer:	To cook in liquid just below the boiling point.
Springform pan:	A round pan with removable bottom. The side are clasped together and can be unclasped and removed after cheesecake, cake, or torte has been baked.
Toasting hazelnuts:	To toast and skin hazelnuts, spread shelled nuts in one layer on baking sheet and toast in a preheated 350 degree oven for 10 to 15 minutes or until lightly colored. Wrap the nuts in a dish towel and let them stand for 1 minute. Rub nuts in a towel to remove as much of the skins as possible. Discard skins and let nuts cool.
Toasting nuts:	Toasting brings out the flavor in all nuts. *To toast:* preheat oven to 350 degrees. Spread in a single layer on flat baking sheet. Toast 5 minutes; check. Continue toasting and checking every 4-5 minutes so

they won't burn. As soon as they begin to color, they will toast quickly. Pine nuts take about 7 minutes, nut pieces take about 10-14 minutes, and nut halves take longer.

Truss: To tie, lace, or sew together an opening in poultry or meat.

Water bath procedure: A large heavy stock pot or water canner is needed along with glass jars and lids. Sterilize empty jars in dishwasher or in water canner.

For water canner method: Fill canner with hot water at least 1 inch above tops of jars. Bring water to boil and boil 10 minutes. Remove jars with tongs and drain on clean dry towel. Keep water in canner for processing foods in jars.

To process foods in jars: fill hot jars with cooked hot food. Jars should not be completely filled, leaving some headspace. Add lids and tighten. Canner should be half full of water. Place over medium high heat and bring to 180 degrees. Load with filled jars using tongs. Water level should be about 1 inch above jar tops; add more boiling water if needed. Process the time requested in each recipe. Remove jars and cool to room temperature.

Wheat berries: Wheat kernels.

Whole grain barley: Barley kernels that have not been pearled, which removes the outer layers. Use of a special type of barley is needed for this. It has a high nutritional value and may be used in place of pearled barley, but needs a longer cooking time. Also known as hulless barley.

Whisk: To beat with a whisk until blended and smooth.

Zest from citrus fruit: The oily, colorful part of the peel of lemon, orange, lime, or grapefruit.

SELECTED BIBLIOGRAPHY

America's Spectacular Northwest. Washington D.C.: National Geographic Society, 1982.

Barr, Tom, *Portrait of Washington.* Portland, Oregon: Graphic Arts Center Publishing Company, 1980.

Flaherty, David C., and Sue Ellen Harvey. *Fruits and Berries of the Pacific Northwest.* Edmonds, Washington: Alaska Northwest Publishing Company, 1988.

Hinchman, Robert. *Place Names of Washington.* Tacoma, Washington: Washington State Historical Society, 1985.

Johansen, Dorothy and Charles Gates, *Empire of the Columbia: A History of the Pacific Northwest.* New York: Harper and Brothers, 1957.

Kirk, Ruth and Carmela Alexander, *Exploring Washington's Past.* Seattle, Washington: University of Washington Press, 1990.

Morgan, Murray. *Skid Road, Seattle: Her First 125 Years.* Sausalito, California: Comstock Editions, Inc., 1951.

Petersen, Keith and Mary E. Reed. *Discovering Washington: A Guide to State and Local History.* Pullman, Washington: Washington State University Press, 1989.

Phillips, James W. *Washington State Place Names.* Seattle, Washington: University of Washington Press, 1971.

Sale, Roger, *Seattle Past to Present.* Seattle, Washington: University of Washington Press, 1976.

Schwantes, Carlos A. *The Pacific Northwest: An Interpretive History.* Lincoln, Nebraska: University of Nebraska Press, 1989.

Washington Agricultural Statistics. *Olympia, Washington: State Department of Agriculture, 1991, 1993.*

INDEX